Mark Virkler has written ye⟨...⟩ ⟨...⟩ead. Not only must read, but must study ⟨...⟩ ⟨...⟩hen asked, I was happy to endorse his new book. ⟨...⟩ ⟨...⟩ze was that I too really need to review and go through this ⟨...⟩ ⟨...⟩arefully. Mark takes us on a deep dive into understanding not only the various ways to appropriate physical healing, but even more importantly, it is also a study on maintaining spiritual and emotional health and well-being. Carol and I plan on using this tool for daily devotions to draw our hearts even closer to the heart of God. Read it and allow the Lord to heal you physically, emotionally, and spiritually.

John Arnott
Founder, Catch the Fire Ministries

Mark Virkler wrote a book that I wish I had been able to use when I had a chronic illness years ago. There are too few voices in the body of Christ teaching or going after the miraculous healing power of God. Worse yet, many of the ones who do end up not having great theology to accompany the gift they are trying to demonstrate. In comes Mark's *Hearing God's Voice for Healing* which will act like a field guide to go after instantaneous miracles but also to have the longevity to keep pursuing healing ⟨e⟩ven when you don't see the signs of it when you first pray. Even if you ⟨ha⟩ve gone after healing gifts before this is a book for you! And it's right ⟨on⟩ time!

Shawn Bolz
Founder, BolzMinistries.com
Author, Speaker, TV Host

⟨He⟩aring God's Voice for Healing is going to help so many people! First, to ⟨set⟩ them free from the shame and confusion of "unanswered prayers," and

most of all to set them on the path not only of healing, but consistently living in divine health.

Wholeness is Father's heart for us, and we know His great promise "I, the Lord, am your healer." Yet that promise is conditional, based on our listening to His voice and obeying His instructions. Indeed, the immediate context of that verse is the story of the bitter waters of Marah. We recall God told Moses to throw a tree into the waters and it made the undrinkable water sweet (Exodus 15:22-26). That is, there was something natural, in nature, that when appropriated in faith and obedience to God's directive released a miracle.

Wow! So there is a part we get to play in the unfolding miracle. There are things we can do to partner with heaven to experience supernatural healing. To understand the revelatory truth that therapeutic "process healing" is biblical and even Christ-like is liberating and empowering, especially when these practical pathways to wellness are so clearly laid out for us to easily walk in. Every good gift is from above, and we want to avail ourselves of all the various gifts of healings God has so graciously supplied.

I am grateful for this balanced and comprehensive resource to inspire us in our own health journey as well as equip us to minister more effectively to others. Healing is complex and this book provides several more missing pieces to the puzzle!

Charity Virkler Kayemb
Founder, GloryWaves.or
Co-author, Hearing God Through Your Dreams and Everyday Ange

In the very extensive and practical guide to healing that Mark has p duced here, he has an important revelation: that God heals both throu instant healing and through therapeutic healing or a term he has coine *process healing*. And we should not consider process healing to be any divine or second rate.

He will bind up our wounds (Psalm 147:3). Binding a wound impli a process healing. Think of a nurse carefully wrapping an injured arn

If the nurse does it carefully, what we receive in the process is the love, nurture, and care from the nurse. Her care touches us. We feel loved and valued.

In the story of the healing of the blind man in Mark 8, Jesus led the man *by the hand* outside the village. And once outside the village, Jesus prayed twice for the man before he was completely healed. This was a process healing. How long would it have taken to lead this man outside the village? Five, ten, fifteen minutes? What would it have been like to hold Jesus' hand for this amount of time? This man would have felt love and care and nurture from Jesus, a love and care that would have touched his soul deeply. I am convinced that he received two healings that day: his eyes were healed, and his soul was healed from shame.

Shame is often a fruit of sickness. We get sick, we carry the shame. We are overweight, we are ashamed. We have poor health, we are ashamed. For the blind man, in the religious Jewish culture of the day, it was thought, "What sin has led to his sickness?" Though this may sometimes be true, it is not always the answer to why we are sick. In that culture the sick were shamed. It's the same today in some religious cultures. And if we are not instantly healed when someone prays for us, we carry double shame.

There is healing of shame when we hold Jesus' hand. When He slowly heals us through process healing, we discover how loving, caring, gentle, and nurturing our Father is, and our souls are healed. We get not only a healing of our bodies, but a healing of our souls as well.

Thank you, Mark, for identifying process healing. And thank you for providing us an extensive list of processes through which the Father heals. Process healing must be taught and experienced in the body of Christ.

Jeff Duncan
Pastor, Catch the Fire Ottawa

Fantastic book! Very comprehensive, compelling, and a great reference. Dr. Mark has written here a brilliant compilation of biblical revelations with fascinating medical affirmations, practical insights, and amazing testimonies that will encourage, guide, and assure you that God's will is healing and divine health for your life.

Dr. Don Paprockyj
Founder and President, Glory Power Ministries

This is a phenomenal, apostolic statement! Love it!

Rev. Peg Yarbrough
Founder and President, Light of Christ Ministries

This book is scholarly as well as spiritual and is the product of Mark's desire to see people saved, healed, and set free. He has a unique style that invites detailed exploration of the material, which when pursued with patience will bring heavenly revelation. Anyone who decides to delve into this wonderful treasure house will find their delight in the Lord increased, and they will surely find a path to their healing.

Rev. Margaret Cornell
Founder and President, Hearing God's Voice UK
Founding co-pastor, Ely Christian Fellowship and author of two books:
Life Shared and *Why Me God?*

Dr. Mark Virkler does it again! The "how-to-guy" has developed a new book on prophetic healing that just hits the nail on the head! After reading this, I really felt my faith had been stirred up and made ready to witness the hand of God at work! A must read!

Dr. Eric McCracken
Associate Pastor, Maplewood Christian Church
Professor, Christian Leadership University

A few years ago, a friend of mine said she had been listening to someone named Mark Virkler about hearing God's voice. As I began to read and listen to him, my life drastically changed. I began to hear the Lord's voice and commune more fully with God. I am now a member of the faculty of Dr. Mark and Patti Virkler's university, Christian Leadership University.

I also have had the pleasure to work behind the scenes to live out a modern-day Habakkuk 2 by converting many of their courses, "making them plain on tablets," so students all over the world may read their works online. I share this only to say I have had the intimate opportunity to read most of their writings and am a special witness of the fruit-bearing in many people's lives as a result of their writings.

Hearing God's Voice for Healing is ideal for both individual and group exploration and will serve as a useful reference for my short bookshelf near my prayer chair. There is an ongoing reminder within the book to tune in to the flow of the Holy Spirit to call down the Lord's strategies and instructions. Drs. Mark and Patti remind us of our part as well, and they include a wealth of their other books and blogs for further review and meditation. May all be blessed and be healed who read and seek the Lord to apply these principles.

Dr. Michelle Kirby
Founder and President, In All Things Ministries
Professor, Christian Leadership University

This book is one of the most thorough resources on healing I have ever seen. As the calling on my life, including ministry and profession, is healing, I have studied the Bible along with numerous resources and courses, to be well-equipped to bring healing into every environment.

Dr. Virkler provides biblical truth and wisdom for supernatural healing, as well as God's design for the stewardship of our health. Not only does this book provide the information and resources to walk in health and healing, in his usual style, Dr. Virkler gives the guidance and practical steps to walk it out.

Everyone will benefit from this amazing resource!

Suzanne Barker, MS, RDN, Ph.D

Hearing
GOD'S VOICE
for HEALING

Hearing
GOD'S VOICE
for HEALING

Practical & Powerful Paths to Divine Health

MARK AND PATTI VIRKLER

DESTINY IMAGE® PUBLISHERS, INC.
P.O. Box 310, Shippensburg, PA 17257-0310
"Publishing cutting-edge prophetic resources to supernaturally empower the body of Christ"

This book and all other Destiny Image and Destiny Image Fiction books are available at Christian bookstores and distributors worldwide.

For more information on foreign distributors, call 717-532-3040.
Reach us on the Internet: www.destinyimage.com.

ISBN 13 TP: 978-0-7684-8047-4
ISBN 13 eBook: 978-0-7684-8048-1

For Worldwide Distribution, Printed in the U.S.A.
1 2 3 4 5 6 7 8 / 29 28 27 26 25

Dedication

To Patti, my wife, to whom I have had the joy of being married for 52 years. Together we built everything that has been built. Patti is a cherished gift and an amazing friend and companion. The merging of our opposite giftings has made the impossible possible, as we have together chosen to follow the Lord wherever He leads.

And to my daughter, Charity Kayembe, who far surpasses me when it comes to Bible knowledge, spiritual boldness, and courageous navigation of the supernatural realm. She and Patti have worked together to refine this book.

Acknowledgements

Many thanks to those first readers who embraced this book and wrote endorsements for it, and to Larry Sparks and Destiny Image for choosing to publish it.

May the Lord carry it on angels' wings to every place it is to go.

Contents

Foreword by Patricia King

I first met Mark Virkler in the 1990s during the outpouring of the Spirit in Toronto. He passionately desired to help hungry believers hear from God for their lives and develop an intimate devotional realm as they richly communed with the Lord in His tangible presence. I was impressed by the way he so easily presented profound truths and after speaking with many who were mentored and taught by him, I was excited for all who would enter new realms of connecting with God in deep, enriching, and life-changing ways.

Too often, believers complicate spiritual invitations from the Holy Spirit that we find in the Scriptures. The Lord created the Kingdom and all its promises to be accessed by childlike faith. He makes it easy for all to engage and encounter. This is what I love about Mark Virkler's book, *Hearing God's Voice for Healing*. Although he is academically brilliant, he has written it for the spiritually hungry and for those with childlike faith.

Accessing all the Lord has for you as a believer requires seeking. If you seek, you will find. Profound truths and mysteries are hidden for true seekers like yourself. This book will teach you how to position yourself to hear from God, walk with God, and respond to all He reveals to you. You will become a wonderful steward of the things He discloses to you as you activate the lessons. The lessons and principles can be applied to so many areas of your life, but in the areas of healing for spirit, soul, body, finance, relationships, and other important areas of life, this book particularly holds vital keys for you.

Hearing God's Voice for Healing is both practical and profound, and I am truly excited for all who read it. Valuable insights, instruction, and mentoring are found in the pages of this book. If you are suffering from chronic ailments, diseases, and infirmities that don't yet submit to God's healing promises, you will discover keys for your breakthrough. If you have a heart of mercy for others who are suffering, this book will be used to equip you to be an effective minister of Christ's healing anointing and power.

The world is very broken, but we know the Savior, Healer, and Deliverer who can bind up the brokenhearted, heal the sick, and deliver the oppressed—and He lives mightily in you. In these days of harvest, Jesus wants to give every blessing He died for to all who desire to receive, and He is looking for those who will carry His message and His mandate. I think that might be you!

> *The Spirit of the Lord is upon Me,*
> *Because He has anointed Me*
> *To preach the gospel to the poor;*
> *He has sent Me to heal the brokenhearted,*
> *To proclaim liberty to the captives*
> *And recovery of sight to the blind,*
> *To set at liberty those who are oppressed;*
> *To proclaim the acceptable year of the Lord* (Luke 4:18-19 NKJV).

Patricia King
Founder, Patricia King Ministries

Introduction by Mark Virkler

"Why not me? I didn't get healed!" Thankfully, there are many paths to experiencing God's healing.

A man approached me during a break in my seminar in Texas. He asked if I would pray for the arthritic pain in both of his knees. I said, "Yes," and had him sit in a chair, and I laid my hands on both of his knees and commanded the pain to leave and for healing to occur. I then encouraged him to do a "Jericho march" around the church five times, while the break was still on. He did and reported back that all the pain had left his legs! We thanked God for His goodness.

However, sometimes the result is, *"Why not me? I didn't get healed. I went forward in the service. I got prayed for. They even laid hands on me, and nothing changed! So now what do I do? Doesn't God love me? Is my sin too great? Maybe God picks and chooses whom He wants to heal. It did not work. I am going to quit believing that healing works today. It is my lot to suffer with this thing. I am so discouraged."*

Sound familiar? Is there an answer to this dilemma? Can I get healed? The answer to these questions is *yes!* You can get healed because it is God's will to heal you, and He has laid out *many paths* to healing in the Bible which we are going to explore. We are going to make this extremely practical, meaning we will teach you how to travel these various paths of healing that God has laid out until you reach your goal of walking in divine health.

So relax, sit back, and enjoy as you dive into this book. Ask the Spirit to quicken to your heart and mind the things He would have you learn and apply as you read. Apply them. Since healing often comes in layers, you can scan this book again and again, asking the Lord to highlight additional concepts He wants you to give attention to. You will receive new insights every time through. His light of revelation will shine brighter and brighter in your heart (Prov. 4:18). Your life will be more and more vibrant as you continually walk more fully in His ongoing revelation (2 Pet. 1:19).

So enjoy the party. Enjoy the process, for life is a process. Always has been. Always will be. Therefore, celebrate the process, so your life is *fun!*

Come on, let's get started and see what we can find out. When you discover a new truth to apply, *stop* and apply the truth before going on. Let His light burst out through you in one more beautiful way.

OK, let the journey begin!

As believers, Jesus has equipped us with various powers for healing.

God provides many ways of healing which we will explore in this book. Above all, remember that an intimate relationship with Jesus is God's number-one priority (Matt. 7:21-23).

> And He called the twelve together, and gave them **power** [*duna-mis*] and **authority** [*exousia*] over **all the demons** and to **heal** [*therapeuo*] **diseases**. And He sent them out to proclaim the **kingdom of God** and to perform **healing** [*iaomai*] (Lk. 9:1-2 NASB95).

> God has appointed in the church...miracles [*dunamis*], then gifts of healings [*iama*] (1 Cor. 12:28 NASB95).

The most obvious insight that stands out in the above verses is that there are *multiple ways* to get healed. I can go after a miracle; and if I do not receive one, then I explore the various gifts of healings available to me. *Both* "gifts" and "healings" are in the *plural* in 1 Corinthians 12:28, meaning there is a good variety of ways to be healed.

- The Greek words describing healing show sickness is a multi-strand problem requiring a multi-strand solution. In the supplements of this book, we offer an exhaustive examination of *each* of the eight Greek words used to describe the healing process. Each word appears to have a slightly different shade of meaning, although there is overlap among them.
- There must be a reason and value in God providing gifts of healings rather than simply miracles. What are these reasons? Why would He do this?
- What is required of me to experience the various modalities of healing God has provided?

It is best if you cover the entire book and then come back to it using it as a resource manual, reviewing sections to help you become more adept in various ministry situations.

- The chapters in the book have more of a topical and story format, so focus on these if that is your best way of learning.
- The supplements are arranged as neatly organized exhaustive Greek word searches, so focus there if that is the learning style you prefer.

Why did I write this book?

I wrote it because I did not feel my prayers for healing and miracles were getting the same results as Jesus, the One I am imitating. Since I believe the Bible is meant to be lived, I felt led to examine the Gospels one more time to see if I could discover what I was missing.

Well, two big things I discovered were: 1) my appraisal concerning the speed and the approach Jesus was using to get people healed was not quite accurate and needed adjusting, and 2) I could become more effective with healing prayer if I saw the biblical basis for the various ways Jesus healed and was comfortable in using them myself. These are things we are going to explore in-depth.

This book is *not* the final word on healing.

"The secret things belong to the Lord our God, but the things revealed belong to us and to our sons forever, that we may observe all the words of this law" (Deut. 29:29 NASB95). Believe and receive the truths revealed to us, and accept that we will never know everything God knows.

Why do I use repetition in this book?

You will note that I repeat the idea of *tuning to flow* over and over and over. Jesus did the same thing as He reiterated over and over that He did nothing on His own initiative but only what He heard and saw His Father doing (Jn. 5:19-20,30; 8:26,38,42; 10:18; 12:49; 14:10; 16:13).

Jesus was speaking to a Middle Eastern culture that did not worship rationalism (reliance on reason), and yet Jesus still felt the need to say again and again, "You don't live out of your reason; you tune to the Father's words and visions." In the Western world, we cannot say this too often as we are completely breaking from the false God of rationalism, where they believe "we can be like God, *knowing* good from evil." This, of course, is satan's lie in the Garden (Gen. 3:5).

So let's celebrate repetition and let it do its work of releasing us from the worship of the false god of rationalism!

I find that even right-brained believers are challenged by the idea that they should tune to flow before they claim a promise in the Bible. That is, they should *allow God to show them* which promise they are to be claiming at the moment they are in. However, upon reflection, they will agree that indeed they have done that throughout their lives, even though they may have never stated this as a principle about how they pray.

Abraham, the Father of Faith, did not just grab a promise to believe. God spoke the promise to him and then gave Abraham the specific vision of the promise fulfilled (Gen. 12:1-3; 15:5-6).

Satan tempted Jesus in the wilderness by suggesting He claim this promise from the Word:

And he led Him to Jerusalem and had Him stand on the pinnacle of the temple, and said to Him, "If You are the Son of God, throw Yourself down from here; for it is written, 'He will command His angels concerning You to guard You,' and, 'On their hands they will bear You up, so that You will not strike Your foot against a stone'" (Lk. 4:9-11 NASB95).

Jesus refused to take the bait, as it would have meant *claiming the wrong promise.* The right Word from God for Jesus to claim was this: "It is said, 'You shall not put the Lord your God to the test'" (Lk. 4:12 NASB95).

The actual instruction that Jesus had received from God and was living at that point was this: Jesus was "led around by the Spirit in the wilderness for forty days, being tempted by the devil" (Lk. 4:1-2 NASB95).

How many times have you heard a Christian recommend that we claim that from the Spirit?

So, yes, I repeat myself over and over and over. "Lord, let us see and declare that *we live and walk **by the Spirit**, not by the memorized Scriptures we pull out of the hat* when we feel we need them." *God* must be Lord of all, including showing us what Scriptures to claim at a given time. When the Spirit reveals Scriptures to us, they look very different than man's interpretation of Scripture. Consider how Jesus opened the Scriptures to the disciples on the Emmaus Road, and they saw everything in an entirely new light (Lk. 24), or how Jesus re-interpreted Paul's theology on the Damascus Road, and Paul completely reversed his thinking and actions (Acts 9).

Why does this book have so many endnotes?

Since I have written numerous books on healing over 30 years or more, I recognize many of the readers of this book will have read some of these previous books. I don't want to bore them by repeating all that information to them and making this book extremely long and cumbersome. On the other hand, I don't want new readers to miss important principles and truths. So I simply provide an endnote as to where an interested reader can go to explore a point more in-depth should they desire to do so.

You will also find an endnote for "Going Deeper" at the end of each chapter. If you want to read more about something discussed in that chapter, please refer to the articles I've referenced there.

My favorite translation of the Bible:

I love the New American Standard Bible and it is what is used predominantly throughout this book. Occasionally I refer to the King James Version, New King James Version, Young's Literal Translation, and The Passion Translation.

Chapter 1

Testimonies of Various Ways God Heals

Please read Supplements A and B for foundational background research that aligns with this chapter:

- Supplement A: Opening the Door to God's Blessings Through Salvation
- Supplement B: Receiving Authority (*Exousia*) from God

Instantaneous Miracles versus Process Healing

Maybe you believe a healing from God must be an instantaneous miracle. At one time I believed that. I also heard that if you did not get healed, it was because you had a lack of faith or sin in your life, or God had some purpose in your remaining sick. Wow! I wonder how many of those ideas are correct.

Is it possible that God uses many methods to heal, and I would do well to be aware of these various approaches and open to God using them so I can cooperate and move in the direction He is guiding me?

Let's begin by hearing some stories of ways God has healed me and my friends.

God speaks concerning steps in health and healing—journaling by Linda Garmon.

"Lord, what are the desires and dreams You have for my health? Am I seeing them, pondering them, speaking them, and acting on them as You desire me to?"

Jesus: "Beloved, My desire for you is that you will live out your days on this earth and fulfill every page that I have written about your life, that your earth life would not be cut short or hindered by disease and pain, for this is part of redemption. My desire is also for us to walk this walk together which requires your participation and sometimes your compliance and submission. Know this, beloved, that satan desires to mute your voice and hinder your walk or stop you in any way he can. Don't be ignorant or indifferent to his devices and tactics. Be vigilant!

"We are partners in this walk. This means you are required to do your part. Listen if I tell you, 'Stop this or start this' or 'Take a break from this.' When you go for your annual physical, ask Me first before accepting any medications, vaccines, or injections of any kind. Do whatever is in your power to walk in divine health, rather than depending on divine healing. If you need healing, that is available to you, but it will still be maintained by doing what you know and learning what you do not know. So learn all you can. Be good stewards."

Forgiving from the heart brought healing to a "pain in the neck."

As I (Mark Virkler) finished a Sunday evening teaching on healing, we began praying for one another for healing. I had everyone in the church break into groups of three to five and pray for a person in their group who had a physical need. I joined a group near the back of the church, and we prayed for a young lady who had pain in her back and shoulder. We had prayed three times for her, and each time she had improved a little bit. I had told people that as long as there was some improvement occurring, pray a second, third, and fourth time.

As we finished the third round of praying and asked for a report, she said, "The pain in my back and shoulder is gone, but I still have this pain in my neck." Well, that triggered the recall of a colloquialism, so I asked the question, "Is there someone in your life who is a 'pain in the neck'?" I could see from the tears beginning to well up in her eyes that this was a word of knowledge that could release the fullness of God's miracle-working power to her.

She nodded yes. I asked, "Are you willing to forgive this person?" and again she nodded yes. I asked if she would like me to lead her in a prayer of forgiveness, and once more she nodded yes. I told her to *picture the person she needed to forgive* and repeat this prayer after me:

"Lord, I choose by Your power and grace to forgive this person in Jesus' name. I ask You to circumcise my heart, remove the pain and broken- ness, and give me a new heart and a new spirit." (Pause...) "Lord, I choose to release this person. I choose to honor him; I choose to bless him in Jesus' name."

Healed: Then we laid hands on her for a fourth time and prayed for healing. Moments later she reported all pain was gone and went to the front of the church to testify about her healing.

Reflection: We needed to refocus healing prayer from praying about the infirmity that was manifest in the body to discovering and removing the underlying emotional roots (in this case, unforgiveness).

How I got from there to here, by Uta Milewski (an example of process healing).

I am intimately aware of what it feels like to struggle to draw life-giv- ing breath into my lungs. This is how I lived for much of the past four decades, but it is not how I live anymore. I want to share my story of how God healed me. This is not a story of instant healing but of my journey in seeking and finding wisdom and grace from the Lord.

In my mid-twenties, I developed allergies and asthma, which eventu- ally resulted in chronic bronchitis (COPD), a health condition that only grows worse rather than improving. Once, I was fighting pneumonia but refused to go to the hospital because I was nursing a baby. I became so weak that my husband Bob had to give me mouth-to-mouth resuscita- tion to keep me alive. Even without the added difficulty of pneumonia, I couldn't breathe if the air was too cold. The simple joy of laughter made me cough.

I tried jogging to get some exercise and improve my health, but I was unable to go more than a few yards before my lungs gave out. I was grateful for Flovent and Proventil inhalers because they enabled me to lead a normal life when I didn't have a cold. In order for them to help me, I had to use them every day without fail, both morning and night. Whenever I caught a cold, my respiratory system overreacted terribly, and it took me weeks to recover, in spite of the meds.

Once I began working in the office of Love Joy Church, I determined not to let sickness keep me from passionately serving the Lord. Countless people, including Pastor Ron Burgio, prayed for me to be healed. On several occasions, I thought God had answered our prayers and healed me because I could go a few days without the medications. Sadly, my respiratory struggles always returned. I continued to pray and read the Bible to find strength for my fight. On many occasions, God used a Bible verse to pull me out of my pit, but my health struggles continued. I wanted God to heal me instantly. I had seen Him heal others, so why not me?

Dr. Mark Virkler once said something to me about asking God for healing that I took to heart, and it changed my life. He said, "If God healed you, but you continued to do the same thing that harms your health, what good would it do?" I realized that I was not taking very good care of myself. I did not make wise choices regarding my food, rest, exercise, or strengthening my immune system through supplements. After struggling with chronic bronchitis for nearly 30 years and asking God for instantaneous healing, I began praying a different prayer: Lord, give me wisdom for becoming healthy.

This new focus on praying for wisdom caused me to make wiser decisions regarding my health. I started going to the chiropractor and doing Pilates. After recognizing that swimming was easier on my lungs than jogging, I began praying for a place to swim that was along my commuting route. Soon, I learned about a new YMCA that would be opening halfway between work and home. I signed up before it opened and began swimming three times a week.

Soon, Bob joined the YMCA as well, and we expanded my exercise program to include the stationary bikes, even though I could not go more than two miles at a time. I began searching for breathing techniques for improving lung function in asthmatics, and I found the Buteyko method. This technique involves taking in slow breaths through the nose rather than hyperventilating through the mouth during exercise or an asthma attack.

After retraining myself in this technique, I was able to stop using Proventil. I learned that embracing the discipline necessary to begin swimming, riding a stationary bike (even if I couldn't go very far yet), and new breathing techniques gave me power I never realized I possessed. Soon I joined a cycling group at the YMCA and continued to become stronger.

After a few years, I no longer suffered from asthma attacks unless I got a cold or bronchial infection. I improved enough that even in the frigid weather of Buffalo, New York, I was able to help Bob shovel the snow from our long driveway. I still used Flovent twice a day to control my lung inflammation.

As I continued praying for wisdom, I considered the connection between the burning in my lungs and my food choices. I noticed that my lungs felt better when I fasted for a few days. When my doctor conducted a blood test for food allergens, I found out that I was highly allergic to cow's milk. Why had no one ever suggested that to me before? I practically lived on cheese, yogurt, and cereal with milk.

I started following a strict dairy-free diet, and it made a huge difference for me. My lungs improved so much that I was able to reduce the Flovent to once a day. In November of 2019, I caught a cold and the infection went into my lungs. It took two months to clear up. The pandemic hit in 2020, which motivated me to start taking multivitamins and D3 to strengthen my immune system. Even though my lung health placed me in the vulnerable population during the pandemic, when I had COVID in November 2020, it did not affect me as much as the common cold I experienced twelve months earlier. This was thanks to the new wise choices I had implemented.

Because we have now moved into an apartment in Indiana, one of the benefits is no longer having to shovel snow from the driveway like we did in Buffalo. However, an even better selling point for the apartment is the stationary bikes that are available in the fitness room on the first floor. Remember that initially I couldn't manage more than two miles? Now I am able to ride almost eight miles a day, five days a week.

The final piece of the puzzle came in April of 2023. To lose a little weight, I started to reduce my intake of refined sugar and carbs. Within a few weeks, I was surprised to find my lung inflammation had lessened greatly. As my breathing function continued to improve, I had days when I forgot to use my inhaler. Bob and I like to go for walks in the park behind our apartment. Before, the steepness of some of the hills along the path forced me to stop in order to catch my breath. I still remember how difficult this path used to be for me, but now I am able to walk right alongside Bob while breathing normally.

My story may not be as shocking or dramatic as an instant healing, but I still see it as a gift from an amazing God. I also believe the fact that my healing took place over decades causes me to be even more grateful than if God had instantly healed me 40 years ago. The appearance of the number 40 in the Bible often indicates a season of testing. God sent rain on Noah for 40 days and nights. The Israelites wandered in the desert for 40 years. Jonah preached that Nineveh had 40 days before God would destroy them. Jesus fasted and fought temptation for 40 days in the wilderness. I wonder if I finally passed my "forty" test.

Skeptics may refute my story and say that God didn't heal me at all. They may say that I could have made all of those changes without prayer or intervention from God. I don't think so. I needed God's all-sufficient grace to be with me all of those years. I needed the encouragement of preaching, Bible reading, friends, and prayer to keep from growing despondent. God is the one who made the impossible possible.

I'm now 68 and still feel amazing! In fact, I feel better now than 40 years ago.

Uta Milewski
Check out Uta's ebook: *God's Heart for You*[1]

Misdiagnosis meant my pain did *not* go away.

Testimony received in an email: While the doctor diagnosed the pain in my shoulders as an overuse of my shoulders, the Lord revealed that it was an "overuse" of my mind/thoughts, sending me spinning over anxieties and fears, deferred hopes, and self-expectations. Through prayer, the great weight and entanglement I have been carrying on my shoulders were lifted off as I released these things to God.

Mark's reflections: Life *only* works if you are hearing and responding to God's voice. He is a Wonderful Counselor Who provides wonderful counsel that heals the anxieties of the heart and mind and restores one to joy and peace. "The kingdom of God is...righteousness and *peace* and *joy* in the *Holy Spirit*" (Rom. 14:17 NASB95).

Notice the centrality of needing to receive revelation?

In the above stories, we discovered that receiving and acting on divine revelation was **key** to receiving healing. Psychologists believe 75 percent of illness has an emotional root, so I turn to the Wonderful Counselor to help me discern this emotional root and remove it, so that His healing power can flow. This should take care of 75 percent of illness!

How about a "prescription": Master the skill of living by the Spirit.

It was quite a battle for me to learn to hear God's voice, see His visions, and receive His revelation so I could live by the Spirit (Gal. 5:25). It is not hard to do. It is very easy. It is just that it is completely different than what my culture and religious background taught me.

This means I had to identify the lies I had been taught, repent of them, rebuke them, replace them with truth, and then learn the skill of walking in this new way of living, which the Bible calls walking by the Spirit (Gal. 5:16,25).

Thankfully, it will not take you anywhere near as much time as it took me, as I have written about what I needed to learn.[2] I guarantee that your life can become fun, meaningful, and joyful! Mine has!

Life is far too precious to squander in fear, anxiety, and pain. What I learned *will* remove the emotional and spiritual strain and pressure in your life and train you to walk by the Spirit.

Wow! Do I want to invest nine months?

In order to master the skills, you need to spend three months learning and integrating each of them. Guess what? You are going to be nine months older nine months from now whether you embrace this teaching or not! Why not learn to *let Jesus heal your heart and mind* over the next nine months, so the rest of your life you can experience His Kingdom realities of righteousness, joy, and peace in the Holy Spirit? You will discover healing springing up through your spirit, soul, and body and then out through your relationships. That is what has happened in my life.

This could be an even better learning experience if you opened your home to your family and friends, watched a video each week, and did the exercises together, praying and ministering life one to another. Why not spark a revival in people's lives and bring transformation to your family and friends? This can even be done through a Zoom group that meets weekly.

There is health and healing in experiencing God's names:

*For I am the Lord, I **do not change*** (Mal. 3:6 NKJV).

*Jesus Christ is **the same** yesterday and today and forever* (Heb. 13:8 NASB95).

Let's review the four keys to hearing God's voice:

These allow anyone to have two-way conversations daily with God, which are captured in two-way journaling (Hab. 2:1-2).

1. **Stillness**: Quiet myself in the presence of God (Isa. 30:15; Eccl. 5:1-2; Ps. 4:4; 46:10; 62:5).
2. **Look for vision**: Picture Jesus Who is present with me (Heb. 12:1; Matt. 28:20; Eph. 1:17-18; Ps. 16:8; Acts 2:25).
3. **Spirit flow**: Recognize His Spirit which is flowing as a River within me and sensed as flowing thoughts, flowing pictures, flowing emotions, flowing physical sensations which light upon me, and flowing power (Jn. 4:14; 7:37-39; Jer. 2:13; Rev. 22:1-2).
4. **Record and act**: In faith, write down what I am receiving and act on it (Hab. 2:2; Rev. 1:9-11). (In live situations you may simply act without first writing things down.)

Summary: I quiet myself down, picture Jesus at my right hand, ask for His input, tune to flowing thoughts and pictures and emotions and feelings, and journal these out using childlike faith.[3]

Another way to state the four keys is: 1) Stop, 2) Look, 3) Listen, 4) Write. Many people in Scripture used these four keys (including Jesus), and together they wrote more than half the Bible.[4] So these four keys are the *standard* biblical protocol for communing with God.

We have provided you with a free download called "Sea of Galilee."[5] This is a five-minute visualized walk with Jesus, where we guide you into stillness, seeing yourself present with Jesus, tuning to flow, and writing down His flowing thoughts and pictures. Let us take you by the hand and coach you into using these four wonderful, biblical keys to set up your morning devotions so you are easily hearing from Him. Soft music will continue to play as you journal out what Jesus is speaking to you.

Going Deeper[6] and Journaling Application

- Lord, what would You speak to me?
- Lord, please remind me of some instantaneous healings in my life as well as some process (therapeutic) healings.
- Lord, what would You speak to me about healing?
- Record what God speaks in a separate notebook or file.

Chapter 2

Instantaneous Miracles Versus Process Healing

Please read Supplements C and D for foundational background research that aligns with this chapter:

- Supplement C: *Dunamis* Is the Power of God and Is Occasionally Translated as "Miracle"
- Supplement D: *Iaomai* and *Iama* Are Words for Power Healing

As you go through the supplements, ask God for His revelation as to what the distinctions are between these various words. See what you get. I believe there are *overlaps* between them, but also *distinctions* between them. It is a fascinating and faith-building meditation to review these supplements.

The Word "Miracle"

Some people are healed instantly through a miracle. I was shocked to discover that there is no specific Greek word for "miracle." The word translated "miracle" is the word *dunamis,* which is most often translated as "power," and only *occasionally* translated as a "miracle." In addition, *semeion* is *occasionally* translated as "a miracle," although normally *semeion* is translated as "a sign." Young's Literal Translation *never* translates *dunamis* or *semeion* as a "miracle." Instead, Young uses the phrase, "a mighty work," or something similar.

How often does the word "miracle(s)" appear in various translations?

- Young's Literal Translation: 0 times (translates *dunamis* and *semeion* as "power" and "sign" respectively)
- King James Version: 37 times
- New King James Version: 16 times (wow, cut it in half!)
- New American Standard Bible: 28 times (splits the difference between KJV and NKJV)
- The Passion Translation: 192 times (wow, over the top!)

Note how Young's Literal Translation handles *miracles* and *gifts of healings* (1 Cor. 12:28):

- New American Standard Bible: "then miracles, then gifts of healings"
- Young's Literal Translation: "afterwards *powers*, afterwards gifts of healings"

Young's replaces the word "miracles" with "powers." In both translations, the words "gifts" and "healings" are each in the *plural*, meaning there are many ways to get healed, so I surely should not reduce healing to one or two approaches. That would be cutting off God's grace for healing me in additional ways that He has prepared.

Translating *dunamis* or *semeion* into the word "miracle" is a *subjective* determination and not something agreed upon by the translators.

It certainly seems like there is a lot I need to learn about power miracles, and *my biggest discovery* was that in one location, Jesus was not able to do any miracles. We will explore why this happened in the next chapter.

There are two main words translated as "healing." They are:

1. *Iaomai* (various forms, 32 occurrences): a few times declared as *instantaneous* healing, which would be powered by *dunamis*. The fact that a few of the healings specifically state they were instantaneous makes one think these were unique and different from the other healings

that took place. Perhaps the others were more progressive. For example, when I used inner healing prayer to remove the anger that was causing my arthritis, my testimony is that I was healed. The arthritis pain left my body! The fuller version of my story is that 50 percent of my pain was gone within one day and all of it was gone within a week. So my statement that I was healed was not wrong; it just didn't include all the details concerning the timing of the disappearance of the symptoms. When covering 33 years of Jesus' life in a Gospel you can read in an hour or two, you are certainly going to be leaving out some details.

2. *Therapeuo* (various forms, 48 occurrences): "therapeutic," more often can be a *process* of healing. There are two unique modalities which are mentioned with *therapeuo* and *never mentioned* with *iaomai*. They are:

- **Anointing with *oil*** (Mk. 6:13 NASB95)—could this include "essential oils"?
- ***Leaves* that bring healing** (Rev. 22:2 NASB95)—could this include "herbalism"?

In addition, laying on of hands (Lk. 4:40) is mentioned much more often in the context of *therapeuo* than in the context of *iaomai*. Question: Could chiropractic perhaps be included within the category of laying on of hands?

Seventeen times as Jesus heals, the Greek word being translated is *therapeuo*. I am not aware of any statement in the New Testament saying *therapeutic* healings were instantaneous. Please refer to Supplement E, especially the very beginning, for an extended Greek definition of *therapeuo*.

When the Stated Story Is Not the *Whole* Story: An Assignment to Complete

When I read in the Gospels that Jesus healed, I assume that is the entire story because that is what is stated. I suppose that Jesus spoke or laid on hands or whatever, and the person was immediately healed. Well, that is not necessarily the case. The Gospel writers were cramming a 33-year life into a few short chapters, so chances are good that details have been left out.

Let's explore the story of the crucifixion, for example. To answer the questions below, you may want to chart all details mentioned in each of the four Gospels and then note what each Gospel writer added or skipped as they told the story.

- Matthew's version of what happened at the crucifixion is recorded in Matthew 27:32-52. Please read it and list each main detail. So, you would think this is the whole story, right?
- Mark's version of what happened at the crucifixion is recorded in Mark 15:21-41. What new details do we discover?
- Luke's version of what happened at the crucifixion is recorded in Luke 23:32-49. What new details do we discover?
- John's version of what happened at the crucifixion is recorded in John 19:16-37. What new details do we discover?

Now that you see the fuller story, does it help you see that these abbreviated stories in the Gospels are only a portion of all that happened? Each author is only putting in the details they sense are important for their readers to read, and each Gospel is written to a different audience. When you put them all together, do you get a fuller picture of the crucifixion event? Do you think that there may still be details beyond what the four Gospel writers describe?[1]

Should I assume this same principle is true when it says, "Jesus healed everyone"? *Would it be wise to understand that statement as a summary of what happened and that there is a lot of detail being left out?* Does it explain the exact approach Jesus took in healing them? Does it describe if Jesus used different methods with different people? Does that statement tell how long it took for each person to be healed? Does it detail if part of the healing was instantaneous and part appeared the next day or the next week? Should I be making assumptions when there are no details to back them up?

Journaling Questions

Lord, what do You want to speak to me concerning the stories I read in the Bible? How am I to look at them? How am I to understand them? Can I understand them through my reasoning alone, or do I need Your revelation? Do I need You to "open Scriptures to me" just as You did the disciples on the Emmaus Road?

Deliverance and oil are classed as *therapeutic*:

*Who had come to hear Him and to be healed [iaomai] of their diseases; and those who were troubled with unclean spirits were being **cured** [therapeuo] (Lk. 6:18 NASB95).*

*Then a demon-possessed man who was blind and mute was brought to Jesus, and He **healed** [therapeuo] him, so that the mute man spoke and saw (Matt. 12:22 NASB95).*

Jesus used *therapeuo* to heal every kind of disease:

*And large crowds came to Him, bringing with them those who were lame, crippled, blind, mute, and many others, and they laid them down at His feet; and He **healed** [therapeuo] them (Matt. 15:30 NASB95).*

Deliverance and anointing with oil were intertwined with *therapeuo* healing:

*And they were casting out many demons and were anointing with oil many sick people and **healing** [therapeuo] them (Mk. 6:13 NASB95).*

Here is an example of Paul doing *two* types of healing in the same situation:

- When shipwrecked on the island of Malta, Paul laid his hands on the father of Publius and healed (*iaomai*) him (Acts 28:8 NKJV). This appears to be an *instantaneous healing.*

- The rest of those on the island who had diseases also came and were healed (*therapeuo*, Acts 28:9 NKJV).

Wow, two different Greek words for healing are being used in the *same* story! This releases us from the pressure that we *must* see an instantaneous miracle.

If we consider healing as encompassing *both instantaneous* miracles *(iaomai)* and *process* healing *(therapeuo)*, then there is no need for a person to be healed instantaneously.[2] It could be either way: a process healing or an instantaneous miracle. That resolves the issue that we need to see 100 percent quick results. I am not aware of anyone who is getting 100 percent immediate results in healing prayer. I sure am not.

If you put your body, soul, and spirit in a healing mode, then God's healing power (*energeo*[3]) is flowing, and the healing/miracle *will* manifest in its own time. This takes the pressure off me expecting that I must get an instant miracle. Instead, I would be saying, "When I put myself in a healing posture, the process of healing *is at work!*"

The posture for both types of healing (miracle and therapeutic) is identical.

If the above premise is true, then I would never walk away from a healing service disappointed that I was not healed. I would understand that healing comes in many forms. I would understand that God has miracles and gifts of healings. The gifts of healings include *therapeuo* healings, which incorporate a host of ways God uses to release healing into my being. We will suggest 28 such remedies in Chapter 11.

So with this in mind, I leave the service excited to spend some time asking God what specific gift of healing He has in mind for me to pursue. As I listen in the Spirit with faith that He does have some wonderful approach in store for me to complete, He explains which gift of healing is appropriate and the steps He would have me take to begin the process. I celebrate these words of wisdom and words of knowledge and begin actively working them out in faith and obedience.

If I get stuck, I do what the Bible says. I go to the elders of the church and together we explore the situation, discovering any sins that are blocking the healing and repenting of them, so that the effective prayer of a righteous man can avail much, and God's healing *dunamis* power flows freely and heals me (Jas. 5:14-16).

This is certainly a whole lot better than walking away from a healing service saying, "I didn't get healed. Why doesn't God love me? Is He playing favorites?" Instead, I am walking away filled with faith that God loves me and has one of His gifts of healings (therapeutic cures) in store for me, and by listening to His Spirit and acting on what He says, healing will flow!

So why is God offering "gifts of healings" rather than a quick, fast miracle?

I suppose there are a lot of answers to this question. Let me offer a few.

Fear made the Israelites wander for 40 years rather than inherit their Promised Land.

When God promised them a land flowing with milk and honey and offered to go before them and prepare the way, they instead listened to bad reports from ten spies. Rather than stepping out in faith, fear ruled, and they were afraid to enter into their inheritance. So they returned from the edge of entering into their Promised Land and entered back into the wilderness to wander for 40 years.

I believe God's promise to heal our bodies (Isa. 53:5) is part of our Promised Land blessings. So what keeps us from entering in?

Fear made me disobedient.

I had a sore back that took *many weeks* to heal. When I asked the Lord to heal it instantly, He clearly said He would not. He said if He did heal it instantly, I would go right back to doing the activity I had been doing that made it sore in the first place. You see, He had earlier told me to quit that activity; but I would not, because it was the way I was currently earning an income.

The Lord had told me to stop it and trust Him to provide. I refused to stop because of *fear*. Therefore, He said it would be a slow healing so *I could learn to obey and trust Him*. So, yes, it was slow; and yes, I learned to obey and trust; and yes, my back did ultimately heal.

Unforgiveness blocks healing.

It is hard to forgive when someone dishes out a *big* hurt to your life. One of my biggest hurts was being fired from the pastoral staff of a large church where I worked. The termination seemed unfair and was extremely abrupt. A call came in at 10:00 at night, and one of the senior-level pastoral staff members invited me to breakfast the next morning.

At breakfast, I sat with three men from the Board, and they informed me they had terminated my job at the church and wanted my office cleared out that day! Talk about anger, rage, and unforgiveness. I cleared out my office and hated them all.

Six months later, I had arthritis in my knuckles and knees (age 40). I realized it was because of my pent-up anger. I prayed and forgave them, but I still hated them. After repeating that cycle several times, I realized that prayer was not working, so I did an *inner healing prayer* in my morning devotions.

I *pictured* the restaurant table, with the three men and me. Using the eyes of my heart I looked around for Jesus. Jesus appeared in the picture (vision) laughing and saying, "Don't you know I set this whole thing up? I have told you for two years to get on the road and teach communion with God and you wouldn't go; so I just threw you out of the nest, so you could learn to fly and get on with fulfilling My destiny for your life."

Jesus went on to say, "You can see them as evil men or as instruments in My hand thrusting you into the fulfillment of your destiny. The first picture will make your spirit, soul, body, and ministry shrivel up. The second picture will cause your spirit, soul, body, and ministry to grow and expand. You get to choose which picture you will gaze upon."

I chose to look at those three men in the scene in my mind's eye as we were sitting around the restaurant table and say to them, "I choose to forgive you, to honor you, to bless you in Jesus' name. Thank you for thrusting me forward into the fulfillment of my destiny."

Within 24 hours of this inner healing devotional prayer exercise, 50 percent of my arthritic pain was gone and within a week it was all gone. I am now 72 with no arthritic pain. Yay, God!

The principles for this kind of deep, heart forgiveness include:

1. Re-enter the scene where the hurt happened.
2. Ask Jesus to show you where He is and what He is saying and doing.
3. Tune to flowing thoughts and flowing pictures and record what Jesus says and does.
4. Act in obedience to what Jesus is showing and speaking.

Definition of *when* a hurt is healed:

Memorize this golden nugget: *A hurt is healed when God has shown you the gift He has produced in your life through the experience.*

The gift He showed me in this situation was that the church leaders threw me out of the nest when I was afraid I could not fly, and I discovered I could fly and that they had propelled me into the fulfillment of my destiny. Always ask God to *show you the gift* (Rom. 8:28), and then post that gift at eyeball level and purpose to *only* look at that new picture from this point on. *Never* gaze back at the old picture (the scene where *Jesus was not present*) which produced sickness and death within you, as that contains a lie, which is "Jesus wasn't there." Picturing a lie is an unbiblical imagination.

The above two—fear and unforgiveness—are the biggies that either block or promote miracle-working *dunamis* to flow. The next chapter will explore these two things in more depth. We must move from fear to faith and from anger to love.

Biblical Examples of Process Healing

The blind man whom Jesus prayed for was fully healed after *two* prayers (Mk. 8:22-26). I can also expect that some healings will take more than one prayer to get the job done.

The tree that was cursed showed nothing immediately, but the next day they observed it had died from its *roots up* (Mk. 11:12-14, 20-26). Therefore, when I pray, I can pray for the root cause to be removed and expect that the manifestation of that will occur in time.

When I prayed and asked Jesus to heal an abnormal heart rhythm that I was experiencing, Jesus said, "It is healed." However, my Kardia testing unit said I still had possible AFib. I asked the Lord how I was to handle this apparent discrepancy. His answer was, "Mark, speak this: My heart beats in perfect sinus rhythm, and the symptoms are disappearing." Notice He did not want me to even use the negative word "AFib." This is what I have done as I believe for the full manifestation of this healing, along with taking any nutrition I have discovered that helps strengthen the heart and, of course, exercising to build and restore the heart muscle and focusing on peace and joy and laughter.

What would be the value of a "process healing" rather than a miracle?

If a smoker is instantly healed of lung cancer and continues to smoke, he will likely develop lung cancer again. Part of healing is establishing the discipline of changed behavior so that any behavior that contributed to the infirmity is removed from our lives and we do not draw the infirmity back to us.

When a demon that has been cast out comes back to see if "his house" is filled with the Holy Spirit or not and finds it not filled, the demon re-enters with seven worse demons (Matt. 12:43-45).

When it comes to claiming God's promises to us, we need to be sensitive to what God is perfecting in us at the same time. The Israelites had a prophetic word from God that He had given them the Promised Land

(Exod. 12:25). However, they were forced to wander in the wilderness for 40 years, because they needed to learn to *believe* that God could and would supernaturally provide for them.

When the spies came back with a report of the giants in the land, they were moved by fear, not faith. Without faith, it is impossible to please God (Heb. 11:6). They ended up failing ten tests in the wilderness (Num. 14:22), so those who were trained to fear needed to die out, and a new generation of people who had seen God's supernatural provision every day for 40 years (manna) could arise. They would have the faith to conquer the territory that God had promised was their land.

If God has promised healing and I am living in fear and doubt, then the *dunamis* power of God which provides the miracle will be hindered by my lack of faith, and, once again, Jesus will be able to do no miracle because of my unbelief.

Once faith is established, we go forward into battle, believing God is with us and being guided by His voice.

We take our land through commissioning, believing, and acting. We are told to be strong and courageous. Be very courageous. Do not turn to the side. Meditate day and night on God's words and do them. Here is the *exact commission* given to Joshua.

> *Now it came about after the death of Moses the servant of the Lord, that the Lord spoke to Joshua the son of Nun, Moses' servant, saying, "Moses My servant is dead; now therefore arise, cross this Jordan, you and all this people, to the land which I am giving to them, to the sons of Israel. **Every place on which the sole of your foot treads, I have given it to you**, just as I spoke to Moses. From the wilderness and this Lebanon, even as far as the great river, the river Euphrates, all the land of the Hittites, and as far as the Great Sea toward the setting of the sun will be your territory. No man will be able to stand before you all the days of your life.*

*Just as I have been with Moses, **I will be with you**; I will not fail you or forsake you. Be strong and courageous, for you shall give this people possession of the land which I swore to their fathers to give them. Only **be strong and very courageous**; be careful to do according to all the law which Moses My servant commanded you; do not turn from it to the right or to the left, so that you may have success wherever you go. This book of the law shall not depart from your mouth, but you shall meditate on it day and night, so that you may be careful to do according to all that is written in it; for then **you** will make your way prosperous, and then you will have success. Have I not commanded you? Be strong and courageous! Do not tremble or be dismayed, for the Lord your God is **with you** wherever you go"* (Josh. 1:5-9 NASB95).

Thankfully, God is *with us* today, everywhere we go. He is Immanuel, God with us (Matt. 1:23; 28:20).

Going Deeper[4] and Journaling Application

Lord, what would You speak to me:

- About miracles and process healing?
- About inner healing?
- About my confession concerning health and healing?
- Record what God speaks.

Chapter 3

Faith and Love: Important Keys to Experiencing *Dunamis* Power

Please read Supplement E: "*Therapeuo* Healing Is More Often *Process* Healing" for foundational background research that aligns with this chapter.

Therapeuo Healing

Therapeutic healing can often be a process but is sometimes instantaneous. Verses with *therapeuo* in them specifically mention the following: laying on of hands, anointing with oil, and leaves which bring healing. We get the word *therapeutic* from this word, so it involves various remedies, which we can easily classify under the category of "gifts of healings." In other places in the Bible, we find recommended many additional cures and remedies.

When we are gathered together as the body of Christ, we pray for people's needs, and these include healings and miracles we wish to take place. Sometimes we sense the spark of divine life flowing amongst us. Sometimes we do not.

What is it that increases the flow of *dunamis* healing power, and what is it that hinders this flow? If I know, I can focus on ensuring the right ingredients are present when we gather or when I am involved in pondering Scripture. Let's explore and see what we can discover.

Faith and Love must both be present for miracle-working power to flow.

The picture I have had in my mind of Jesus is that His power is unstoppable! Jesus healed the sick, cast out demons, and raised the dead. The miracle-working power of God flowed through Jesus unhindered, and over and over it says *everyone* was healed (Matt. 4:24; 8:16; 12:15), at least until Jesus returned to His hometown.

When Jesus could *not* do miracles (but He could still do therapeutic cures):

Is it true that Jesus was not able to do a miracle? Yes! When that happens, you want to find out *why*, because whatever stopped Him from being able to do a miracle will also stop us from doing miracles of healing.

> *And He* [Jesus] *could do no* **miracle** [G1411, *dunamis*—instantaneous healing] *there except that He laid His hands on a few sick people and* **healed** [G2323, *therapeuo*—process healing] *them. And He wondered at their unbelief* (Mk. 6:5-6 NASB95).

So power miracles were not working for Jesus, but therapeutic healings were still possible. Therapeutic is like a cure. We find many cures or remedies (therapeutic healings) listed in the Bible. These might be classified under "gifts of healings" (1 Cor. 12:9). Some examples include:

1. Fasting: health springs forth speedily (Isa. 58:6-8 NKJV). While this verse is speaking to spiritual and national healing, there is also no question that physical fasting improves physical health.
2. A merry heart: good like a medicine (Prov. 17:22).
3. A little wine for the stomach's sake (1 Tim. 5:23).

Many more therapeutic healing protocols will be explored in a future chapter.

Dunamis miracle-working power did *not* flow when faith and love were *not* present.

To help us understand the role of faith working by love, let us explore why Jesus could not do any mighty works (*dunamis*) in His hometown

(Mk. 6:1-6). Even though there was the *dunamis* force/power of the Holy Spirit *present in Jesus* to do miracles, this force needed something to interact with. That something is "faith *working through* love" (Gal. 5:6). Note: "working through" is the Greek word *energeo,* which means "energized by." You can read the phrase as "faith *energized by* love." (*Energeo* is explored in-depth in Supplement F of this book.)

Dunamis power is released as it *interacts with faith and love.* So *dunamis* flows when faith and love are present, and these were *not* present in His hometown. They: 1) did not believe, and 2) they took offense at Jesus (i.e., no love), so *no mighty works* occurred.

> *And they **took offense** at Him. Jesus said to them, "A prophet is not without honor except in his hometown and among his own relatives and in his own household." And He could do no **miracle** [dunamis] there except that He laid His hands on a few sick people and **healed** [therapeuo] them. And He **wondered at their unbelief** (Mk. 6:3-6 NASB95).*

Jesus could not get *dunamis* to work because of no faith or love, but *therapeutic approaches were still possible.*

Faith *and* Love must *both* be present for *dunamis* miracles to occur.

Things that can *increase* the flow of *dunamis* power to heal:

1. Our bodies are designed to *heal naturally* if we give them the proper tools (nutrition, hydration, exercise, and Kingdom thinking: love, joy, peace, thankfulness).

2. Additional power is released when we include *believing prayer* and receive what Jesus provides through Calvary—by His stripes we are healed (1 Pet. 2:24).

3. Additional power is released when we are *listening and obedient* to what God is speaking (*rhema*) to us (Jn. 15:7).

4. Additional power is released when *several come together* in agreement (Matt. 18:19).

5. Additional power is released through the *laying on of hands* (Lk. 4:40).

6. Additional power is released when you *go to the elders* of the church and together confess sins and pray for healing (Jas. 5:15-16).

7. Additional power is released through *deliverance* (Acts 5:16) and inner healing, breaking off generational sins and curses, ungodly soul ties, ungodly beliefs, inner vows, and word curses.[1]

Inner alignment speeds you in the direction you are aligned for.

The Lord spoke to me about the power of governing my heart and mind: "Mark, every word you speak, every thought you think, every picture you imagine, and every belief you hold which is contrary to Scripture takes you *backward* rather than *forward* because it is evil, sinful, and wrong."

> *They...walked in the **counsels** and in the **imagination** of their **evil** heart, and went **backward**, and not **forward*** (Jer. 7:24 KJV).

"Mark, to replace these evil imaginations with godly imaginations I ask you to gain My view of life's events, not by listening to non-illumined newscasters but instead by spending your time meditating on My word[2] and communing with Me[3] and listening to My proven prophets. As My pictures fill your heart and mind, you will increase in Kingdom power, Kingdom authority, Kingdom compassion, and Kingdom healing."

God told me to completely align my inner being by:

- **Thinking** *only* what His Word and His Spirit say (about myself, others, and life)
- **Speaking** *only* what His Word and His Spirit say (about myself, others, and life)
- **Picturing** *only* what His Word and His Spirit say (about myself, others, and life)
- **Believing** *only* what His Word and His Spirit say (about myself, others, and life)

- **Feeling** *only* God's heart for the situation at hand (about myself, others, and life)

Examples of evil and godly imaginations:

Even though the hand of God had brought the Israelites miraculously out of Egypt, they seemed to forget His provision for them. When faced with challenges, instead of remembering His care for them in the past, they *imagined* themselves dying in the wilderness (e.g. Ex. 14:11; Ex:16:3, Num. 20:4). Finally, that is exactly what happened.

On the other hand, when David stepped forward to fight Goliath, he called to mind how the Lord had saved him from the lion and the bear in the past. He could clearly see how the Lord would deliver Goliath into his hand and the dead bodies of the Philistine army would be given over to the birds of the sky and the wild animals of the earth (1 Sam. 17).

We have the same choice. If we see only the wickedness that seems to rule, we may imagine a future of turmoil and destruction and we will be overcome by evil. But if instead we remember God's promise that "of the increase of His government and peace there shall be no end" (Isa. 9:7), if we believe it, see it, speak it, and act upon it, He will overcome the darkness.

Worry is simply picturing satan's lies, which produce fear, sickness, and death. We are to be picturing God's truths which produce peace, love, faith, and healing. God promised that *"The steadfast of mind [yester, "imagination" in the Hebrew] You will keep in perfect peace because he trusts in You"* (Isa. 26:3 NASB95).

Yester (H3336) occurs nine times in the Bible. It is defined as "imagination" which "frames up" one's reality. The NASB translates it as "imagination(s)" five times (Gen. 6:5; Deut. 31:21; 1 Chron. 28:9; 29:18) and as "frame(d)" two times (Ps. 103:14; Isa. 29:16).

Therefore, *a steadfast imagination produces an emotional response of perfect peace, which in turn frames up and creates my reality of health and vitality.*[4] It is when our imagination is filled with godly pictures that we live in perfect peace.

We all meditate (ponder, picture, anticipate) all day long. Let's stop meditating on lies that are contrary to the Bible and the Spirit and instead meditate *only* on God's truth. Then we go forward (faith, hope, love, life) rather than backward (fear, hopelessness, anger, death).

It is better to picture Jesus at your right hand (Acts 2:25; Ps. 16:8) than to picture Him *not* there.

It is better to picture yourself as decked out in Christ's robe of righteousness (Phil. 3:9; Eph. 4:24) than to picture yourself as a filthy sinner.

It is better to picture what the Bible says is true than to have an evil imagination and be picturing the opposites and going backward.

The Hebrew word translated as "meditate" in Joshua 1:8 is *hagah* (H1897). It occurs 24 times and includes as part of its meaning "to imagine," according to *Strong's* and *Brown-Driver-Briggs*. So we are to imagine the Bible as our truth, and we live in these imaginations.

The bottom line is that pictures are very powerful. They frame up our reality. They grant us emotional peace, which turns on our immune system, which in turn keeps us healthy. Truly, a picture is worth a thousand words. I must be aware of what I am picturing at all times, for those images are producing either life or death within me. They are framing up my reality!

A Seven-Step Process for Godly Meditation

The various Hebrew and Greek words that are translated as "meditate" and "meditation" in the Bible occur in around 60 verses. Here is one such occurrence:

> *This book of the law shall not depart from your mouth, but you shall **meditate** on it day and night, so that you may be careful to do according to all that is written in it; for then you will make your way prosperous, and then you will have success* (Josh. 1:8 NASB95).

Meditation is defined as "*God's Spirit utilizing every faculty of my heart and mind, bringing forth revelation which ushers in transformation.*"

Meditation constitutes a *full alignment* of all faculties of my inner being on revelation coming from the Spirit as He illuminates Scripture and reveals truth.

1. **Write:** I copy the verse I am meditating on onto a piece of paper or 3x5 card and keep it with me to meditate on, memorize, and mutter throughout the day(s), as instructed in Deuteronomy 17:18. I also record this verse in my meditation/journal (which can be written, typed, or verbally recorded).

2. **Quiet Down:** I become still in God's presence, loving Him through soft soaking music[5] (2 Kings 3:15-16), praying in tongues[6] (1 Cor. 14:14), or putting a smile on my face and picturing Jesus with me (Acts 2:25). I tune to His *flowing* thoughts, pictures, and emotions (Jn. 7:37-39).

3. **Reason:** "Come let us reason *together*" (Isa. 1:18), meaning the Spirit guides my reasoning process. I ask, "Lord, what do You want to show me from this verse?" As I tune to flowing thoughts, revelation from the Holy Spirit bubbles up within me, illuminating the verse.

4. **Speak and Imagine:** I ponder the Scripture, personalizing and speaking it to myself softly over and over again until I can say it with my eyes closed. As I repeat the Scripture, I allow myself to see it with the eyes of my heart. I note what the picture is in my mind's eye as I repeat the Scripture.

5. **Feel God's Heart:** While seeing the above picture, I ask, "Lord, what does this Scripture reveal about Your heart toward me?" I feel His heart's passion, and I journal it out.

6. **Hear God's *Rhema*:** I picture myself in this Scripture story. I ask, "Lord, what are You speaking to me through this Scripture?" I tune to flowing thoughts and flowing pictures (God's voice and vision), and I record this dialogue in my two-way journaling.

7. **Act:** I accept this revelation, repenting of any sin that is opposite of it and roaring at any obstacle that stands in the way of implementing it. I then speak it forth and act on it.

The Holy Spirit guides the above process, leading to more or less emphasis on any of the various steps, according to God's desires for the present moment and the personal needs one has. We remain dependent upon Him throughout. For example, I may need more or less time to quiet myself in His presence or more or less time in Spirit-led "reasoning," or more or less time in speaking it, feeling God's heart in it, or doing two-way journaling about it, or roaring at the enemy to get his lies out of my head and his hands off my being. I allow the flow of the Holy Spirit to guide me through the steps of this meditation process.

A beautiful example was sent to me by Linda of her meditation upon Luke 2:25-38 (the story of Simeon and Anna in the temple):

Linda: "What an amazing experience, Lord. I am still overwhelmed with what I felt. I saw Simeon holding Jesus as an infant, worshipping God for the fulfillment of a promise that God had given him. While he is holding baby Jesus, his old friend, Anna, walks up and sees him holding Jesus, weeping and worshipping; and Anna knows immediately that this is what she had been praying and fasting for all of her life. Anna wraps her right arm around baby Jesus as Simeon is still holding Him; then her left hand is extended toward heaven as she worships, too. I am a bystander, but I walk over and ask permission to hold Jesus. Mary and Joseph nod, and I sob as the most wonderful gift ever is placed in my arms. Thank You, Lord. I love You."

Jesus: "You are welcome, beloved. I felt the same way when I held you in My arms when you were born anew."

The Results of Bible Meditation

- Our *hearts burn* within as He walks with us, opening Scriptures to us (Lk. 24:32).
- We are *transformed* as we look and see what Jesus is doing (2 Cor. 3:18).

Principle: Meditation is the proper way to approach Scripture as it is mentioned more than 60 times!

Going Deeper[7] and Journaling Application

- Lord, what would You speak to me about faith working through love?
- Are all my inner senses in alignment?
- Is there anything blocking the flow of Your power?
- Are there things I am to do to increase the flow of Your power?

Chapter 4

Get in Spirit

Please read Supplement F: "I Release Divine Energy: *Energeo*" for foundational background research that aligns with this chapter. *Energeo* is the flow of *active energy*, which is the anointing of the Spirit.

In Spirit

At this point in my discoveries of what would be the key parts of a prophetic healing protocol, I would say that the *three* most important ingredients to experiencing the flow of God's *dunamis* healing power would be: 1) being tuned to my spirit 2) having faith, and 3) expressing love. This chapter will focus on defining what it is to be in the Spirit and learning to easily and quickly be in the Spirit. It should not be hard, and it should not take long. It has to be easy enough for children to do (Lk. 18:15-17). Ultimately, being in the Spirit *becomes your lifestyle* as you live and walk by the Spirit (Gal. 5:16, 25).

- **Be in the Spirit**: This is where I hear what God is saying, see what He is doing, feel the flow of divine energy pulsating through me, receive a vision of the healing in process and ultimately being completed (Rev. 1:10-11; Hab. 2:1-2; Lk. 8:46).
- **Fuel Faith** by hearing what God is saying and seeing what God is doing (Gen. 12:1-5; 15:5-6).
- **Fuel Love** by seeing and feeling God's compassion toward all, including myself (Matt. 14:14).

The priority of living from our hearts and not our heads:

The Western world trains us to live from our minds. The Bible tells us to live and walk by the Spirit (Gal. 5:25). So, we have two cultures colliding and clashing. Stepping out of the Western culture and adopting a biblical worldview and experience is a major directional transformation in one's life. It involves understanding that there are two opposing ways of living: 1) relying on my mind to lead or 2) relying on my heart to lead. The Bible also clearly states, "Do not lean on your own understanding" (Prov. 3:5 NASB95), and God's thoughts are higher than man's thoughts (Isa. 55:9), and that we know truth by the Spirit (Jn. 16:13). Wow, quite a different worldview than rationalism, which tells me to rely on reason to establish truth.

Once I understand that, I will need to choose the correct path and practice it until it becomes the natural way I live (abiding in Christ). Once I tune to the flow of the Spirit, I receive God's perspective, word of knowledge, word of wisdom, and discerning of spirits, as I have the mind of Christ. Life is greatly enlarged as the Creator's anointing and creativity begin flowing through me. I am now living and wading out into the River of God.

This correct path may be more easily accessed by right-brain individuals as they are created by God to be more naturally intuitive and aware of flowing pictures and flowing thoughts. For example, I suspect this lifestyle was easier to adopt by the beloved disciple John than it was for Peter. I am more like Peter. My wife is more like John. Regardless, we can *all* learn to live and walk by the Spirit and hear God's voice (Jn. 10:27; Gal. 5:25).

Being tuned to the Spirit is something I do to prepare for a ministry session, and it is also a *lifestyle*.

A description of John being in the Spirit:

John said, "I was *in the Spirit* on the Lord's day, and I heard behind me a loud *voice* like the sound of a trumpet, saying, '*Write* in a book what you *see*" (Rev. 1:10-11 NASB95). John then wrote 22 chapters of spiritual encounters with heavenly hosts.

Being in the Spirit involved quieting down, tuning to his heart and the voice and vision of God within his heart (i.e., flowing thoughts and flowing pictures), and recording this flow in a journal. In short: "Stop, look, listen, write," or, said another way, "Stillness, vision, flow, journaling."

OK, I can do that!

Jesus living in the Spirit:

Just as we have the Holy Spirit within us to guide us, Jesus had His Father in Him, guiding Him (Jn. 10:38).

> *I do nothing on My own initiative, but I speak these things as the Father taught Me. And He who sent Me is with Me; He **has not left Me alone**, for I always do the things that are pleasing to Him. ...I speak the things which I have seen with My Father; therefore you also do the things which you heard from your father* (Jn. 8:28-29, 38 NASB95).

For Jesus, being in the Spirit meant tuning to His Father's voice and vision within (flowing thoughts and flowing pictures). Jesus always did what His Father within was directing Him to do, so the Spirit was never grieved, and power was always available to Jesus. The religious leaders were listening instead to the voice of their father, satan.

We are all listening to some inner thoughts and pictures, either from the Holy Spirit or an evil spirit. This is a reality-altering view for the Westerner, who is accustomed to believing, "If the idea is in my head, then it is my idea." In reality, we are a vessel to be filled with a spirit, preferably the Holy Spirit, but before salvation it was evil spirits (1 Thess. 4:4; 1 Cor. 6:17; Eph. 2:2; 2 Tim. 2:26). Jesus even told the religious leaders of His day that they were listening to the wrong spirit, which was the devil (Jn. 8:44).

It's all about what the Spirit does:

> *It is the **Spirit who gives life**; the **flesh profits nothing**; the words [*rhema*] that I have spoken to you are spirit and are life* (Jn. 6:63 NASB95).

The first of six foundational doctrines we are to embrace is to stop doing *dead works*. A dead work is something I come up with, such as an Ishmael, where I try to fulfill God's purposes using my own plan. God will not accept *my* plan (Gen. 17:18-19).

God only wants *live works*, things that are birthed from His River, the Holy Spirit flowing within us. Therefore, I must be in Spirit and operate from my spirit which is in union with His Spirit (1 Cor. 6:17).

Before I pray for a miracle of healing power to be released, I *must* be in the Spirit, because that is where God's power and energy flow.

It is almost incomprehensible to the Western mindset that things I come up with (using my own strength) profit nothing, and it is *only* those things that I receive from the flow of the Holy Spirit within that have value. This revelation requires repentance from dead works to be the first thing we must learn as new believers. That is why Hebrews 6:1-2 lists it as the first of six doctrines or experiences I must have in Christ.

Repentance from believing I can independently do things on my own apart from God is foundational to living a Christian, Spirit-anointed lifestyle! I suggest you journal about this and ask God to give you a revelation concerning this phrase *repentance from dead works*.

Tuned to the Spirit

Everything I need by way of Kingdom emotions, Kingdom knowledge, and Kingdom power is available to me through the flow of the indwelling Spirit, so I do not need to crank these up as a *striving of my flesh*. I tune to the Spirit and simply ask that they flow. Wow! So much easier!

I don't work up a love for my enemies. I ask, "Jesus, please circumcise my heart and remove the anger and hatred I have and put Your love into my heart for this person." Then I fix my eyes on Jesus, tune to flow, and feel anger draining out and love bubbling up within me. Thank You, Lord! Wow, a supernatural miracle as I receive a transformed heart!

I use the same process when I need increased faith. "Jesus, please circumcise my heart of doubt and unbelief and let Your gift of faith well up within me." Wow! I experience myself changing. Of course, I am picturing what I am saying as I am praying since I know that pictures are the language of the heart. Try it. You will *love* it! So much easier than struggling to change by using your own self-effort.

Now I have faith working by love, and *both* are born of the Spirit!

Getting into the Spirit

Was it faster or easier for John to get in the Spirit than it was for Peter? I expect so, but we can all learn to live and walk by the Spirit (Gal. 5:22-25).

How exactly do I *get in* the Spirit as John was in Revelation 1:9-11? We do the same four things we find Habakkuk and John doing to get in the Spirit (Hab. 2:1-2):

1. **Become still**—quiet my thoughts (Ps. 46:10; 62:5).
2. **Look for vision**—picture Jesus Who is with me (Heb. 12:1; Matt. 28:20; Eph. 1:17-18; Acts 2:25).
3. **Tune to flow**—the River of God that is flowing within me (Jn. 7:37-39); flowing pictures and flowing words bubble up.
4. **Record and act**—in faith, write down what I am receiving and act on it. (In live situations I may simply act without first writing things down.)

I quiet myself down, picture Jesus at my right hand, ask for His input, tune to flowing thoughts, flowing pictures, flowing emotions and feelings, and minister from their leading. This is very simple and very childlike. Yes, I do need to become childlike to enter the Kingdom (Mk. 10:13-15).

Technically speaking, you are shifting from left to right brain functions, from rational thinking alone to the inclusion of heart flow, from alpha brainwaves to beta brainwaves. Discover how God has designed you by downloading a free Brain Preference Indicator Test.[1]

I am more left-brained and lived in pure logic for years before I intentionally allowed my right brain and heart to flow. Now I trust I function more holistically, accessing my whole brain and heart flow. I feel and see *dunamis* power flowing and accomplishing its work (more in Chapter 8).

1. Ask for, look for, see, and feel the power/energy/*energeo* of God present and entering, restoring, and healing. We see power as light entering the body (Hab. 3:4). We watch what we see God doing and continue watching through to the end.
2. As we witness the healing action completed, we may speak, "It is done, it is done, it is done."
3. Explore Supplement F on *Energeo* for additional detail on feeling this divine power flow within.

How long does it take to get in the Spirit?

It becomes easier the more you practice it. Things that can assist in tuning to the Spirit (besides the initial four steps of becoming still, looking for vision, tuning to flow, and writing) include:

- Anointed worship music (2 Kgs. 3:15)
- Pray in tongues (1 Cor. 14:2,4)
- Sing in tongues (1 Cor. 14:15)
- Take a walk in the cool of the day (Gen. 3:8)
- Stop striving (Heb. 4:9-11)

For me, I stop striving by putting a big smile on my face, picturing myself as a child with Jesus (Matt. 18:3), or laying my hands on my heart as this focuses my attention downward out of my head and toward my heart (Prov. 4:23).[2] Speaking in tongues is yielding your vocal cords to flow.[3]

Eventually, you will learn to live by the Spirit all the time rather than living by your mind or the strength of your flesh for portions of the day.

You have trained yourself to live and walk by the Spirit. You have broken free from Western rationalism and returned to the worldview of Jesus. "Lord, birth this lifestyle of spiritual dependence in each of us, we pray, in Jesus' name."

Is this quieting down time an awkward silent time during the prayer session?

A minute of silence is not awkward if you announce, "We will first connect with our spirits and sense what God is saying and doing. We can do this through simple silence, looking with the eyes of our hearts for Jesus to be present with us, tuning to flowing thoughts and flowing pictures, and the sensation of flowing energy (heat, tingling, warmth), or even flowing feelings which light upon our bodies."

During the prayer time, make sure to instruct the person you are praying with, "It is extremely important that anytime you sense any of these, share with me what you are sensing, as this helps keep me informed about what the Spirit is doing in you, and that helps me focus my prayers for you."

Blocks that will hold back God's anointing:

1. **Sin**—makes a separation between you and your God (Isa. 59:1-2).
2. **Legalism**—He will hear our prayers when we remove the yoke of legalism from our midst (Isa. 58:9).
3. **Pointing the finger**—If we keep a critical attitude, He will not answer (Isa. 58:9).
4. **Speaking vanity**—When we continue to speak evil, lies, or wickedness, we prevent the Lord from hearing and answering us (Isa. 58:9).
5. **Religious form**—If our expressions of worship are merely for show or empty habits, they do not touch God's heart (Isa. 58:5).

If I am abiding in Christ (which for me involves picturing and conversing with Jesus at my right hand, Acts 2:25; Ps. 16:8), all of the above five issues are automatically dealt with. This simplifies the process of trying to do away with five sinful behaviors. I am simply doing one righteous behavior. When the light of Jesus is present, darkness, in all its various forms, flees. No need to try to push darkness out of the room. Instead, simply invite light in and darkness disappears because I am walking in the light (1 Jn. 1:7).

As we walk in the Spirit's anointing, life is blessed:

> *The Lord will continually guide you, and satisfy your desire in scorched places, and give strength to your bones; and you will be like a watered garden, and like a spring of water whose waters do not fail. Those from among you will rebuild the ancient ruins; you will raise up the age-old foundations; and you will be called the repairer of the breach, the restorer of the streets in which to dwell. If because of the sabbath, you turn your foot from doing your own pleasure on My holy day, and call the sabbath a delight, the holy day of the Lord honorable, and honor it, desisting from your own ways, from seeking your own pleasure and speaking your own word, then you will take delight in the Lord, and I will make you ride on the heights of the earth; and I will feed you with the heritage of Jacob your father, for the mouth of the Lord has spoken* (Isa. 58:11-14 NASB95).

Going Deeper[4] and Journaling Application

Lord, what would You speak to me about:

- Getting in the Spirit?
- Removing blockages to Your anointing?
- My flesh accomplishing nothing?

Chapter 5

Kingdom Emotions Produce Kingdom Health

Please read Supplement G: "*Hugies* Means to Be Made Whole" for foundational background research that aligns with this chapter. *Hugies,* "make well," describes the result of the healing process.

Emotions—YUCK!

I was taught emotions were soulish and unreliable. Since my goal is to be spiritual, I chose to cut off all my emotional responses. Stuff those emotions; bury them! The problem is that emotions buried alive never die. They just fester and express themselves in illnesses. Besides, God is the One who created our emotions so they can't be that evil. The Bible even says we have emotions placed in our *spirits* by God (Ezek. 3:14).

The Kingdom *is* emotions: joy and peace in the Holy Spirit (Rom. 14:17)!

So fine, it is time for me to chuck my erroneous beliefs about emotions and explore what the Bible says about them. What we will discover in this chapter is that we are called to live in the Kingdom emotions of love, joy, peace, mercy, forgiveness, thankfulness, gratitude, hope, and compassion and that these promote health throughout our entire bodies.

Emotions are at the root of most illness.

You can do an online search for "emotional basis for disease" and get limitless articles confirming the fact that unresolved emotions result in pain, sickness, and infirmity.

According to Occupational Health and Safety news and the National Council on compensation of insurance, up to 90% of all visits to primary care physicians are for stress-related complaints.[1]

Stress causes headaches, depression, heartburn, insomnia, rapid breathing, weakened immune system, risk of heart attack, high blood sugar, fertility problems, stomachache, erectile dysfunction, low sex drive, missed periods, and tense muscles.[2]

Wow! That covers symptoms from one's head to their feet, meaning stress creates overall destruction in one's body! *All types of stress affect one's health and must be neutralized.*

- **Emotional** stress (fear, worry)
- **Chemical** and electromagnetic stress (toxins/energy)
- **Physical** stress (bodily trauma)

Emotions turn our immune system on or off.

Kingdom emotions turn our immune system *on* and produce health. These are joy, peace, love, forgiveness, mercy, compassion, thankfulness, and gratitude.

We are *not* to live by emotions that turn *off* our immune system and destroy our health. We are told not to fear, forgive everything against everyone, take every thought captive, do not let the sun go down on our anger, and do not hate (Matt. 6:14; 10:31; 2 Cor. 10:5; Eph. 4:26; 1 Jn. 3:15).

I encourage you to do an internet search of these words: "emotions and immune system." You will find that many studies have been done showing that emotions will turn our immune systems *on or off* depending on the emotion. We must know that a strong, well-functioning immune system is what keeps us healthy. A weak, offline immune system allows all sorts of diseases and illnesses to overtake us.

Biblical Perspectives

Of course, what the Bible says is more important to us than what any other expert may say. So let's take a look. Does the Bible link thoughts, sin, and emotions to physical disease and physical health?

> *My **eye** is **wasted** away from **grief*** (Ps. 31:9 NASB95).

Job became very ill:

> *For what I **fear** comes upon me, and what I **dread** befalls me* (Job 3:25 NASB95).

My health prospers *as my soul prospers* (3 Jn. 1:2). Disease is coupled with iniquity:

> *Who pardons all your **iniquities**, who heals all your **diseases*** (Ps. 103:3 NASB95).

Sin produces guilt which produces sickness:

> *When I **kept silent about my sin**, my **body wasted** away through my groaning all day long. ...My **vitality was drained** away as with the fever heat of summer* (Ps. 32:3-4 NASB95).

> *There is **no health** in my bones **because of my sin**...and the light of my eyes, even that has gone from me* (Ps. 38:3,10 NASB95).

On the positive side:

> *A **joyful** heart is good **medicine*** (Prov. 17:22 NASB95).

> *A **joyful** heart makes a **cheerful face*** (Prov. 15:13 NASB95).

*The **joy** of the Lord is your **strength*** (Neh. 8:10 NASB95).

*A **tranquil heart** is **life** to the body, but **jealousy** is **rottenness** to the bones* (Prov. 14:30 NASB).

So yes, the Bible clearly shows there is a relationship between my emotions and my health.

God tells us to maintain positive emotions in every situation.

My new life is in Christ. I acknowledge that I am dead to selfish responses, and I tune to the Spirit within who gives me Christ's responses of love, joy, and peace (Gal. 2:20; Rom. 8:4-5). No anger, judgment, bitterness, or vengeance is allowed, as it quenches the Spirit's power to heal:

> *See that no one repays another with evil for evil, but always seek after that which is good for one another and for all people. Rejoice always; pray without ceasing; in everything give thanks; for this is God's will for you in Christ Jesus. **Do not quench the Spirit*** (1 Thess. 5:15-19 NASB95).

Here is an example of power being released as Kingdom emotions are expressed while suffering injustice:

> *But about midnight Paul and Silas were praying and singing hymns of praise to God, and the prisoners were listening to them; and suddenly there came a great earthquake, so that the foundations of the prison house were shaken, and immediately all the doors were opened and everyone's chains were unfastened* (Acts 16:25-26 NASB95).

We can give thanks in everything (1 Thess. 5:15-19) because we believe that:

God causes all things to work together for good to those who love God, to those who are called according to His purpose (Rom. 8:28 NASB95).

Let no unwholesome word proceed from your mouth, *but only such a word as is good for edification according to the need of the moment, so that it will give grace to those who hear. Do not grieve the Holy Spirit of God, by whom you were sealed for the day of redemption. Let all* **bitterness and wrath and anger and clamor and slander be put away** *from you, along with all malice.* **Be kind** *to one another, tender-hearted, forgiving each other, just as God in Christ also has forgiven you* (Eph. 4:29-32 NASB95).

Watch over your heart *with all diligence, for from it* **flow the springs of life** (Prov. 4:23 NASB95).

In summary, we process our emotions with God *before going to sleep* by asking God to heal our hearts, give us new hearts, and restore us to Kingdom emotions of joy and peace (Rom. 14:17).

Emotional states that release Kingdom power are achieved by living in the Spirit.

The fruit of the Spirit is *love, joy, peace, patience, kindness, goodness, faithfulness, gentleness, self-control* (Gal. 5:22-23 NASB95).

This results in gratitude, thankfulness, compassion, mercy, forgiveness, anointing, and revelation; and your immune system is turned on as God's Spirit fills you.

These emotional states do not need to be worked up through an *effort of my flesh*. Instead, I tune to the Spirit and ask Jesus to circumcise my heart of any ungodly emotions and for the Holy Spirit to birth within me Kingdom emotions. I pause and smile as I feel God doing this supernatural work within me. This is Spirit-fruit pouring out of me.

> *God has chosen you from the beginning for **salvation** through **sanctification by the Spirit and faith in the truth**. It was for this He called you through our gospel, that you may gain the glory of our Lord Jesus Christ* (2 Thess. 2:13-14 NASB95).

Emotional states that release demonic power are experienced by living in the flesh.

> *The deeds of the flesh are evident, which are: immorality, impurity, sensuality, idolatry, sorcery, enmities, strife, jealousy, outbursts of anger, disputes, dissensions, factions, envying, drunkenness, carousing, and things like these* (Gal. 5:19-21 NASB95).

This results in fear, guilt, shame, depression, abandonment, and loneliness, and your immune system is turned off and demonic darkness envelops you. "Those who practice such things will not inherit the kingdom of God" (Gal. 5:21 NASB95). These people have entered into the *path to destruction*:

> *With all the deception of wickedness for those who perish, because they did not receive the **love of the truth** so as to be saved. For this reason God will send upon them a **deluding influence** so that they will believe what is false* (2 Thess. 2:10-11 NASB95).

They often function in a deranged way, lacking any capacity for clear reasoning abilities. Logic does not move them. Binding demons and releasing the Spirit to convict them is the best recourse when interacting with them.

Health improves as one's soul/emotions prosper.[3]

Sanctification is from the *inside* out.

> *Now may the God of peace Himself sanctify you entirely; and may your spirit and soul and body be preserved complete, without*

blame at the coming of our Lord Jesus Christ (1 Thess. 5:23 NASB95).

The anointing flows when we live in peace and *harmony*.

> *Behold, how good and how pleasant it is for brothers to dwell together in unity! It is like the **precious oil**.... For there the Lord commanded the **blessing**—life forever* (Ps. 133:1-3 NASB95).

Unforgiveness: The Greatest Cause of Affliction

Bill Johnson states: "I think that for believers, unforgiveness is the greatest cause of affliction."[4] Unforgiveness does produce stress in one's body.

> *Is anyone among you sick? Then he must call for the elders of the church and they are to pray over him, anointing him with oil in the name of the Lord; and the prayer offered in faith will restore the one who is sick, and the Lord will raise him up, and if he has committed sins, they will be forgiven him. Therefore, confess your sins to one another, and pray for one another so that you may be healed. The effective prayer of a righteous man can accomplish much* (Jas. 5:14-16 NASB95).

The Bible's wonderful solution to stress:[5]

> *The steadfast of **mind** ["imagination" in the Hebrew] You will keep in perfect peace because he trusts in You* (Isa. 26:3).[6]

If I **clean up my imagination/picturing**, I move from stress to peace. We picture Jesus at our right hand (Acts 2:25; Ps. 16:8; Heb. 12:1-2) and invite Him to speak and show us what He is doing in every situation we are visualizing. We are transformed "while we look" (2 Cor. 3:17-18; 4:17-18). Be aware of what you are visualizing at all times, and take captive any picture that does not have Jesus present in the scene (as that visualization is an evil imagination, taking you backward). *This is not optional*. It is critical for physical, emotional, and spiritual health.

Inner healing, as illustrated in the story of getting fired from my job in Chapter 2, is the best means I know of to walk me through heart-level forgiveness and removal of stress. *Use this* in your daily devotions. Do it every day, if necessary, until you are at peace within.

Praying in tongues reduces stress and builds the immune system, as does smiling, exercising, and ten minutes of relaxed, slow breathing (five seconds in through your nose and five seconds out through either your nose or mouth).

Re-focus prayers from physical healing to resolving emotions.

Since the Bible confirms that there is a link between emotions and health, we should assume that 85 percent of those with whom we pray for physical healing will need healing of their thoughts and emotional life as a precursor to their bodies being healed.

Understand the principle that every system in your body is negatively affected by stress and it promotes a host of physical problems.

This is a startling revelation and means I need to re-focus my prayers for physical healing to: 1) first heal the emotional unrest which is the root cause of the infirmity; 2) once emotions are restored, I would cast out any demons that had attached themselves to these once-darkened areas; and, 3) finally, I would pray for healing of the body parts that had become damaged by this digression into darkness.

The biggest emotional stressors are guilt, fear, rejection, unforgiveness, and anger.

Let's go back to my earlier story of the pain in a lady's neck being healed. We discerned the pain in her neck was caused by a person whom she needed to deeply forgive. As soon as she forgave from her *heart*, healing was released. Remember, heart faculties involve picturing and tuning to flow. So she *pictured* the offending person and the situation; and while in that picture, she stated, "I choose to forgive you in Jesus' name. I release you. I honor you, and I bless you in Jesus' name."

When we have pain in our bodies, we now know that 75 to 85 percent of such pains are caused by emotional dis-ease. My number-one approach for the last 20 years to bringing healing by releasing emotional and spiritual stress is by using the seven prayers that heal the heart, which was first ministered to me by Kay Cox while I taught in Australia. In just two hours I experienced amazing heartfelt freedom, and so I wrote a book about the process she used with me.[7]

Remember the principle: "Emotions are guided by the pictures I gaze upon."

Gazing *only* at the new pictures God shows will give me *continuous* Kingdom emotions with resulting health in my body, soul, spirit, and interpersonal relationships.

A new habit must be formed to maintain healing.

After experiencing emotional healing of a strained relationship, I must form a new habit that consists of thinking *only* the thoughts that God has about the person and only *holding pictures* that God has about them. This keeps my heart clean from reverting to harboring emotional discontent. This allows me to walk in the light. This can be accomplished by reminding myself of what God has shown me about this person and how God is showing that this tension is to be resolved.

How to do ever-deepening emotional housecleaning which results in increased vitality:

1. **Step one** for me was learning to hear the voice of our Wonderful Counselor, so He can *counsel me daily.*[8]
2. **Step two** involved *journaling specifically about my emotional issues* and receiving divine revelation and perspectives that transformed my limited viewpoints.[9]
3. **Step three** was applying *seven complementary prayers* that removed generational roots and demonic influence.[10]
4. **Step four** is letting God reveal emotional upset through my dreams at night.[11]

I strongly encourage you to allow the Holy Spirit to show you how He wants to work in you right now to bring healing to your spirit, soul, and body.

Going Deeper[12] and Journaling Application

- Lord, bring to my mind a situation that is causing stress in my life or a scene where I need to forgive either myself, an event, You, or someone else.
- Jesus, please enter this scene and show me what You are doing and what You are speaking.
- Follow Jesus' lead and be healed.

Chapter 6

Relational Five-Step Prayer Model by John Wimber

Please read Supplement H: "Every Example of Casting Out Demons in the New Testament" for foundational background research that aligns with this chapter. Supplement H: *Ekballon pneumati akatharto* ("casting out an unclean spirit") brings instantaneous change.

This chapter is written with the view that you are praying for a client and utilizing these truths. If you are praying for yourself, then consider yourself as the client receiving these instructions. Remember that very often there is an increase in healing effect when you go to your spiritual leaders and have them pray with you, so never shy away from taking this step (Jas. 5:14-16).

Many years ago, John Wimber came up with a five-step template that he used for healing prayer. I have benefited from this five-step approach over the years and want to share it with you, as I believe these steps have great value. We will begin this chapter with a discussion of what constitutes a heart-level prayer, followed by a healing testimony provided by Rev. Don Paprockyj, and then close this chapter with Wimber's five-step model.

Heart-Level Prayers

Heart-level prayers use the language of the heart.

- **Flow**: "out of his *heart* will *flow*" (Jn. 7:38 NKJV).
- **Imagination**: "Keep this for ever in the *imagination* of the thoughts of the *heart*" (1 Chron. 29:18 KJV).

- **Emotions**: "He was *grieved* in His *heart*" (Gen. 6:6 NASB95).
- **Meditation**: "I will *meditate* with my *heart*" (Ps. 77:6 NASB95).

Make sure all prayers are heart-level prayers.

A heart-level prayer utilizes the language of the heart which includes flowing thoughts, flowing pictures, and emotions and often results in feeling a bodily sensation. So we slow down as we pray. We utilize the language of the heart and instruct the client to look for and expect flowing thoughts, flowing pictures, flowing emotions, and bodily sensations to occur and to report to you as these things are occurring.

It is best to encourage the client not to speak during the prayer session but to experience through the senses of his heart and sensations in his body what God is doing and revealing. As a counselor, I generally keep my eyes open so I can observe and detect through the client's bodily manifestations what is happening. I also keep the eyes and ears of my heart open (flowing pictures and flowing thoughts), so I can sense guidance directly from the Spirit and then release that into the prayer time.

We ask the Holy Spirit to guide these prayer times. We see each thing we are doing and saying (picture/visualize). Forgiveness is deepened when you are picturing the person's face and the situation where the hurt happened, and speaking directly to them from this scene. "I choose in Jesus' name to forgive you, to love you, to honor you, to bless you, and to release you." This is one example of how we use pictures, flow, and emotion in our prayer times to make it heart-level rather than simply head-level.

Principle: Prayers are most effective when *applied directly to the point when the hurt happened*. So, for example, if I am praying to cut off generational curses, the point when they entered me would be when I was a baby in my mother's womb. Therefore, I picture myself as a baby in my mother's womb. I picture the curse (as flowing negative energy) coming from my father toward me, and I picture the cross of Christ standing between me (the baby in the womb) and this negative energy flowing from my father. I see and speak that this energy is hitting the cross of Christ, falling to the ground, powerless at the foot of the cross. I then see and speak for the blessings of Calvary to cascade down over the baby, and I bless him with life. I bless him with life. I bless him with life. I command, "Come alive, come alive, come alive." I see the baby (myself) coming alive with the life of Jesus. Flow is present in all of this. Flow is the anointing of the Holy Spirit. Flow is the River of Life that sets the captive free.

This is one example of the combined principles of using heart prayers and applying the prayer to the point when and where the hurt happened. In this case, I will repeat the entire prayer for my mother's side of the family. This way I am assured that any curses coming from either side of my family line have been cut off.

All prayers begin with forgiving the person involved, and often we add, "I also forgive myself for my participation in this issue, and I forgive You, God, for allowing this to happen in my life." (It's not that God has done anything wrong, but I may be holding a grudge against Him anyway.)

Forgive everything against everyone, as this releases God's power.

> *Truly I say to you, whoever says to this mountain, "Be taken up and cast into the sea," and **does not doubt in his heart,** but believes that what he **says** is **going** to happen, it **will be** granted him. Therefore I say to you, all things for which you pray and ask, believe that you **have received** them, and they will be granted you. **Whenever you stand praying, forgive, if you have anything against anyone,** so that your Father who is in heaven will also forgive you your transgressions. [But if you do not forgive, neither will your Father who is in heaven forgive your transgressions]* (Mk. 11:23-26 NASB95).

The above verses teach us so much about healing prayer:

1. You need to command the miracle.
2. You need heart faith (requires utilizing the language of the heart— flow, pictures, emotions).

3. Believe what you command by seeing it *already received*, and it *will* be granted to you.

4. Forgive everyone: self, others, God.

The verse directly before the above verses provides another powerful truth—we need God's *gift of faith* to well up within us. Young's Literal Translation puts it this way: "Have faith *of* God" (Mk. 11:22 YLT). A smoother rendition of this verse would be, "*Have God's faith.*" To make this happen, I simply *ask for the gift of faith*, tune to flow, and feel faith rise up within me. I thank Him for it.

The Bible is clear: *I do not work up faith.* It is a *gift* from God: "For by grace you have been saved through faith; and that not of yourselves, it is *the gift of God*" (Eph. 2:8 NASB95).

Don Paprockyj provides the following testimony of healing:

It is fascinating that 85 percent of our sicknesses could be mind-related. According to the "pain in the neck" example you gave and Bill Johnson's quote, "I think that for believers, *unforgiveness* is the greatest cause of *affliction*," it seems unforgiveness is the main issue.

This reminds me of when my wife and I were in South Africa in 2014 ministering through our churches. Hilda, the wife of one of our church pastors, was eight months pregnant and lost all feeling in her legs and could not even move her toes. She went to the hospital and while there, the doctors could not detect a heartbeat from the baby for at least a week. They said the baby would be born dead soon. I was taking the Prayers That Heal the Heart course at the time, and I was leading people in many services and individually to break generational curses of immorality and witchcraft, and to forgive those needed. We were seeing people healed from pains all over, even crippling pains.

I led Hilda in prayer to break these generational curses of immorality and witchcraft. My wife and our lead pastor's wife had their hands on Hilda's stomach as we prayed. I then asked Hilda if there was anyone she had not forgiven. She said yes and then forgave the person. At that instant, my wife felt a kick in Hilda's womb, the first movement of the baby in over a week. Then Hilda started wiggling her toes for the first time in a while. A week later, the baby was born completely healthy and has been normal ever since. Hilda was also completely healed soon after. The baby is named Brilliant. Some of the other women patients in the room with Hilda told us they were praying along with us, and they were feeling better as well. Bless the Lord!

The Relational Five-Step Prayer notes are very helpful references. I remember learning this prayer model years ago at a Randy Clark conference, but the model here seems to have been enhanced with added interview questions and greater emphasis on the client stating if anything is happening during prayer. This will be very helpful.

Knowing the different types of words of knowledge can confirm hearing from the Lord—albeit in a peculiar manner (e.g., pain in a certain part of your body, hearing or vision of a number, etc.)—which can help ensure that healing takes place. (More on this in the next chapter.)

What are the steps in Wimber's healing prayer model?

1. **Interview**: Build trust and discover what needs healing.
2. **Diagnosis and Prayer Selection**: Determine what prayer approaches are to be used.
3. **Prayer Ministry**: Apply the prayer selection(s).
4. **Stop and Re-Interview**: Discover what the client is experiencing to better focus your prayers.
5. **Post-Prayer**: Give instructions on how to maintain victory.

Step 1: Interview: Build trust and discover what needs healing.

Honor the person and build trust by getting the person's name and asking what they are seeking healing for. Ask how long they have had the condition, and have them ask God, "Lord, what occurred in my life shortly before this condition appeared?" Tell them to tune to flow and share what pops into their mind.

Everyone is to stay tuned to flow throughout the entire prayer encounter. You can pray aloud saying, "Lord, lead us in this prayer time. Guide us in the way we are to pray, the questions we are to ask, and the answers we are to give. Cover us, our families, and our properties with the blood of Jesus, so that no attack of the enemy can touch us in any way."

Steps 2 and 3: Diagnosis, Prayer Selection, and Prayer Ministry.

As you discern the root cause of the disease, you can select the prayer approach, or approaches, that will deal with that. Following are some common approaches.

Emotional dis-ease:

Emotional issues play a role in the vast majority of illnesses. The biggies include unforgiveness, resentment, guilt, and shame. The proper prayer approach for this is "inner healing," which is inviting Jesus to show up in the picture in our mind of the trauma (if rape, then Jesus shows up *after* the trauma, so the client is *not* retraumatized). Instruct the client to picture the scene of the hurt for only *one second*, and then look around for Jesus, because *He was there*. Our goal is to receive revelation from Jesus.

A preliminary step that makes this easier and safer is to have the client meet Jesus in a comfortable place where they have met Jesus in the past. Once the client re-enters that scene, instruct them to tune in to flowing thoughts and pictures as you invite Jesus to take the client from that scene to the scene where the hurt happened.

Once the client affirms that Jesus has done that, you pray saying: "Jesus, show (client's name) what You were doing and speaking when that situation occurred." The client continues to watch and listen as you encourage him to keep his eyes on Jesus and tune in to flowing thoughts and flowing pictures. You take notes on what the client is describing in the unfolding scene. You lead the client in honoring and acting on what Jesus is revealing (being comforted by His touch, forgiving the perpetrator, etc.).

You close this scene by asking Jesus to show them the *gift* He has produced in their life through this event (Rom. 8:28). Record this gift, as they describe it, and have the client *thank God for this gift.*

Instruct them that from now on, whenever they go back to this scene in their minds, they always see the scene where *Jesus is present* and thank Him for the gift He produced in their life through the painful event. This causes the pain to be dissolved and replaced with thankfulness and gratitude. The client has just experienced the truth that "emotions are the byproduct of the pictures we gaze upon."

Finish by commanding the demons that attached themselves to this heart wound to leave in Jesus' name. (The demons' names could be unforgiveness, resentment, guilt, shame, etc.) Then fill the area the demon has left vacated with the Holy Spirit by simply speaking, "I welcome You, Holy Spirit, to enter this area and fill it with light and bring it completely under Your control."

Getting unstuck:

If the person gets stuck in the painful trauma and you cannot move forward, then have them go back to the safe place where they began with Jesus at their side in a comfortable setting.[1]

Natural causes:

Accidental injuries or carcinogens can cause illness. Command in Jesus' name that the trauma resident in the cells of the body from the accident or injury be released. Then release the peace of the Holy Spirit to that area of the body. Command the injury to be healed in Jesus' name. Then command the attached demons to be dismissed in Jesus' name. Teach the client any lifestyle changes that will detoxify their bodies and ways they can strengthen their immune system so that it functions at 100 percent capacity.

Genetic causes:

Command the DNA to be rewritten and to come in line with heaven's pattern and be normal. "Chromosomes, change, become perfect in Jesus' name."

Generational sins and curses:

Break the sins and curse(s) by having the client picture their parents (one at a time) and say, "I forgive you for passing this on to me. In Jesus' name, I choose to release you, to honor you, and to bless you."

Then have them picture themselves as a baby in their mother's womb, and you lead them in a visionary prayer that they repeat after you: "I place the cross of Jesus Christ between me and all sins and curses flowing toward me from my parents. I command this negative energy to halt at the cross of Christ and fall to the ground powerless at the foot of the cross. I pray for the blessings of Calvary to cascade down upon that baby in the womb. I bless you with life. I bless you with life. I bless you with life."

Seeing and feeling each step is important.[2]

Afflicting spirits:

Demons are connected with most illnesses, so assume once you have dealt with the primary issue (the root issue which demons often attach to), you will then be able to easily command any demons connected to this wound or infirmity to leave in Jesus' name. Jesus would often cast out demons as He was healing people. We are to do the same. Once the root has been resolved, the legal right for the demon to be present is removed, and the demon(s) comes out rather easily.[3]

Lifestyle issues:

Improper rest, poor diet and dehydration, a lifestyle of stress, lack of exercise, and gluttony all contribute to illness and disease. One needs to repent of these sinful behaviors and learn how to treat their body with the honor and respect it deserves since it is a temple that God lives in (1 Cor. 6:19).[4]

Step 4: Stop and Re-Interview

As the client shares the ongoing flowing thoughts, pictures, emotions, or feelings they are experiencing, you then know precisely where God is active within them and what God is doing. This allows you to focus your prayer *more perfectly on that spot* or that activity. Not only should the client share these things when you stop praying and re-interview them, but they should be encouraged to "interrupt your prayer time" *to express what is happening.* Again, this helps the client and counselor stay aware and focused on what God is doing, so prayer can be focused accordingly.

I know when someone was casting several demons out of me, the thought lit upon my mind that I needed to forgive my dad for a certain event. So, I simply spoke aloud as she was praying and said, "Dad, I forgive you. I honor you; I release you; I bless you, in Jesus' name."

The prayer counselor was mature enough to know that God had just spoken to me, that I was acting on God's instruction, and that by doing this step of forgiveness God was removing a legal right that the demon was using to stay connected to me and not come out. This deliverance session was successful!

In Mark 8:22-25, Jesus interviews the blind man, and the report is that he sees men as trees walking. So Jesus prays a second time, and the man sees clearly. It is *not* wrong to pray a second time. This does not show a lack of faith. Healing often occurs in layers. Expect this and flow with it.

You can re-interview several times and pray several times. Keep praying as long as each prayer brings increased freedom and the Spirit is leading forward. Stop praying when: 1) the client wants to stop, 2) no more progress is being made, or 3) they are fully healed.

The interviews may cause you to ask additional questions to get to additional roots. Stay tuned to flow and follow the spontaneous thoughts, ideas, and pictures coming to you. They are revelations from the Holy Spirit.

Step 5: Post-Prayer: Suggestions and follow-up instructions or exhortations

Listen to the Lord as to what instructions to send the client home with. Share these with the client. Never share your thoughts, as our thoughts are not His thoughts (Isa. 55:8-9). Only share what is coming to you by flow. Teach them to never look back at old pictures of a hurtful scene, but *only* look at pictures where Jesus appears in them, ministering His grace.

Teach the client to resist demons when the demons whisper with their spontaneous thoughts, "We're back." Tell the client to rebuke the demons in Jesus' name, command the demons to be gone, and to fix their eyes on Jesus and His revelation to them.

Encourage the client in the lifestyle changes that are appropriate in the pursuit of ongoing health. Listen to God. He will tell you what to say to minister life to them, not accusation, judgment, legalism, or death.

When healing power is flowing, expect to feel some heat and tingling. When demons are coming out, expect to feel a release. If they move and do not fully come out, then have the client repent again of the sin and tell the demons they no longer are welcome, as the client is going to live in righteousness in this area from now on; and the client then commands the demons to leave now in Jesus' name. These are wedges that force a separation between the demon and the person.

Then you command the demons out in Jesus' name. If they still resist, ask God what they are still attached to that gives them a legal right to remain. Tune to flow and receive His answer and then pray and remove that legal right and once again command the demon to leave. Once the demons have no legal rights that allow them to remain, they will flee.

Journaling Application

- "God, what would You like to heal today?"
- "Lord, show me the root cause of this infirmity."
- "What specific step(s) am I to take to remove this root cause?"
- Take the step(s) He has told you to take. When confirmation is needed, submit your leadings to spiritual advisors.
- Watch John Wimber teach.[5]

Chapter 7

Words of Knowledge Increase the Faith Level

One way to raise faith in a healing service is to have a word of knowledge called out, saying God wants to heal something specific. A person with that particular issue will reach out in faith to receive the healing. You can have them raise their hand or come to the front. This makes it easy for several people to lay their hands on them and come into agreement for healing.

People believe and understand that when a word of knowledge is given, it is Jesus standing there addressing the infirmity. Their increased faith can cause an instant miracle without anyone even praying for them.

Ways to Receive a Word of Knowledge

One way the Holy Spirit may make you aware of someone's need that He wants to address is by allowing you to suddenly feel pain in a specific part of your body such as your knee. Simply say, "I believe God wants to heal someone's knee right now. Anyone with knee pain, reach out in faith for what the Lord wants to do for you."

Rather than experiencing pain, you might see a picture or word on the inner screen of your mind that tells you what God wants to heal. It may only appear for a split-second, but if you speak in faith, the Lord will touch bodies.

Or you may not even get a picture. Simply a word or thought may appear in your mind of a disease or organ or other need. Share your impression along with your faith that God is moving.

Some people have dreams of what God wants to heal either in their own bodies or in someone they will be meeting shortly. This, too, is a way to receive words of knowledge.[1]

Or perhaps a number may appear in your mind. Do not try to interpret what the number means. Simply speak it out and ask if it means anything to anyone. You may be amazed at Lord's creativity!

Examples of very simple prophetic pictures that were seen, and the results they bore:

A woman in the congregation had no salivary glands and had to carry water with her all the time. When the leader said that he saw a water bottle, she knew this vision was for her, and she received her healing.

A person received a picture in their mind of a white stallion. When they shared this as a word of knowledge, a woman in attendance came forward. She had once been horseback riding and a white stallion had fallen on top of her, causing many injuries that had become chronic issues and remained unhealed. After prayer, she was healed of the injuries related to that accident.

A prophet simply saw the number nine. There was a person who had suffered a back injury requiring the placement of nine screws in his back. He accepted the prophetic word as being for him, received prayer, and was healed of the constant pain he had been experiencing. It is important to remember that numbers can have various meanings, so do not try to interpret what they mean.

Another minister saw a mechanic working on a car engine. There was a mechanic in the audience who had had a radiator he was repairing blow up and burn his hands. He joyfully received this vision for himself and received healing as he was prayed for.

A recommended pattern for receiving words of knowledge:

1. Become still in the Lord's presence.
2. Ask God for words of knowledge concerning what He wants to heal.

3. Tune to *flowing/spontaneous* thoughts, words, pictures, or pains that suddenly appear in your body. These are coming from *flow*, the River of the Holy Spirit who *flows* within you (Jn. 7:37-39). These are revelations from God.

Ways to humbly deliver your word of knowledge:

None of us is perfect, and we do not always perfectly hear or understand what the Lord is saying to us. This is especially true in the area of prophecy and words of knowledge which are addressed to other people. We never want to place ourselves in a position of authority because of what we believe we hear from God. Humility is the hallmark of those who truly hear God's voice.

Therefore, especially as you are learning to walk in the prophetic, be careful how you share what you believe you are receiving. Speak in a natural voice using contemporary language. Instructions such as, "This word may be for one person or several people" can encourage everyone who is suffering from an infirmity to reach out in faith. If you are speaking to a specific person, you can take the pressure off them feeling like they must respond in a specific say by saying something like, "I am learning how to hear from God. If what I say bears witness in your heart that it is true, receive it; but if it does not, let it go."

Practical suggestions for ministry times:

God is the Healer, and He knows how best to minister to each individual. Some people may be healed before you even pray for them. For others, you may pray for 20 minutes before you can see things happening. Continue watching and praying until the work is done.

Sometimes it is not appropriate for you to lay your hands on the place that needs healing. This is especially true when praying for someone of the opposite sex. In that case, they can lay their hand on the spot of the infirmity, and you lay your hand on their hand.

Seven steps to mastering any new skill (e.g., word of knowledge)[2]

1. Have a passionate intention to succeed, whatever the cost.
2. Have a clear vision from God, so you know His will concerning the area.
3. Master the key skills necessary to succeed in the area. Then move on to the next skill God wants you to master.
4. Seek coaching from experts. Allow them to teach you the finer points.
5. Commit time to becoming proficient—acknowledge successes and failures.
6. Learn together in community; as iron sharpens iron, so one man sharpens another.
7. Release God's anointing through the gift.

Remember that words of knowledge accompanied by healing can convince a person that God is real and completely change the course of their life. What an honor that God has given us the opportunity to partner with Him in ministering His healing power!

Going Deeper[3] and Journaling Application

- "Lord, do You have a word of knowledge for me now?" Tune to flow, with your eyes on Jesus, and write.
- "What is the skill You want me to master now?"
- "What step would You have me take today to move into mastering and ministering words of knowledge?"

Chapter 8

Practical Guidelines as We Minister Healing

I am passionate about "how to." I have a passion for being as biblical, spiritual, and practical as possible when I describe in detail how one steps into Christian spirituality in every area; and in the case of this book, specifically in the area of healing. For me, the more practical we can be, the easier it is for a person to follow the steps and move forward to victory. So here is a chapter of practical steps one can take.

Specific guidelines for healing sessions (to use with self-healing and with others):

1. Healing is accomplished from a place of unconditional love!
2. *Fear, doubt, and disbelief* are the most powerful blocks to any healing. They can be in the heart and mind of the one ministering healing or the one receiving healing.
3. Joy, gratitude, and love are key emotions that carry healing power. You need to genuinely care for people to be effective.
4. Call upon God for wisdom and guidance throughout the healing. He *will* answer.
5. Be specific in what you are requesting in the healing.
6. Take a moment to quiet yourself and tune in to the Spirit.
7. Remain in the Spirit until you witness the miracle completed.

How We Step from the Flesh to the Spirit

1. We **disconnect** from the flesh, which includes self, ego, fear, doubt, disbelief, tribe consciousness, personal desires and passions, religious dogmas, and theologies. The easiest way to do this is by simply doing step two.

2. We **connect** to the Spirit within, which is the River of God that *flows* (Jn. 7:37-39).
    *   His **voice** is sensed as flowing thoughts (while your eyes are fixed on Him).
    *   His **visions** are sensed as flowing pictures (while your eyes are fixed on Him).
    *   His **emotions** are sensed as flowing feelings (while your eyes are fixed on Him).
    *   His **power** is sensed as flowing energy, warmth, and tingling (while your eyes are fixed on Him).

3. Living from the Spirit becomes **easier** as we practice it. The ultimate goal is to live and walk by the Spirit (Gal. 5:16, 25), which is also called abiding in Christ (Jn. 15). This can be accomplished by continually seeing Jesus at your right hand (Acts 2:25), asking for the Spirit's input, and tuning to flow.

Honor the pattern of the apostles and pray to be re-filled with the Holy Spirit (Acts 4:31).

The apostles prayed:

> *"Grant that Your bond-servants may speak Your word with all confidence, while You extend Your hand to heal, and signs and wonders take place through the name of Your holy servant Jesus." And when they had prayed, the place where they had gathered together was shaken, and they were all **filled with the Holy Spirit** and began to speak the word of God with boldness (Acts 4:29-31 NASB95).*

This was a *re-filling* as some in this group were filled in Acts 2:1-4.

It is spiritually strengthening to put on the full armor of God (Eph. 6:10-18).

I pray and picture the following: "In Jesus' name, I present my entire being to God to be filled by the Spirit. I see You, Holy Spirit, in union with my spirit, filling every part of my being." I lay my hand upon each part of my body as I speak:

1. I speak to my **mind**: Be the mind of Christ by receiving God's *flowing thoughts.*
2. I speak to my **eyes**: See visions by seeing God's *flowing pictures.*
3. I speak to my **vocal cords**: Speak the oracles of God by saying what *flows naturally.*
4. I speak to my **heart**: Release Christ's compassion, extending *mercy* toward myself and others.
5. I speak to my **belly**: Experience *power* through your *union* with the Holy Spirit. Release God's *creative flow.*
6. I speak to my **feet**: Be a peacemaker by walking in *peace and grace toward all.*

Thank You, Jesus. It is done, it is done, it is done!

Pictures

Pictures increase faith, which in turn increases miracle-working power. A picture is worth a thousand words. When God gave Abram a picture of the promise fulfilled (millions of stars representing millions of descendants), faith erupted within Abram (Gen. 15:5-6).

When flow takes over a godly imagination, you are *stepping from* a godly imagination into a divine vision. Ministering out of vision is the power-packed goal.

Emotions are byproducts of pictures, so ask God to bring to your attention ungodly pictures you are gazing at (i.e., any picture that does not include Jesus Christ—Heb. 12:1-2), so you can repent of it. Ask Him for a replacement picture that has Jesus in it. Now gaze only on this new picture.

Emotional problems such as anger, grief, hatred, or personal tragedies often require inner healing to process fully and completely.[1]

Possible pictures: Some starting points to prime the pump:

1. **Picture One**: The Spirit filling: As I reverently speak the prayer to be filled with the Holy Spirit, I can watch the energizing power of the Holy Spirit, Who is joined to my spirit, filling me with God's light, energy, and power and then bursting forth from me.

2. **Picture Two**: "Lo, I am with you always" (Matt. 28:20 KJV): I see Jesus at my right hand (Acts 2:25), ministering alongside me. When necessary, He is roaring together with me at the adversary we are encountering (Joel 3:16).

3. **Picture Three**: I see the River of Life, flowing clear as crystal, pouring out from the throne of God and of the Lamb. Next to this river, I see the Tree of Life whose leaves are bringing healing, breaking every curse (Rev. 22:1-4).

Begin the healing prayer once you are filled with the Spirit and quieted in His presence.

1. Ask the client what they want before offering to pray for healing (Jn. 5:6-14).

2. Ask permission from the client to pray for their healing. This brings the client into the healing process, and through that, they are giving their body permission to heal.

3. "In Jesus' name, I command that this (specific illness) in (client's name) be resolved according to God's wisdom and power. Show me,

Lord, what You are doing. Thank You, Jesus! In faith, we receive Your revelation."

4. Continued observation causes continuing transformation—you are to witness the unfolding miracle, so keep observing until the miracle is complete.
    a. The client speaks forth what they are seeing or feeling.
    b. Obey any instructions God is giving you (it will come as flowing thoughts or pictures).
    c. The longer you stay with this vision, the easier it is to give birth to the good things God has intended for you and, thus, experience His promises to you.
    d. Do not let your mind wander. The healing may be instant or it may take several minutes.
    e. As you sense God's miracle-working power surrounding you, you come into perfect wholeness and balance.

5. Quantum physics affirms that simple observation changes the outcome.[2]
    a. A witness in court tells what they have observed. We are witnesses (Acts 1:8).
    b. In prophetic healing prayer, we are witnesses watching what the Spirit is doing as He heals, and we are telling what we are seeing, feeling, and observing.

6. Find out the pain level of the client when you begin praying (1-10 with 10 being the worst), and then ask what the pain level is when you finish praying. Generally, it will have fallen, which is extremely encouraging.

Facilitators of the Anointing

We want to be the most effective vessels of the anointing of the Holy Spirit as we can be, both to bring healing to others and to receive His healing in our own bodies. There are keys in the Scriptures to how we can increase the flow of the anointing through us.

God has given each of us unique gifts and ways of expressing Him. When we join with others who have different gifts, we experience the synergy of a multi-gifted team (Eph. 4:7-11). Our weaknesses are another's strengths and together we can accomplish so much more than we can alone. For example, since my strength is teaching, whenever I am called upon to minister healing, I try to have a visionary seer—a prophet—working alongside me. I am able to offer much more effective ministry when teamed up in this way.

Further, if we do more than simply work side by side toward a goal, if our hearts are blended together in a bond of love and we are in one accord, the power and anointing of God flow freely (Acts 2:1-2; 4:24; Ps. 133:1-3).

Group soaking prayer is a powerful tool that I have used for many years and have seen some level of healing manifested every time.

Guidelines for Group Healing Soaking Prayer

1. Gather around a client with several people laying their hands on the client.

2. Everyone receives and sends (especially through their touch) God's unconditional love, compassion, and healing power to the client, seeing it pulsate through every cell of the client's being, doing only and exactly what God desires to do.

3. Anyone can pray, sharing words of wisdom or words of knowledge.

4. Silence is welcome and fine.

5. Witness (watch) God's light, love, and power filling every cell.

6. Throughout this filling the client may report what they are feeling and sensing.

7. The normal length is 15 minutes. This can be repeated as needed.

Since we walk in ever-increasing light, we can assume healing comes in layers.

> *But the path of the righteous is like the light of dawn, that **shines brighter and brighter** until the full day. ...My son, give attention to my words; incline your ear to my sayings. Do not let them depart from your sight; keep them in the midst of your heart. For they are life to those who find them and health to all their body* (Prov. 4:18-22 NASB95).

Common unbiblical beliefs to repent of so healing power can flow freely.

We have already talked about the effects of our emotions on our health, and the fact that our emotions are the products of the pictures we hold in our minds. But where do those pictures come from? Frequently it is our beliefs that generate the things we imagine. We believe something to be true, so we picture how that "fact" impacts our lives. This is why it is so important that we be aware of even the unconscious beliefs we hold and be absolutely committed to embracing only the truth and rejecting any belief that is contrary to the revealed will of God.

In my counseling and prayer ministry to the sick, I have heard several unbiblical beliefs expressed frequently by people seeking a touch from God. These ungodly beliefs must be brought to the Light, repented of, and rejected if the healing power of Truth is to be released.

1. My sin is unforgivable.
2. I deserve to be sick.
3. I must be punished.
4. I am separated from God.
5. It's in my genes.
6. I am gaining something I want through this sickness (compassion, attention, a disability check).

7. The doctor told me I would die soon of this disease.
8. I want to die.

Blocking beliefs such as these must be replaced with revelation truth from God. Ask Him to reveal to you the beliefs, emotions, and/or pictures that are preventing you from receiving healing. Repent of them, remove them, and replace them with God's beliefs, emotions, and pictures which are contained in His promises and revelation to us.

Deliverance is a big part of the healing process.

It is also important for us to remember that of Jesus' 41 prayers for healing, 13 included prayers for deliverance. Surely, since He is our example, deliverance must be a central part of our healing ministry as well. Repentance of sin removes the legal rights for demons to be present, and then deliverance comes easily.[3]

Going Deeper[4] and Journaling Application

Lord, what would You speak to me:

- About putting on the full armor of God?
- About specific practical steps You would have me take when praying for healing?
- About ministering soaking healing prayer with a group?

Chapter 9

Peg Yarbrough's Spirit-Led Approach to Healing

Rev. Peg Yarbrough is a friend of mine who has focused on healing prayer for many years of her life, so I asked her if she would share her approach.[1] Her answer is below. It is practical, spiritual, and heart-warming. You will see in her description that she is utilizing the principles we have taught in the first eight chapters of this book.[2]

Seven Spirit-Led Steps

Principle: Truth be told, I have ministered healings, including casting out demons, thousands of times, and no two are alike.

1. Opening prayer:

The first thing I do is pray for Jesus to be present in both our hearts, for a hedge of protection, and thank God for His gift of healing.

2. Building trust:

If it is someone I have never met, I ask Jesus to show me how to build their trust, so they feel free to open up completely with me.

Jesus told me years ago to ask questions. Get specific. What do they want/need?

3. Big meetings with high faith:

In a large, formal meeting with teachings and music, the "temperature" (faith) can run high; I can often minister in a few minutes and see the results.

a. If it is physical, I ask the recipient to do something they could not do before the healing: bend their leg, see clearly, have no pain, etc.

b. In a one-on-one counselor/healer situation, when we are not in that spiritually "charged" atmosphere, these sessions/encounters usually take one hour plus. The Lord is always present to heal, but the person with a need must also have trust in order to receive their healing.

4. One of the main goals, in that situation, is to "till the soil."

a. Build trust that God *will* heal them.

b. Remove anything that is subconsciously keeping the person from receiving the gift of healing from the Lord.

c. I ask the client to keep their eyes closed throughout the session in order to keep out as much external distraction as possible.

d. When I do multiple sessions with one person, we get to the results much quicker each time.

e. Once trust is built, they start seeing consistent results.

5. Peeling the onion:

a. Rarely with anyone is it just one thing.

b. We are body, soul, and spirit. They did not get messed up overnight, so it can take time. In reality, it usually takes several sessions to see major deliverance on all three levels—body, soul, and spirit.

c. If at all possible, I only ask simple questions, such as, "Ask *Jesus* to show you..." "When you think of your current situation, what emotion comes to mind?" That is always a negative emotion. They are here because they have a problem/need. And we build from there. Then we can get into past traumas, generational curses, word curses, soul ties, forgiving someone—you never know.

6. Always, always, always, Jesus is the great Counselor; not me!

a. My preference is to only ask questions and let Jesus speak directly to the client's spirit, and then they tell me what He said to them. I let Jesus do the counseling, I just keep the ball rolling. (I invite them to picture Jesus with them in a safe, loving place, and see what thought flows into their mind.)

b. Some folks have a very hard time getting into the flow, so when all else fails, I will ask *Spirit*-guided questions, and ask the client if Jesus is telling them yes or no. That often shakes things free so they can now hear Him and get in the flow themselves. It is kind of like priming the pump.

c. Frequently I ask the Lord to show them where the negative energy/spirit/belief was stored in their body. This is often very powerful as we cast out the darkness, and Jesus fills that place with light, healing, a new godly emotion, and often a new cellular vibration that affects the whole body positively. It is all connected. Always fill the empty "hole" with light, or seven more wicked will come back to roost. We fill it and seal it.

d. If I make any suggestions at the end, it is only inspired utterance! I work diligently to stay out of the way with my "solutions," my guess-work, and what I would do in their situation; all those are dead-end streets. I do not know anything; Jesus knows everything.

7. The greatest thing for me is to have zero judgments and overflowing love, *patience*, and compassion.

a. You cannot rush Jesus at work.

b. I am almost always surprised by what Jesus speaks to the client. It is usually something I would not have guessed in a million years. I find all of this quite thrilling—to participate in watching the Lord do His thing in their heart and soul. It is utterly fascinating.

c. Sometimes I thought a session was dead in the water, and we were getting nowhere, and then 30 or 40 minutes into the session, something would break loose. It is like a puzzle suddenly coming together, and then—it is great *joy*, and their healing comes to pass! Again, patience is the word of the day.

Reflections

If possible, I like to see the client, rather than just talk by phone, because you can see on their face when Jesus has touched them. It is often tears of joy, genuine relief, or just a huge smile!

I could talk about healing for days on end. I am constantly remembering healings I had forgotten I was part of, and they come back to my memory and bless me all over again. Or someone will call or email me and say, "You changed/saved my life 40 years ago...."

At some point, I usually have clients repeat after me something that Jesus showed them during the session, the blessing, because the Bible plainly says, "Believe in your heart, and confess with your mouth!"

There is something powerful about speaking a blessing over yourself.

For me (Peg) it is:

1. Fix our eyes on Jesus.
2. Pray—build *trust* in the promises of God.
3. Ask the person, "What do you want the Lord to do for you today?" This sets their expectation.
4. From there, I never know what is going to happen! I just stay relaxed and go with the flow of Jesus' plan.

No two healings are ever alike.

- If someone is going to passionately go into the healing and deliverance part of ministry, I say, *"Expect the unexpected!"*

- Have lots and lots of *patience*—do not rush the Lord.
- For decades I have studied every single healing Jesus did, studied them in-depth; and the one thing I learned is that every healing is different and unique!
- Everyone's life experience is different and unique, so that is the way I roll.
- It is all very intuitive.

Healing is part of proclaiming the Kingdom.

> *When Jesus had called the Twelve together, he gave them power and authority to drive out all demons and to cure diseases, and he sent them out to proclaim the kingdom of God and to heal the sick* (Lk. 9:1-2 NIV).

Healing, both giving and receiving, is one of many ways we proclaim the Kingdom of God. Isn't that wonderful? To God be the glory!

Uncovering lies that block the flow of *dunamis* healing power:

Find the lie and you will find the why. When looking for lies that are hindering the flow of healing power, you need to discover the original lie. Then follow Jesus' voice as you remove it and replace it with truth. This is a homerun.

Examples of limiting beliefs that restrict the flow of God's healing power:

1. I do not trust God (which is code for he/she is afraid of being disappointed). They do not usually say those words out loud; they just want to avoid getting to the nub of the problem.
2. Why would God do that for me?
3. Miracles went out with the apostles!
4. I am not righteous enough.
5. I am not good enough.

6. God will do that for them, but not for me.
7. I have never seen a miracle.
8. What if God fails this time?
9. And a million more...

Examples of emotions that restrict the flow of God's healing power:

1. Shame (is probably number one).
2. Unforgiveness or resentment, especially when aimed inward!
3. Guilt.
4. Fear of being disappointed: "What if this does not work?"
5. Afraid of getting honest with themselves or others.
6. "If Jesus takes this away, who will I be?" The problem/disease is so much a part of them that they are *afraid* of who they will be without it.
7. Even though the issue is painful, toxic, limiting, or destructive, it is still the "them" they are used to, wagging this pain around and having become "comfortable" with it.
8. I have had people who did not want to be healed because they would *lose* their Social Security or military disability benefits.
9. Afraid of losing *attention* that their addiction, sickness, etc. is bringing to their life.
10. Afraid to face life without their "crutch."
11. Afraid of what the *new* them would look like (I hear this one a lot.)
12. "I am not ready to give up that part of me yet."

Repressed memories restrict the flow of God's healing power.

People never cease to surprise me. Very few are deeply self-aware; we wear masks even with ourselves. Getting to the truth is often shocking and painful. Thank God we have Jesus in our midst to walk us through and heal the hurt.

A major sickness is usually triggered by a traumatic event that causes it to manifest in someone's life, but it is also an indicator of deeper contributing strands that go back years in a person's life that have never been dealt with and cleaned out. So, if the trigger reoccurs, the disease will also come back until the root is taken out. The lie-based thinking could go back to in utero! And it often does. The people who do the deeper work get the most long-lasting results. Homeostasis in body, soul, and spirit is a journey.

As new problems arise in my own life, I still go back for more inner healing myself. I do not need as much as I did in my 40s when Dr. Wade introduced me to this. Back then I had 40 years of lies and bad habits to deal with, but I still need "tune-ups" from my trusted counselors. I value them greatly to keep living in homeostasis.

Going Deeper[3] and Journaling Application

- Lord, what would You speak to me from Peg's testimony about Spirit-led healing?
- How would You have me be more Spirit-led as I pray for healing for myself and others?

Chapter 10

A Spirit-Led Protocol for Claiming God's Promises

How do I go about claiming the promises in the Bible? Do I demand them? Do I declare them? Do I proclaim them? Do I pick the promise, or do I ask the Holy Spirit to bring the right promise to my mind and for Him to tell me how to speak it and apply it properly? Do I ask Him if there are any specific changes He wants me to make in my life, so this promise can be realized? I journaled asking the Lord what He would say, and here is what I received.

Journaling: "Lord, what about claiming Your promises in the Bible?"

Mark, if a promise is made directly to you (the Church), it is for you. However, the steps to properly apply it and experience it are available through conversing with Me. My Kingdom is more than written promises. It is a relationship between you and your God, the King of Kings and the Wonderful Counselor.

For sure you would seek My wonderful counsel in the proper selection and application of any promise I have made to you. As man's thoughts are not God's thoughts, you cannot properly apply a verse any better than satan did when He tempted My Son in the wilderness. Satan offered the wrong verse at the wrong time and in the wrong way.

When you select a verse and seek to apply it and fit it into your life, it is much different than Me selecting the verse for you and showing you how to apply it. If I were *not* with you always, then, yes, you would need to do this on your own. However, I have said: "Lo, I AM with you always." This means you can come to Me at all times, receive living words, and do living works at all times, rather than *dead* works. The ability to do a miracle in My name, outside of intimacy with Me, does not impress Me, nor does it make you saved or My child or on the way to heaven (Matt. 7:21-23).

Learning how to release spiritual power is one thing, and anyone can learn that, Christian or non-Christian.

However, what I am seeking is *fellowship, intimacy, communion, living works, and you birthing things from My divine initiative*, not from man's initiative. I created mankind so I could have fellowship with them. That is still My passion and My desire. Do not do anything on your own, and yes, that even includes claiming My promises.

Would you claim a promise Patti made to you and demand it of her, or would you enter into an intimate caring discussion with her and see how that promise can be best carried out in the current circumstance? Patti is not a statue that you would ignore. She is a person whom you love and are intimate with. You do not *use* the promises which she has made to you. You enjoy discussing everything with her. You enjoy the fellowship. You enjoy the love. You enjoy the intimacy, and her provisions to you flow from that, and not from you claiming a promise she made to you. Provision comes through love, sharing, intimacy, and *ginosko*. (*Ginosko* is the Greek word for intimate knowing and is used when a husband knows his wife and they bear a child.)

The reason I told those who had the power to do miracles and cast out demons in My name that they were bound for hell is because they *did not ginosko me*. They were not in fellowship with me. They had learned rules for releasing power and were living out of the expression of those rules and not out of intimacy with Me. Therefore, I said to them, "Depart from Me; I never was intimate (*ginosko*) with you."

Mark, I desire you to abide in Me, walk in Me, live in Me, celebrate our times of intimacy together, and live through them, not apart from them.

Behold, I have spoken. Behold, it is to be done.

*Not everyone who says to Me, "Lord, Lord," will enter the Kingdom of heaven, but he who does the will of My Father who is in heaven will enter. Many will say to Me on that day, "Lord, Lord, did we not prophesy in Your name, and in Your name cast out demons, and in Your name perform many miracles?" And then I will declare to them, "I never **knew** [ginosko] you; depart from Me, you who practice lawlessness"* (Matt. 7:21-23 NASB95).

Response to the Above Journaling, from Peg Yarbrough[1]

Mark, you hit the nail on the head! So many people do not understand that spiritual power is a spiritual law/gift. A gift is yours to do with as you choose. Once a person taps into how to use it, they can use it for selfish, even demonic reasons (Simon the Sorcerer). Satan can counterfeit all the manifestations of the Spirit! But they will not bring good to mankind; they come at a high price to the receiver.

I know the Bible says, "Whatsoever you shall ask in my name, believing, you shall receive it." I agree the "in my name" points to *ginosko*, a continuing, growing intimacy, and communion with the Lord. Some folks decide what promise they "need" to claim, say it over and over, and never get their answer. Saying is not the same as having faith. That is the key that unlocks the door.

I am at the point in my life where I realize I do not even know what to ask for, because God knows my heart better than I do. So I ask Him, "Lord, what do I ask for?" And I look to the Comforter to bring to my heart's remembrance whatever Jesus is saying I need, and He lets me know (Jn. 14:26). Then I lock in on that.

I am still trying to figure some stuff out; for example, it seems to me that God will bend over backward to show Himself strong to "babes in the Word." But as we mature, "to whom much is given, much is required" (Lk. 12:48). It seems like He expects more trust as we grow in grace. Perhaps the Father wants us to grow more and more God-dependent! The depth of intimacy between us is my choice.

I am trying to get a handle on this, but it seems like the more we know *ginosko*, the more God expects us to simply trust Him on a deeper level. Take the training wheels off. To me, it is kind of like expecting more out of your 40-year-old son than out of your toddler or teenager.

Once Papa shows me what I need, I focus on that promise or *rhema*. Then, the more intimate and relaxed we get with Him, the more freely we can receive. Second Corinthians says we grow from glory to glory in the face of Jesus Christ. One cannot have relationship without deep conversations, "face to face," heart to heart. Hence, our need for the four keys to communion with God.

But we all, with open face beholding as in a glass the glory of the Lord, are changed into the same image from glory to glory, even as by the Spirit of the Lord (2 Cor. 3:18 KJV).

Wow! Being born again is sonship. Deciding to move into that place of deep trust, that Papa really loves us beyond measure and, therefore, we completely trust Him—that is fellowship.

The following day, Peg sent over more reflections:

I gave a lot of thought to, "Can we claim any of the promises of God?"

That all depends on what your definition of *claim*. A lot of folks believe because they go to a chapter and verse, pick out a promise, and say it over and over and over, it belongs to them because they said it a bunch of times. This is kind of like in the witchcraft field called incantations. The promise does not come to pass because of incantations or repetition! Jesus warned against that in Matthew 6:7. He said not to think you are going to get something because you say it over and over, but pray like this: "Our Father" and focus on heaven and heaven's provision. We need to ask what the Lord is saying that we actually need.

So the understanding lies in the word *claim*, which comes back to your word *ginosko*. It is not looking so much at the promise as it is focusing on the Promisor! When I go to the bank to cash a check, and I know the money is in my account, I do not have one iota of a doubt they are going to hand me my cash. It is not the check, the piece of paper. It is what's behind the paper. God is behind His *rhema*; He's got the goods and never disappoints!

When you know in your heart of hearts that the words of their Promisor are yes and amen; they are true, and they are meant for you; it is your "account," and Jesus filled it to the brim—it is that attitude of heart that brings the promise of God into manifestation/concretion.

I think we get religion confused with relationship, and that is the real problem. It is also the real answer when we get it right. Relationship is the key.

Mark's Response Back to Peg

I fully agree with this.

And my addition is, while I am saying, "Our Father Who art in heaven," I am to be lifting my eyes to the heavens and seeing Him and acknowledging His holiness ("hallowed be Thy name").

Then I tune to flow and let the Spirit begin revealing to me things, and I speak forth what I am seeing: "Thy kingdom come, Thy will be done." So healing prayer is ministering from flowing thoughts, flowing pictures, and flowing emotions (i.e., His River of Life). I am sharing in what He is doing in this situation and at this specific moment. At this point, my heart and spirit are engaged, not just my mouth. The eyes of my heart, ears of my heart, and the emotions of my heart are participating. I am in the Spirit and reverently in His presence as I minister. I have now moved from a head thing and a mechanical thing to a reverent, heart, devotional, intimate (*ginosko*) encounter.

Since His words are spirit and life, and the flesh profits nothing (Jn. 6:63), I have just stepped from the flesh that profits nothing, to *rhema*, which is flowing from the Holy Spirit. I have stepped from death to life, from religion to relationship. Now I am doing nothing on my own initiative, but only what I hear and see my Father doing. This is Christianity! This is how Jesus lived (Jn. 5:19-20, 30; 8:26, 38). This is what releases the Kingdom!

Pastor Margaret Cornell Shares How She Receives *Rhema* Words for Healing[2]

In thinking about how I receive Scriptures—first, since "all of the promises of God are yes and amen for us in Christ," I cannot see why anyone would have a problem with claiming them. However, I think the Holy Spirit must be the "Highlighter" and be involved in the process. I think where people go wrong is in snatching a word with head knowledge rather than allowing the Spirit to lead. Having said that, if they meditate on the verse and get true revelation, God can use it!

Margaret shares examples of claiming God's promises:

The Flu

I had the flu and felt terrible. I went to bed and started to play Kenneth Hagin's healing Scriptures on tape. After turning the tape over several times and only half listening, a Scripture jumped out.

The sun of righteousness will arise with healing in its wings; and you will go forth and skip about like calves from the stall" (Mal. 4:2 NASB95).

Immediately I had no symptoms in my body. I lay there for a while thinking that it is odd that I do not feel sick anymore. I got up and loaded the dishwasher, which surprised a friend who knew I had been very unwell. She said, "I thought you were sick." I said, "Yes I was, but now I am well."

Direction for a Major Move

Another time my husband and I were seeking God about moving to Ely to start a church. We both agreed that we would fast and seek God in our daily readings from the Church of England Lectionary. That week God spoke to us both highlighting very meaningful Scriptures, so we made the move!

Changing Jobs

Another time we were praying about Tony leaving full-time work to be a paid pastor. I had a ladies' group whom I asked to pray in a downstairs room while I went upstairs and asked God for three Scriptures. I knelt down and listened. I clearly heard three Scripture references, not knowing what they were. Each of them confirmed definitively that it was time for Tony to be full time. Tony also received his own Scriptures.

Resolving Cancer

When I was diagnosed with cancer, I knew I needed a key Scripture to take hold of. So during the week I kept very quiet as I listened. One day I looked on my bookshelf and found a book by Jerry Savelle which I leafed through. I was surprised to see a program by him on the Christian channel that very day.

When I listened, it was the same message as in the book. The Scripture that leapt out was:

There is no one like the God of Jeshurun, who rides the heavens to help you, and in His excellency on the clouds. The eternal God is your refuge, and underneath are the everlasting arms; He will thrust out the enemy from before you, and will say, "Destroy!" (Deut. 33:26-27 NKJV).

I knew that was my word, and I would speak to the cancer frequently saying, "Cancer, my God is destroying you." After doing so many other things, this was the final piece that did destroy the cancer.

Scripture Verses Arising as I Sang in the Spirit

I had a period of time when I was in extended worship every day. After an hour or two of singing in the Spirit and walking around my garden, eventually Scripture verses arose in my heart. I declared them over situations I was in and received results.

Impounded Dog Returned

I was in our kitchen at the church center. A church member came in very upset, telling me that her sick dog had been impounded by the RSPCA, and she was accused of cruelty. I knew this could not be a true accusation and began to pray in tongues. Despite there being many people in the room who would probably not understand, a word rose within me and I shouted: "No weapon formed against you will prosper and every tongue rising against you in judgment will be refuted. This is your inheritance as a servant of the Most High God" (see Isa. 54:17). The dog was soon returned!

While Praying Over Someone with Fibromyalgia

Suddenly a Scripture I had not thought of for years leaped into my mind, and I spoke with authority: "When I passed by and saw you weltering in your blood, I said to you in your blood live...I speak life into your blood" (see Ezek. 16:6). This ended with good results.

Kidney Stone

In 1978, I'd had a kidney stone removed with a big operation. There was no keyhole surgery then! I was really sick and feeling terrible; but we had recently heard about confessing the word of God, and I was struggling to do it rather feebly, just muttering it to myself because it sounded such a lie! That night to my amazement Jesus came into the room, stood at the bottom of my bed, and touched my feet. The power of God shot through my body, and I was completely healed and sent home the next day. I am sure He came to honor His word.

Selling Our Home

Another time we were selling a house and did not realize the people wanting to buy it were trying to trick us. However, as I prayed God said, "Your house is amid treachery and deceit." We took authority, and they withdrew.

Then another man came and made an almost unbelievable offer. He, too, was false so we stood in faith again. Eventually a lady came, glanced round the house quickly, and said, "Yep, we'll have it," and that was it!

Others Have Given Me Scriptures That Brought Cleansing and Health

I went to the Lighthouse, where my son now pastors, for a wedding. Two of his elders, Joseph and Constance (Nigerians), prayed with me after the service; and as a result, I do feel much better.

They began by giving me a Scripture, and they said, "The scepter of wickedness shall not remain in the land allotted to the righteous" (see Ps. 125:3). Well, it went off in my spirit like a bomb, and I received it.

Joseph also said that when Giles told him about "my condition," he had cried out and said, "Oh no, no, no, no, no, the devil will not have the last word in her life!" Immediately my spirit soared, and I said in agreement, "I agree; the devil will not have the last word."

Joseph then took a bottle of water, just an ordinary bottle of filtered water, and he said, "I am praying over this; and when you drink it, it will cleanse your system supernaturally of all the toxins put in it by the chemotherapy and anything else."

The next morning, my urine was a terrible color and smelled, which it does not normally, and I declared, "Gosh, there are those toxins!"

It is an amazing story of how God has brought wisdom and people into my life to help and support my life until my healing manifests.

Mark Suggests This Seven-Step Model for Receiving Faith-Building *Rhema* and Visions

Here is a life model I adopted about 40 years ago. I use this simple model for everything: healing, walking in health, living in victory, joy, and peace, and fulfilling my destiny. Following is the story of how this was birthed in my consciousness and what the seven steps are.

After reading about Dr. David Yonggi Cho's church of 1 million people in Seoul, South Korea, and Kenneth Hagin's miracle-filled ministry, I knelt at the altar of my church and in prayer said, "Lord, I want to do great things for You. I want to see miracles released through my life. How does this happen?"

As I pondered that question, in a flash God showed the following to me. It was a combination of strategies that Cho and Hagin were using. I have lived out of this revelation ever since. By following a few simple steps, God has birthed miracles as well as an international ministry out through me, which is far beyond my wildest imagination. I pray He does the same for you as you let God fill all five senses of your spirit with Himself.

Filling all five senses of your spirit with God creates inner alignment!

Abraham is called the Father of Faith (Rom. 4:11-16). I believe that this means that he models all the key steps that we need to take if we desire to be children of faith. The Bible says we can cast mountains into the sea if we do not doubt in our hearts (Mk. 11:22-24). We want to understand how to have heart faith so we can see miracles released through our hands. We want to speak to mountains in our lives (i.e., sickness, poverty, demons, etc.) and see them removed! So let's see what we can learn from the Father of Faith. How did Abraham grow so strong in faith?

Step 1: Faith begins with a *spoken word* from the Lord.

God spoke a promise into Abraham's heart.

> Now the Lord **said** to Abram, "Go forth from your country, and
> from your relatives and from your father's house, to the land which
> I will show you; and I will make you a great nation, and I will
> bless you, and make your name great; and so you shall be a bless-
> ing; and I will bless those who bless you, and the one who curses

you I will curse. And in you all the families of the earth will be blessed" (Gen. 12:1-3 NASB95).

So when we need a miracle, we go to God in prayer and ask, "Lord, what do You want to say to me about this situation?" We listen for His voice, tuning to flowing thoughts, and we write down what He speaks back to us.[3]

Step 2: God adds a *vision*, a picture of the promise fulfilled.

God showed Abraham a vision (Gen. 15:1):

> *And He took him outside and said, "**Now look** toward the heavens, and count the stars, if you are able to count them." And He said to him, "So shall your descendants be." **Then he believed** in the Lord; and He reckoned it to him as righteousness* (Gen. 15:5-6 NASB95).

We say a picture is worth 1,000 words. According to the above verses, I would say the Bible agrees. You will note that as soon as God gives Abraham a picture of the promise fulfilled, the next verse tells us, "*Then he believed.*" So I understand that in order to have miracle-working faith, I need two things from God: I need God to speak a *rhema* word to me, and I need God to show me a picture of this *rhema* word fulfilled.

> *Lord, what does my healed body look like? What will I be able to do when You have restored me to full health? What does Your blessing of prosperity look like in my life? What does total freedom and release look like? Can You show me pictures of these things? Thank You, Lord!*

Once we have received a *rhema* word and a vision from the Lord concerning His promises and provision for any area of our lives, then conception has taken place. We are now pregnant with the purposes of God for that area of our lives.[4]

Step 3: We *ponder* this *rhema* and vision from God—nothing else!

> *And not being weak in faith, he **did not consider** his own body, already dead (since he was about a hundred years old), and the deadness of Sarah's womb. He **did not waver at the promise of God through unbelief,** but was strengthened in faith, giving glory to God, and being fully convinced that what He had promised He was also able to perform. And therefore "it was accounted to him for righteousness"* (Rom. 4:19-22 NKJV).

As with Abraham, we must choose what we are going to look at and what we are going to believe. Abraham could have looked at the weakness of his aged body and said, "Reality is, I cannot reproduce anymore," but instead he chose not to consider (ponder and picture) his weakness but, instead, to ponder and picture only the promise and vision of God.

So, I choose carefully to daily, continuously ponder and see only God's promised blessing to me, and not lack or need. As God spoke to me, "Whatever you fix your eyes upon grows within you; whatever grows within you, you become." This changed my life. I no longer look at disease, self-effort, lack, weakness, or law. Now I only fix my eyes on Jesus (Heb. 12:1-2; Acts 2:25; Ps. 16:8) and His spoken promises and visions to me; and these grow within me, and I step into these realities. I am healed! I am blessed! I have favor everywhere I go! I release effective ministry to those I touch! I have a blessed marriage and family! Thank You, Lord, for these amazing gifts!

What do you see in your mind's eye: lack or fullness, disease or health, division or unity, rejection or acceptance? We ponder and see something all the time. Make sure you are only seeing God's promises to you in every area of your life! We choose to meditate on God's promise and visions to us in both our morning and evening prayer meditations, as well as throughout the day (1 Chron. 23:30). I would recommend a 5- to 15-minute prayer meditation of thanksgiving morning and evening where you speak the promises God has made to you in the various areas of your life. Filling your heart and mind with His divine light causes darkness to flee.

Step 4: We *speak* the *rhema* and vision God has spoken to us.

When Abraham was 99 years old (Gen. 17:1) and had no children by his wife, God asked him to speak a word of faith and call the promise into being:

> *No longer shall your name be called Abram, but your name shall be Abraham; for I have made you a father of many nations* (Gen. 17:5 NKJV).

The name *Abraham* means "father of a multitude," so now every time Abraham speaks his name aloud, he is confessing God's promise to him. Abraham was convinced that "God...calls those things which do not exist as though they did" (Rom. 4:17 NKJV), and "by faith we understand that the *worlds were framed* by the word of God, so that the things which are seen were not made of things which are visible" (Heb. 11:3 NKJV).

In the same way, our spoken words become the directives that *frame* the creative miracles we are going to see. *Breath* and *spirit* are the same words in the Greek and Hebrew languages. When we speak what God speaks, the spiritual energy/realities that have been growing within us through our daily meditations on God's *rhema* and vision pour out with our spoken words and create that which we frame with the words of our mouths. Death and life truly are in the power of the tongue (Prov. 18:21)!

God will tell us what words to speak. We do not need to come up with them ourselves. We ask God what He wants us to speak about our situations, and He will tell us. God said to Abram, "Your name shall be Abraham," so God told Abram exactly what to say and, incidentally, God waited a period of time before telling Abram to confess this new name. So we always keep God in the center of the process. We do not need to be doing things on our initiative. Our only desire is to live as Jesus did, out of divine initiative (Jn. 5:30).

So shall My word be that goes forth from My mouth; it shall not return to Me void, but it shall accomplish what I please, and it shall prosper in the thing for which I sent it (Isa. 55:11 NKJV).

Now that I have God's direction as to what to confess, how to confess it, and when to confess it, I need to speak it boldly, decree it, declare it, believe it and envision it. This is crucial in the birthing of a miracle.

Step 5: We *act* on the *rhema* and vision God has spoken to us.

Faith without works is dead (Jas. 2:17). "Take up your bed and walk" (see Lk. 5:24). We decide to get up and walk. We decide to walk on the water, to take risks, aware that God must and will come through. As long as our eyes stay on the Lord, our faith is intact, and the miracle happens. Peter walked on the water as long as he looked only at the Lord Jesus Christ. When he looked at other places, fear entered in, which disconnected him from the power of God, and down he went (Matt. 14:29-31).

Abraham "grew strong in faith" (Rom. 4:20 NASB95), which brought him to the place of instant, total obedience to God's ongoing directives to him. He acted, circumcising his family on the very same day God commanded him to do so (Gen. 17:23), his wife became pregnant immediately following, and within one year Isaac was born (Gen. 22:1-2).

We, too, grow strong in faith through daily, prayerfully reviewing in our hearts and minds the *rhema* and visions of Almighty God, and in the fullness of time, He brings forth a miracle (Gal. 4:4).

Step 6: We *die* to self-effort.

The fullness of time—hmmm. It only took 24 years for Sarah to become pregnant! "Personally, God, I do not want to wait 24 years for anything to happen. I prefer it to happen within 24 minutes or 24 seconds of the time You speak it." His answer back to me was, "Who writes the rules of the universe, you or Me?"

"Fine, You do."

So many times, miracles require an incubation period before they are released from the invisible, spiritual world into the visible, physical world. I need to make sure that, while I wait, I stay tuned only to God's voice and vision and do not come up with my own ideas of how to make things happen (Gen. 16:1-2). If I do, I will be birthing an Ishmael, which will not be accepted by God (Gen. 17:18-19). I must die to all self-initiated behavior (Jn. 14:10) and only do those things I hear and see the Father doing (Jn. 8:26, 38). Wow! This is a counter-cultural way of living. Lord, teach me to live this way, I pray.

Step 7: In the fullness of time, *God brings forth* the miracle.

> *And the Lord visited Sarah as He had said, and the Lord did for Sarah as He had spoken. For Sarah conceived and bore Abraham a son in his old age, at the set time of which God had spoken to him. ...Abraham was one hundred years old when his son Isaac was born to him* (Gen 21:1-2, 5 NKJV).

Wow! It only took 24 years for this miracle to get started, and the full manifestation of it (i.e., the earth being blessed through Abraham's seed) occurred 1,500 years later when Jesus was resurrected from the dead! Yikes, now I do not like the rules of the universe. However, I only have two choices: one is to say, "Yes, Lord," and the other is to become angry and bitter and fall away from the living Lord. Of course, whatever is not of faith is sin (Rom. 14:23).

Okay, Lord, I believe, and I am willing to go to my grave believing in the *rhema* and vision You have given to me. I will be a worshipper until the day I die, and then I will continue worshipping You for all eternity.

A summary of the seven-step model of ministering from the Holy Spirit's direction:

1. Faith begins with a *spoken word* from the Lord.
2. God adds a *vision*, a picture of the promise fulfilled.

3. We *ponder* this *rhema* and vision from God—nothing else!
4. We *speak* the *rhema* and vision God has spoken to us, according to His directions.
5. We *act* on the *rhema* and vision God has spoken to us.
6. We *die to self-effort*.
7. In the *fullness of time, God brings forth* the miracle.

Mountain-moving faith is conceived by a *rhema* and vision from God, which, when incubated through pondering, speaking, and acting, births a miracle in God's fullness of time.[5]

For healing to occur you need to: 1) be in inner alignment, 2) use vision and observe the healing process through to its finish. You watch God's energy flow; and as it touches body parts, they are healed.

Abraham saw the miracle completed (millions of stars representing the millions of children he would have). Gazing upon this finished work raises faith, drawing the miracle into full manifestation.[6]

Going Deeper[7] and Journaling Application

- Lord, what would You speak to me about how I am to claim Your promises?
- Lord what would You have me learn from the steps Abraham took in becoming the Father of Faith?
- Lord, what am I to be decreeing today?

Chapter 11

Twenty-Eight Therapeutic Healing Protocols

Finally Set Free!

Cindi writes: "I am 67 and my hobby and passion since my 20s has been nutrition and health. But I never felt confident that some of what I have been interested in was okay, because there is so much New Age thought; and when you go shopping, you see a lot of different looking and thinking people. So I was uncertain if I was in areas a Christian should not be. Your teaching on various health approaches has set me free to be who I am, a Christian who has studied and loved the alternative stuff that is not drugs and allopathic, with a desire to help people feel better. Thank you so much."

Mark writes: "Cindi, you are welcome. Thankfully, we do not gauge things by whether New Agers do them or not. New Agers drive cars. I am not going to decide to not drive a car just because a New Ager does. No, we gauge things by whether they are compatible with Scripture, produce life, and the Spirit of Truth within us affirms this is a direction we are to go in. All 28 therapeutic modalities below meet these conditions, so be at peace and enjoy!"

Therapeutic healing would fall into the category of gifts of healings: *"God has appointed in the church...gifts of healings"* (1 Cor. 12:28 NASB95).

Foundational study: Supplement E: *Therapeuo* Healing Is More Often *Process* Healing.

What therapeutic methods could produce a fairly quick response?

Over half the times in the Gospels, the word translated as "heal" is *therapeuo*, and we normally think of these as cures or remedies, which are not necessarily quick. This raises the question, "Could any of these *therapeuo* remedies generate a rather quick response?"

Yes, the following could all produce a fairly quick healing response:

1. **Deliverance**: When a demon is cast out, the change can be instantaneous, especially if you do the follow-up prayer of commanding any bodily damage done by the demon to be healed in Jesus' name.
2. **Inner healing**: When Jesus shows up in a painful scene and shows you what He is doing, that brings peace and release, which in turn removes stress, the major cause of disease.
3. **Repenting for judgments and anger**: Forgive everything against everyone, the Bible says, or you will be turned over to the tormentors (demons). Leading people in heart prayers of forgiveness, where you picture the person and the scene of the pain, and say, "I choose to forgive you, to honor you, to love you, and to release you in Jesus' name" offers great immediate release of stress and frees one to experience deliverance from the tormentors (demons).
4. **Laughter**: Laughing removes stress, resulting in healing.
5. **Breaking curses** can bring an instantaneous spiritual and physical release.
6. **Herbs**: In the Bible, a branch immediately turned bitter water to sweet.
7. **Speaking life**, not death, over yourself.
8. **Confessing sins** one to another.
9. **Praying in tongues** releases stress, builds the immune system, and energizes one's spirit.

I can easily testify that when I did inner healing prayer to deal with my anger, I was healed of my arthritis. That testimony doesn't mention how long the healing took, but if you ask for that, I will tell you: 50 percent of the pain was gone in 24 hours, and within a week all the pain was gone. So, saying I was healed is true; however, it does not address the *time involved* for the healing to become fully visible. Most often the Gospels do not address the time involved, other than in a few cases they specify it was immediate. I suppose the fact they specify some were immediate indicates that others were not.

Twenty-Eight Therapeutic Modalities

Since one of the Greek words translated as "healing" is *therapeuo*, here are 28 therapeutic healings that are either specifically mentioned in the Bible or compatible with Scripture. This is just a sampling. If I fall ill, I explore any option compatible with Scripture to restore my health.[1]

When fighting off illness, prayerfully scan down through the list below asking God to reveal to you the gifts of healings He wants you to apply (1 Cor. 12:28). Then apply them. *Never quit* until you have reached your goal of *complete health!* Do not settle for infirmity. I have personally used the approaches below and found them helpful in restoring and maintaining my health.

Explore the endnotes, especially for this chapter! To simplify your reading, I have put information about additional educational resources and my personal recommendations of products for the various categories into the endnotes. They are packed with vital information that can be lifesaving! Take the time to check them out.

#1: God's design is that our bodies heal themselves.

A cut will always go to work healing itself. The cut never stops to ask if it is God's will. We never need to ask if it is God's will to heal. It is! Jesus never asked if it was God's will to heal anyone. So know that time will heal, especially if you give your body the nutritional tools to work with and an atmosphere of emotional peace (Phil. 4:7).

Three foundational keys to physical health are: 1) building the immune system, 2) detoxifying the body and soul, and 3) nourishing the cells. Any activity that contributes to one or more of these three activities promotes health.

I once read the introduction to a 900-page book on cancer treatments written by medical doctors and recommending allopathic approaches to healing. In the introduction, the doctors indicated that *if you have a strong immune system, cancer cannot develop.* Unfortunately, they did not go on to say what could be done to strengthen the immune system. So, here is a list of things I know of that make the immune system stronger and more resilient: love, laughter, joy, peace, speaking in tongues, fasting, internal cleanses, nutrition, hydration, and exercise. (This is just a sampling.) It is imperative that we do these so our immune systems are strong and can ward off disease and illness!

#2: Casting out demons promotes health (Matt. 8:16; 10:1, 8; Mk. 1:34; 6:13).

Jesus healed many by casting out demons. Assume this will be a normal part of at least one-quarter of those you pray for. It was for Jesus.[2]

#3: Break generational curses.

> *You shall not worship them or serve them; for I, the Lord your God, am a jealous God, visiting the iniquity of the fathers on the children, on the third and the fourth generations of those who hate Me* (Exod. 20:5 NASB95).

Use heart prayers, picturing the cross of Christ between you (as a baby in your mother's womb) and the streaming generational sins and curses flowing toward you. Command them to halt at the cross and fall to the ground powerless at the foot of the cross. Then speak for the blessings of Calvary to cascade down over that baby in the womb.[3]

#4: Heal Dissociative Identity Disorder.

There is a unique prayer approach developed by Rev. Bob Lucy that heals fractured hearts, a condition common in those who have experienced satanic ritual abuse. Bob's prayer ministry can take place over the phone or in person, and it is extremely effective.[4]

#5: Commanding residual trauma to be released from our cells promotes health (Mk. 11:22-23).

Lay your hands on the area affected by the trauma and speak, "I command the memory of the trauma from this (*name whatever the trauma was)* to be released from these cells in the name of the Lord Jesus Christ. Trauma, be gone. Trauma, be gone. Trauma, be gone in Jesus' name. I speak peace and restoration to these cells in the name of Jesus. Cells, be restored to your normal, natural function in Jesus' name" (repeat three times). You can pray these prayers for any lingering infirmity. The traumas can be left over in your body from an event, a sickness, a rash, a broken bone, etc. Remember that prayer from your heart includes the use of flowing pictures, flowing words, and flowing emotions, so follow the flow as you pray (Jn. 7:38-39; 5:19-20, 30). As you speak, picture Jesus doing the speaking and His hands being laid on these traumatized cells.

#6: Herbs are for the service of mankind.

> *He causeth the grass to grow for the cattle, and **herb** for the service of man: that he may bring forth food out of the earth* (Ps. 104:14 KJV).

> *The **leaves** of the tree were for the healing of the nations* (Rev. 22:2 NASB95).

> *Use a little **wine** for your stomach's sake* (1 Tim. 5:23 NKJV).

> *The Lord showed him a **tree**; and he threw it into the waters, and the* [bitter] *waters became sweet* (Ex. 15:25 NASB95).

Herbs are God's medicine. Herbs are anti-fungal and anti-bacterial and come from the leaves, bark, and roots of trees. Take them as necessary.[5]

The energy vibrations present in herbs can also be put into a homeopathic remedy.

German lifespans vs. U.S. lifespans:

Doctors in Germany can prescribe herbs (therapeutics), and German men live *five years longer* than U.S. men. German healthcare cost per person is *half* of the U.S. Germans did not throw out herbs and homeopathic treatments when pharmaceuticals were introduced. The U.S. went 100 percent pharmaceutical and threw out herbs, homeopathic remedies, etc.[6]

#7: Fasting/cleansing promotes health.

Fast and your health *"shall spring forth speedily"* (Isa. 58:6-11). Water and juice fasts for three to ten days are excellent means for your body to rest, detoxify, and heal.[7]

#8: Emotional wholeness promotes health (Prov. 17:22).

Psychologists believe 85 percent of illnesses have an emotional root. A joyful heart is good medicine. Laughter is healing. You remove the psychosomatic roots of diseases by growing in faith, hope, and love (1 Cor. 13:13), which displace the opposites of fear, hopelessness, and anger. Recognize that dis-ease in your soul produces disease in your body.[8]

Faith is a powerful healing and creative force (Mk. 9:23-25; Gal. 3:5; Jas. 5:14-16). You can grow in faith by asking God to speak to you concerning your healing and show you a vision of yourself healed; then ponder this, speak it, and act on it, and it shall come forth (Mk. 11:22-24).[9] Faith is increased by 1) asking for the gift of faith, 2) growing in revelation knowledge, and 3) exercising the faith one has. Often, through experience, individuals grow into a specific faith/anointing to heal one type of infirmity. Some examples from recent healing evangelists include goiters, blind eyes, or barrenness.

#9: Praise and worship promote health.

It allows you to enter before God's throne room and soak up His presence and light and healing love and power (Rev. 5:11-14; Exod. 34:29; Hab. 3:4).[10] Patti Virkler shares the following testimony concerning one aspect of the healing power of praise and worship.

> I tend toward high blood pressure, so I try to check on it regularly to be sure it is under control. The other day when I was grocery shopping, I used the machine in the pharmacy to check it out. As I sat there with my arm in the brace, I was just looking around at the people and reading the information on the machine. The numbers came in at 149/83. Well, that certainly was not what I was expecting or wanting! I had been feeling fine, and I did not want to accept the numbers as accurate; so when the machine offered the option of re-testing and finding the average, I went with it. The second time it was testing, though, I closed my eyes and silently sang a worship song to the Lord. I was amazed to see that the numbers had decreased to a much healthier 125/79! Not only do we please the Lord when we worship Him; we bring life to our physical bodies.

According to Dr. Benson's book, *The Relaxation Response*,[11] the relaxation response is "a physical state of deep rest that changes the physical and emotional responses to stress (e.g., decreases in heart rate, blood pressure, rate of breathing, and muscle tension)." Guess what? It is also typical that wholehearted participation in throne room worship will produce this relaxation response, as will abiding in Christ.

Worship involves a heart of appreciation. The Institute of HeartMath has shown that expressing gratitude and appreciation have a positive impact on your heart rhythm.[12]

And cardiac surgeon Dr. Steven Gundry has gathered research showing that singing builds your immune system.[13]

#10: Rest.

Both a good night's sleep[14] and living in Sabbath rest promote health (Gen. 2:3; Lev. 16:31; Mk. 2:27; Heb. 4:1-11). Living in Sabbath rest is resting from your labors and realizing God is the One who blesses and increases the work of your hands, and it is He who provides all your needs. You learn to "rest" in His arms as you walk through life.

#11: Death and life are in the power of the tongue (Prov. 18:21).

Every word you speak is an instruction to your body. For example, "You make me sick to my stomach" means you will have a sickly stomach. "You are a pain in the neck" means you will have a painful neck. You can speak God's healing promises.[15]

#12: Godly imaginations take you forward.

> But they hearkened not, nor inclined their ear, but walked in the counsels and in the imagination of their evil heart, and went backward, and not forward (Jer. 7:24 KJV).

Picturing things contrary to Scripture (evil imagination) takes me backward. Picturing biblical truth (godly imagination) takes me forward. I must be constantly aware that my eyes are fixed on Jesus (Heb. 12:1-2), and I am tuned to flow and see Him in action in every picture I gaze upon in my mind. This produces health and life!

#13: Anoint with oil.

> Is anyone among you sick? Then he must call for the elders of the church and they are to pray over him, anointing him with oil in the name of the Lord (Jas. 5:14 NASB95).

Biblically, of course, anointing with oil is often used to represent or demonstrate the anointing of the Holy Spirit. But is it possible that the healing properties of essential oils could also be suggested as a way to minister *therapeuo?* A great book on this is *Healing Oils of the Bible,* by David Stewart.[16]

#14: Confess sins one to another.

> *Therefore, confess your sins to one another, and pray for one another so that you may be healed. The effective prayer of a righteous man can accomplish much* (Jas. 5:16 NASB95).

Ask God to show you any sin that has allowed this infirmity into your life. (Read Deuteronomy 28 and Proverbs 17:22.) Do not be shy about confessing sin. We have all sinned and fallen short of the glory of God (Rom. 3:23); there is none righteous, no not one (Rom. 3:10, 20). Confession brings healing. We need to be free to admit that we are sinners saved by grace. It is not of ourselves; it is a gift of God. We are the weak ones. He is the strong one. It is okay to be weakness fused to strength. That is the way it is. So we find our perfection *in Christ,* rather than in ourselves. Trust me, everyone else has sinned, too. Confess your sins to your spiritual counselor, then see yourself decked out in Christ's robe of righteousness which you put on by faith (Phil. 3:9).

#15: Roaring at the enemy defeats the enemy.

> *For thus hath the Lord spoken unto me, Like as the lion and the young lion roaring on his prey...so shall the Lord of hosts come down to fight for mount Zion, and for the hill thereof* (Isa. 31:4 KJV).

See Jesus and yourself roaring together at the blocks the enemy has put in your path. Since you are always picturing something, this is a biblical picture to gaze upon and engage yourself in emotionally as you roar to demolish the enemy holding you back. Get intense! Emotions are energy in motion.

You can roar together with God at the infirmity, commanding it to be gone in Jesus' name, and watching it dissipate into thin air. We start with a situation that has set itself up against the rule and reign of God in our lives. In Isaiah 31:3, the Egyptians looked to the strength of their army as their god. So the true God was going to come and roar at this army, this false "reality" set up by satan, and fight against it and destroy it (Isa. 31:5).

That is exactly what the Lord wants us to do over the ungodly situations in our lives. These situations could be a lingering sickness, infirmity, sin, fear, doubt, unbelief, anger, poverty, disunity, etc. Anything in your life that is contrary to the Word of God is an enemy that the Lord of Hosts wants to destroy.[17]

#16: Wash using running water.

Now when the man with the discharge becomes cleansed from his discharge, then he shall count off for himself seven days for his cleansing; he shall then wash his clothes and bathe his body in running water and will become clean (Lev. 15:13 NASB95).

Interestingly, the practice of handwashing was lost and then re-introduced to medicine in 1846 by a brave medical resident in Austria, Ignaz Semmelweis. He experimented at the childcare clinic where he worked, asking doctors to wash their hands between assisting patients. Patient deaths immediately fell by *90 percent*. Rather than be rewarded for this insight, Semmelweis was ridiculed by the doctors, fired from his hospital, made professionally unemployable, and was eventually driven out of Vienna entirely. He died broke in Hungary, in a psychiatric hospital, after suffering a severe beating by asylum guards.

This story is an example of the observation attributed to George Orwell, that, "In a time of universal deceit, telling the truth is a revolutionary act."

#17: Exercising promotes health.

"Bodily exercise profits" us in this life (1 Tim. 4:8 NKJV); and, of course, spiritual exercise profits for both this life and the next. "Use it or lose it" is one of our mottoes. God has designed our bodies to move. Movement increases both blood flow (which provides vitality to the cells), and also flow of lymph, which is the activation of our immune system. In addition, muscle strength is increased, the body is toned, and overall health is established and maintained. Check out the books *Foundation: Redefine Your Core, Conquer Back Pain,* and *Move with Confidence* by Dr. Eric Goodman and *Pain Free* by Pete Egoscue.

All sorts of exercise programs and equipment are available. It would probably be wise to ask the people you know who are most fit what they have found and what they do.

#18: Eat a healthy diet.

Our passion is to eat clean, organic, unprocessed, locally grown whole foods. Anything man messes with is not as good as what God created. Dr. Josh Axe offers a great overview of various healthy diets and exercise plans on his website.[18] One specialized healing diet that has been used successfully for more than 75 years is the Budwig Diet.[19]

#19: Take enzymes, vitamins, and antioxidants.

We take a digestive enzyme[20] with everything we eat. We take lots of vitamins, and the two primary places we order from are R-Garden[21] and Life Extension.[22]

#20: Drink clean, healthy water.

When God wants a descriptive word for His healing qualities, one of the terms He uses is "water."

> *And he showed me a pure river of **water of life**, clear as crystal, proceeding from the throne of God and of the Lamb* (Rev. 22:1 NKJV).

> *Life will flourish wherever this water flows* (Ezek. 47:9 NLT).

You want to be drinking clean water. For many, that means purchasing bottled water. The other alternative is to put water purifiers on the faucet where your drinking water comes out. It is also wise to have a purifier on your shower head, as breathing in chlorine is not healthy. An internet search for water filters will give you many options. Purchase one that takes out 99 percent of most everything.

#21: Drink single file aligned water.

The molecular structure of water is chaotic, but Nobel Prize winning research tells us that in order for water to be optimally absorbed, it needs to be in single file alignment (SFA). This exceptional characteristic has been found in remote mountain streams which are still pristine and untouched by manmade interventions.

For example, people in one region near the nuclear disaster at Chernobyl *did not get cancer*. Scientists went to the location and upon investigation, discovered what made them so resilient was their unique water source. Careful analysis revealed there was nothing unique *in* the water; it was the *structure* that was different. The molecules were not in a chaotic state, but in single file alignment.

Because our bodies are over 60 percent water, and water is a universal solvent in which millions of reactions within our bodies occur daily, it is no wonder it has such life-giving capabilities. This type of single file aligned water is what we drink in our home and the ultra-hydration has improved our health in astounding ways.[23]

#22: Breathe pure air.

Air is filled with contaminants. An internet search for air purifiers will give you many options. We have used one from Austin for years.[24]

#23: Use EMF protection.

As our screen time increases, so does our exposure to harmful electro-magnetic radiation and 5G technology. We want to neutralize these damaging effects and guard ourselves from the dangerous electromagnetic fields that bombard us daily.

As the heart is to our circulatory system and the lungs are to our respiratory system, so the biofield is to our energetic system. We can use beneficial frequencies to strengthen our biofield and measurably support our body's energetic system. We have tried various EMF protection over the years and the best we have found utilizes patented and proprietary technology, verified with third-party research, and muscle tests stronger than any we've used before.[25]

#24: Tapping: Emotional Freedom Technique

Emotional Freedom Technique, EFT, is a God-created physiological technique that allows us to experience liberty and choice about our feelings and how we experience them. It involves tapping gently on acupressure points of the face and upper body. This tapping can release pent-up emotional stress, via the neurological system, of daily and long-term events and memories. You can experience emotional freedom by tapping into God's peace and joy today.[26]

#25: Hear God's voice.

Deuteronomy 28 is a chapter of blessings and curses for those who listen to His voice and obey it and those who do not.[27] God's covenant of healing declared in Exodus 15:26 states four prerequisites to living in health, and these include hearing His voice and obeying it, and reading His statutes and keeping them.

#26: Soak in healing prayer (Hab. 3:4; Heb. 1:3; Col. 3:16).

This approach to healing is to do a 15- to 20-minute soaking prayer where two or three people lay hands on the client and soak them in the healing presence of God. Each prayer counselor prays as they are led during the 15 minutes. There can be periods of silence during the prayer time. Each person is to see the power of God as light flowing through their hands into the person's body, transforming it. The client also maintains a receptive mode by seeing the power of God entering him, transfiguring the damaged area, and restoring it. Everyone stays tuned to "flow" and responds as the Lord is directing them.

The prayer team sits in comfortable positions around the client during the 15- to 20-minute "divine radiation treatment." It is preferable if the team of pray-ers includes a person who has been healed of the same infirmity as the one being prayed for (which means they will have great faith). Another prayer counselor is someone who currently has the same infirmity (which means they will have great empathy). The third is a close friend (which means they will have great compassion). We have found this almost always results in improvement in either the client or those doing the praying, or both!

#27: Praying in tongues promotes health.

It edifies your being and energizes your spirit. An energized spirit energizes one's body also (1 Cor. 14:2,4). Brain specialist Dr. Carl Peterson, M.D. conducted a study at ORU in Tulsa, Oklahoma, on what happens in the brain when one prays or speaks in tongues.[28] He found that as we pray or worship in our heavenly language, the brain releases chemicals that give a 35 to 40 percent boost to the immune system, promoting health and healing. In addition, this secretion is triggered from a part of the brain that has no other apparent activity and is only stimulated by our Spirit-led prayer and worship!

#28: Great chiropractic care aligns the body's structure.

Since 70 percent of the messages from the brain to an organ in the body can be cut off by slight misalignments in the spinal column, many organs are not receiving complete messages from the brain and are functioning at a fraction of their capacity. This can be remedied by chiropractic care.[29]

Many, many more modalities promote health.

Add to this list those approaches you have discovered that have released a new level of health for you. Share these gifts with others. In the endnotes I have provided links to a few more resources that look promising to me and that I have used or would explore further should I have the need.[30]

Seven "Diagnostic Tools" for Discovering Root Causes of Infirmities

#1: Divine revelation:

You should always pray and ask God, "What is the root cause of this infirmity and what should I do now to bring forth healing?" Then be aware of the "divine chance encounters" that come your way (i.e., flowing thoughts and pictures, comments people make, the information you "accidentally stumble across" during the day, dreams you have at night, etc.). Some specific questions to ask: "Lord, is there anything I am doing (thoughts, behaviors) that is contributing to this infirmity?" Respond in repentance to any thoughts He gives you. Since the key sins that produce dis-ease in our souls are anger, fear, and hopelessness, ask God to show you any way any of these negative attitudes are present within you. Then choose to release them in prayer to God and ask for His opposites to replace them, which are His abiding realities of faith, hope, and love (1 Cor. 13:13). You can prayerfully scan down over the list above of 28 gifts of healings and *see what jumps out at you, and begin there.*

#2: Removing root causes of the infirmity promotes health (Lk. 6:43-44):

The Bible teaches that if you have a "fruit," it comes from a "root." So we ask God to reveal to us the root cause of the infirmity (i.e., fruit) that we are experiencing. With this knowledge, we can effectively deal with it and remove it. Ask, "Lord, what happened in my life at the time this infirmity showed up?" Relax and tune to flow and see what bubbles up by way of spontaneous thoughts or pictures. Then properly address the response you receive. One lady received the answer that the fungus growing on her hands began two years ago when she took a new job in a pill factory and constantly had her gloved hands in pills as she sorted them.

I have found asking, "Lord, show me the root of this infirmity" *to be the most effective question I can ask*. Receive and act on words of wisdom and words of knowledge (1 Cor. 12:8). These words from God can help you discern the root causes of infirmity, as well as the steps God wants you to take to receive their healing. They release God's purpose from heaven, which brings forth healing.

#3: Qest4:

I have owned a Qest4[31] unit for several years and we use it daily. According to their website: "The QEST4 bioenergetic system takes centuries of homeopathic wisdom and combines it with cutting edge quantum physics to produce unique and individualized results you won't find anywhere else. Everything in existence possesses a unique energetic blueprint or 'signature.' Utilizing a digital version of these energy patterns, the QEST4 allows you to interface with the 'innate intelligence,' gaining invaluable insight and information, allowing you to create personalized solutions."

However, this is a very expensive unit (currently priced at about $15,000).

#4: Muscle response testing:

Learn to do muscle response testing (MRT) on yourself or a friend and test yourself to confirm what products your body desires most and what is no longer needed or necessary. You can use MRT to compare one product to another, to check out foods, or to confirm the root causes of an infirmity. MRT allows your body to communicate back to you its current needs. Books that deal with MRT include *Health Mastery Through MRT*.[32] This lays out a scientific and biblical basis for MRT and provides about 40 points on the body to test all major organs. Anyone can learn how to use MRT, and it's free![33]

#5: Life Line Screening:

Life Line Screening[34] is a non-invasive testing service that brings high quality equipment and trained technicians to public buildings in local communities. Screening is designed to help prevent cardiovascular disease, sudden stroke, bone loss, etc.

#6: *Trusted* online experts I access all the time for therapeutic remedies:

Type an affliction, disease, or condition into the search bar on the websites of each expert here: DrAxe.com, LifeExtension.com, GreenMedInfo.com, Mercola.com, Dr. Schulze,[35] CWGMinistries.[36]

#7: Utilize two to three quality health counselors:

My first requirement is that my health counselor model health and look healthy. They need to believe the infirmity *can* be healed and offer approaches for healing it. I expect them to be able to provide testimonies of others who have taken their advice and been restored to health. If their suggestions are not providing me with at least slightly improved health within a month, I am likely to seek out others who may be able to help me. I always go with the most natural and spiritual approach possible. Their philosophy concerning how to restore health needs to be compatible with my philosophy. My philosophy on health care is that I will use Western medicine (allopathic medicine, MDs) for trauma care, and naturopathic and spiritual counselors for everything else.

Where Do I Begin in Restoring Health to My Body?

Always begin restoring your body to health by discovering and removing the *root cause* that has disrupted your body's natural God-given healing energies. See "Step 2" in the Gifts of Healings: 7 Step Model[37] for an expanded delineation of how to do this. Next, give your body the tools it needs to heal itself by working on enhancing your body's digestion, hydration, improving nutrition (organic foods and nutrition which is not messed with by man), and cleansing the colon and body organs, as these simple steps will solve many health issues.

But, why do I have to do all this?

Why not just live as Daniel in the Old Testament? That would be fine. He ate an organic healthy diet that did not include the king's rich food which Daniel said defiles the body (Dan. 1:8, 12). The seeds that grew his food were not GMO (genetically modified) seeds. And his environment did not have all the toxins in it that we have today. His food was unprocessed and largely uncooked. His water did not have chlorine or fluoride in it. The air was not filled with chemical and electrical pollution. He most likely walked a great deal every day. So by all means, this is a wonderful option for those who want to pursue it. If you do not, then the above gifts of healing are probably things you will need.

My testimony of a torn ligament being healed:

I was dancing during worship in a church service and tore a ligament in my knee, which took more than two years to fully restore. Since I did not know what would be too much pressure for the knee to handle, I re-injured the knee three or four times during the first three or four months, making the initial tear even worse.

The healing steps began with asking God why it happened and if there was anything I needed to repent of. He said, "Pride and judgment," as I was judging the folks in the service who were *not* entering into worship. So I repented and asked people to pray many different times for miraculous healing of my knee. I would then try doing things I was unable to do, thus demonstrating my faith, and clearing the way for healing. Using vision, I saw it healed, I spoke that it was healed, I went to sleep seeing it healed, and it simply got re-injured and worse over the first three or four months.

I put Deep Tissue Ointment and Healing Salve, healing creams that I purchased from two of my favorite websites, on my knee. I went to my chiropractor, and he helped quite a lot; because I was walking with a limp, I threw my back out of place, so now both my knee and my back hurt. I wore a knee brace day and night because even rolling over at night would re-injure my knee.

By "chance" (i.e., a divine chance encounter), while I was reading a health book, I came across a practice called Active Release Technique or "ART" and through a footnote in the book, I found a website where I could put in my zip code and find a certified ART practitioner near me. We had just moved to Florida and were looking for a new chiropractor. I discovered a chiropractor who practiced ART.[38] He examined me and discovered muscles with adhesions in my hip on my left side (it was the right knee that was injured). He assumed the seized-up muscles were putting additional strain on the opposite knee and that had greatly contributed to the torn ligament. He broke the adhesions in the muscles and restored much greater flexibility to my body. I was back to bouncing out of bed in the morning with no soreness or stiffness *in my back*. Awesome, as this was the way I woke up in the morning for all of my life, until the last couple of years.

However, as the chiropractor worked on breaking the adhesions in my muscles, my injured knee developed a searing pain across the front of the kneecap. The thought came to me (i.e., God speaking) to ask myself, "What nutrition does a ligament need to heal?" With a bit of online research, I was reminded of something I had known, which was that glucosamine was good for ligaments. So, I took glucosamine, and within a week the searing pain was greatly reduced, and within three weeks it was mostly gone. After six to eight weeks, when I checked using Muscle Response Testing, my body told me my knee no longer needed glucosamine, and glucosamine was now registering as a product that was weakening my body and not strengthening it, so I stopped taking it.

I felt about 90 percent better, but still felt an inner weakness inside the knee. It was like my knee was saying to me, "Don't take long, strong strides, or something inside may catch and get damaged." As I was reading another book on health, the author commented that he had recommended magnets be placed on a person's knee for 10 days, and by day 10, the knee problem would be completely healed. Really! I had never heard of wearing a magnet, day and night, for 10 days! So I dug out my magnets, and using an Ace bandage, wrapped the magnet to my knee for about 18 hours a day for the next 10 days—and lo and behold, the inner weakness continued to be reduced!

Well, since I had reinjured my knee already a few times, it was a bit nerve-wracking to decide to take the long forceful strides that I once used to take. However, I realized I needed to carefully put this healing to the test to see if it was finally complete. It had now been two years since the initial injury.

I tested my knee out by playing a game of tennis with Jasmine, my granddaughter, and found the healing was about 98 percent complete! Yay, God! I had used His miracle-working power, and His many gifts of healing, and restored a damaged ligament which some had suggested I may need to live with for the rest of my life.

I worked on the remaining 2 percent until 100 percent restoration of my knee was realized. I went back to muscle testing to see if I needed more of the magnet, more nutrition, more healing, or more of whatever. I found through muscle testing that a 6.5-inch magnet would be better than the 4.5-inch one I was using, so I switched to the 6.5-inch magnet and wore it on the side of my knee every night. Since my bottle of glucosamine had been completely used up, I went to Vitamin World and muscle-tested what they had on the shelf and tested very strong to their glucosamine sulfate. I continued with these two steps until I reached 100 percent healing of my knee.

Now, at age 72, I can tell you my knee is completely healed with no pain and with full flexibility. Thank You, Lord! You see, I have chosen to reject the idea that I need to live with infirmity since God has promised me health as His covenant child (Ex. 15:26). So I *fought* for health and *believed* for health and *acted* upon every tip He gave me as I moved along, and health was restored!

Below are the infirmities Patti and Mark put up with for years before we discovered (or fought for) the solution. The solution that finally worked is listed after each affliction:

- **Constant colds**—breaking off generational Masonic curses
- **Indigestion**—enzymes, probiotics, HCL, and SFA water
- **Loose stools**—lactose intolerant, so take Lactaid or no dairy consumption
- **Headaches**—chiropractor adjustments from an Atlas Orthogonal Chiropractor, thinner pillows

The choice is ours. We can become complacent and accept infirmities, limitations, and weaknesses, or we can radically declare that we are healed *and fight until the healing is fully manifest in our lives*. I urge you to be radical and never quit, not until you are walking in the fullness of health and strength that God has promised you. Never accept anything other than God's best for your life! Then glorify Him in His multiplied gifts toward you.

Make your decision and confess it aloud to yourself, your close friends, and the Lord:

> *I choose to walk in divine health by applying both miracles and gifts of healings until my health is completely restored. By the power of the Holy Spirit, I will press in until I am walking in the fullness of health.*

Abraham fulfilled his destiny at age 100 when Isaac was born (Gen. 21:1-2). At age 72, there is still a large part of the mission God has given to Patti and me[39] to be fulfilled. We continue to focus intensely on health, so we can live long enough to fulfill the destinies God has given us. Our prayer is that the Lord would put within you a passion to take charge of your health so that you, too, can live long enough to fulfill the destiny God has given you!

> *If you want to do something, you will find a way.*
> *If you do not, you will find an excuse.*

Going Deeper[40] and Journaling Application

- Lord, what would You speak to me concerning the role of therapeutic cures?
- Is there any therapeutic cure You want me to apply now?

Chapter 12

Planted by the River and Bearing Fruit Continually: A Summary and Review

The Bible offers us an astounding picture of what our anointed lifestyles are to look like. It is breathtaking. Talk about a Promised Land of blessings! Let's take a look at it, so we can hold it in our imaginations and let it frame up our reality. It is a picture of God's amazing gifts, anointings, and blessings being poured out into our lives through the Holy Spirit.

A Picture of Our Anointed Lives

> *Then he showed me a river of the water of life, clear as crystal, coming from the throne of God and of the Lamb, in the middle of its street. On either side of the river was the tree of life,* ***bearing twelve kinds of fruit,*** *yielding its fruit* ***every month;*** *and the leaves of the tree were for the* ***healing of the nations*** (Rev. 22:1-2 NASB95).

God has an always-flowing river whose sparkling streams *bring joy and delight* to His people. *Life will* ***flourish*** *wherever this water flows* (Eph. 5:25; Ezek. 47:9; Ps. 46:4 TPT; Rev. 22:1-2). Living by the Spirit means we are moment-by-moment immersed in and living from God's fountain of life.

Once I own this beautiful picture in my heart, mind, and imagination, can I then define the principles of life in Holy Spirit well enough to know how to step into this anointed lifestyle?

God has created laws that govern the physical and the spiritual worlds. We will spend this chapter on precise definitions of the laws of the Spirit, so we can clearly explain them and intentionally walk in them allowing us to release the Spirit's revelation and power to heal. All the laws we will examine are laws I have used successfully for years and written about in my books. I am thrilled to share them with you, so you can prosper. Following is a summary of key principles from my 50 books.

The simplest summary of the Spirit-anointed lifestyle is to "abide in Jesus" (Jn. 15:1-15).

Live *fully in the present* moment, *seeing Jesus* at your side, *asking for* His input, and *receiving* it through flowing ideas, pictures, emotions, and energy. Honor and act on this flow.

By doing the above, we are moving from our head to our heart, from left to right brain, from man's thoughts to God's thoughts, from satan's lie in the Garden to restoration of divine walks with God, from emptiness to fullness, from aloneness to companionship, from shallowness to completeness, from rationalism to Spirit encounter, from a branch cut off from the tree that can do nothing to fruitfulness.

Abiding in Christ is the *only meaningful lifestyle*. It is the lifestyle prescribed by Jesus and exemplified by Jesus as He lived continuously out of the flowing revelation of His Father Who was abiding in Him. It is worth taking the time to fully master this lifestyle. What other lifestyle is worth living?

Foundational Scriptures underlying the need for a Spirit-anointed lifestyle:

> *Abide in Me, and I in you. As the branch cannot bear fruit of itself unless it abides in the vine, so neither can you unless you abide in Me. I am the vine, you are the branches; he who abides in Me and I in him, he bears much fruit, for **apart from Me you can do nothing*** (Jn. 15:4-5 NASB95).

If you abide in Me, and My words [rhema, i.e. the things Jesus is speaking right now] **abide in you,** *ask whatever you wish, and* **it will be done** *for you. My Father is glorified by this, that you* **bear much fruit,** *and so prove to be My disciples. Just as the Father has loved Me, I have also loved you;* **abide in My love.** *If you keep My commandments, you will abide in My love; just as I have kept My Father's commandments and abide in His love. These things I have spoken to you so that My joy may be in you, and that* **your joy may be made full.** *This is My commandment, that you* **love one another,** *just as I have loved you* (Jn. 15:7-12 NASB95).

If it is true that I can *do nothing* apart from abiding in Jesus, then I am passionate about defining what that looks like in every area of endeavor.

The Bible likens the Holy Spirit to wind and water—so what can I learn from these images?

Wind

When the day of Pentecost had come, they were all together in one place. And suddenly there came from heaven a noise like a **violent rushing wind,** *and it filled the whole house where they were sitting. ...And they were all* **filled with the Holy Spirit** *and began to speak with other tongues, as the Spirit was giving them utterance* (Acts 2:1-2,4 NASB95).

Water

"If anyone is thirsty, let him come to Me and drink. He who believes in Me, as the Scripture said, 'From his **innermost being will flow rivers of living water.'"** *But this He spoke of* **the Spirit,** *whom those who believed in Him were to receive* (Jn. 7:37-39 NASB95).

The wind and water symbols both involve "*flow*," so living in flow is going to be a *big key!*

I find it fascinating that in a short 25-year span, water and wind were harnessed to release power. In 1881, it was discovered that water could be controlled to create electricity. In 1903, the Wright brothers learned how to cooperate with the laws of wind and air to be able to fly.

Man has been around for thousands of years, yet within just 25 years, wind and water were harnessed to propel us forward into a more abundant lifestyle.

At the same time, power was released in the spiritual realm as the Azusa Street revival broke forth in tongues and healing in 1902. I can't help but wonder if the revelation of these three sources of power in such a short period was simply a coincidence or if it was the hand of God moving to demonstrate spiritual truth through physical patterns.

Prior to these discoveries that there were principles and laws governing the flow of wind and water, people didn't believe that such things were possible. Yet these discoveries changed the world!

Today there are people who believe that there are no laws governing the spiritual world and that no one can know or teach how to hear God's voice or release a miracle or prophecy. But I believe that there are spiritual laws that can be discovered and applied to change our lives and to change the world.

Precise Definitions Promote Advancement

Precise definitions have allowed us to harness the powers of the physical world.

Because of precise definitions of the force of *gravity* combined with a precise application of the force of *aerodynamics*, planes were created allowing man to fly successfully without crashing.

Likewise, I want to be able to soar in the Spirit successfully and continuously without crashing.

Precise definitions allow us to soar in the Spirit.

If we can establish clear, accurate definitions of spiritual realities, the Spirit can lift us to new heights of spiritual activities, which can include hearing God's voice, seeing His visions, interpreting His dreams, and releasing His healing power and revelatory gifts, and more.

Below we will *review and consolidate* many of the definitions and principles discussed in this book. Please take the time to ponder them, meditate upon them, and integrate them into your lifestyle, so you can soar in the Spirit every moment of every day.

Choose to master a *precise understanding* of how to live by the Spirit and a *clear intention* to do so (Rom. 8:5-6, 13-14).

A. I Move from Thinking on My Own to Spirit-Led Reasoning

Western rationalism is a *reductionist* worldview that neglects the Spirit.

Rationalism is defined as relying on reason to establish truth. It ignores the Spirit. The Bible tells us to rely on the Spirit to guide us into all truth (Jn. 16:13). Thus, rationalism is a *faulty* epistemology (system for knowing).

When man uses his mind *himself*, the result is man's un-anointed, analytical reasoning, which is rebuked by Jesus three times in the Gospels (Matt. 16:5-12; Mk. 2:5-12; 8:15-18 KJV). The Bible says: "For as the heavens are higher than the earth, so are My ways higher than your ways and My thoughts than your thoughts" (Isa. 55:9 NASB95).

Our minds are to be yielded to the Holy Spirit.

*"Let us reason **together**," says the Lord, "though your sins are as scarlet, they will be as white as snow; though they are red like crimson, they will be like wool"* (Isa. 1:18 NASB95).

The only command in the Bible to reason is to reason *together* with God (Isa. 1:18). This *Spirit-led reasoning* involves letting the Spirit's *flow* guide our reasoning process. Divine creativity, wisdom, revelation, intimacy, and healing are realized this way.

Flowing thoughts *come from the vision being held in our minds.* We purify the flowing thoughts that come as our eyes are fixed on Jesus. We can picture Jesus at our right hand just as King David pictured the Lord at his right hand (Ps. 16:8; Acts 2:25; Matt. 1:23).

Notice in Isaiah 1:18 that godly reasoning includes picturing. *"Though your sins are as scarlet, they will be as white as snow; though they are red like crimson, they will be like wool."* When God reasons, He uses pictures: "sins as scarlet" is an image of *my need*; "white as snow" is a picture of *His provision* which meets my need. Thus, godly reasoning involves two back-to-back pictures—the first of my needs and the second of God's provision. Great preaching uses the same strategy.

Since *emotions are byproducts of pictures,* we will also be experiencing God's emotions if our reasoning includes picturing God's pictures of His provisions in our lives.

I discern three sources of the thoughts in my mind:

1. **My thoughts** come from my reasoning process and are sensed as cognitive, *connected* thoughts, which I build through my own reasoning.
2. **The Holy Spirit's thoughts** are spontaneous thoughts that line up with the names and character of God. These include Wonderful Counselor, Prince of Peace, Comforter, Teacher, Creator, Healer, and Giver of Life.
3. **Evil spirits' thoughts** are spontaneous thoughts that line up with the names and character of satan, which include accuser, adversary, liar, destroyer, condemner, thief, and murderer.

We choose *only* the Holy Spirit's thoughts—take every other thought captive to Christ (2 Cor. 10:5)!

If Jesus did not reason on His own (Jn. 5:30), then we are not to reason on our own. Whenever I have the option of using one of my faculties *myself* or tuning to flow and allowing the Holy Spirit to utilize it, I always choose the Holy Spirit. I believe this provides me with a huge edge to succeed.

B. I Move from Me Picturing to Spirit-Guided Pictures (Dreams and Visions)

Pictures have extraordinary power over us. "A picture is worth a thousand words." I must picture truth and not lies.

> [They] *walked in the counsels and in the imagination of their **evil** heart, and went **backward**, and not **forward*** (Jer. 7:24 KJV).

A godly picture that takes me forward could be: "Lo, I am with you always" (Matt. 28:20). An evil picture that takes me backward could be: "We became like grasshoppers in our own sight" (Num. 13:33).

Here is a godly picture that takes me forward: "I can do all things through Him who strengthens me" (Phil. 4:13). This evil picture takes me backward: "I cannot do _____" (Num. 13:31).

I live gazing upon godly pictures—pictures which *include Jesus* in them (Heb. 12:1-2).

Live in pictures of things God declares are true. Examples include seeing Him with me (Acts 2:25; Ps. 16:8; Matt. 28:20); seeing that He has provided "more than enough" (Deut. 28:1-14); seeing His Spirit joined to my spirit (1 Cor. 6:17); seeing my new shining heart (2 Pet. 1:4), my clean heart, my empowered heart (Ezek. 36:26); seeing myself wearing Christ's robe radiating His righteousness and reflecting His glory as I walk through my day (Gal. 3:27). *Picturing these truths will empower us* to be the overcomers we are called to be. Seeing myself as a miserable sinner will take me backward, even if I am confessing, "I am the righteousness of God in Christ Jesus." The picture has more power and wins.

"The steadfast of *mind* ("imagination" in the Hebrew: *yetser)* You will keep in perfect peace because he trusts in You" (Isa. 26:3). *Worry* is picturing satan's lies rather than God's truths.

We all meditate all day long (ponder, picture, anticipate). Let's stop meditating on lies that are contrary to the Bible and the Spirit, and instead meditate *only* on God's truth. Then we go forward into faith, hope, love, and life rather than backward into fear, hopelessness, anger, and death.

The eyes of our hearts are the faculty that is used to receive divine visions.

Picturing is a faculty of the *heart* (i.e., "every *imagination* of the thoughts of his *heart*," Gen. 6:5 KJV).

1. **Evil imagination**: picturing demonic things (Jer. 16:12 KJV)
2. **Vain imagination**: picturing what I want (Rom. 1:21 KJV)
3. **Godly imagination**: picturing things God says are true (1 Chron. 29:18 KJV)

Ask and look for visions from God that will grant wisdom concerning the issues before you. Divine visions *begin* when flow takes over a godly imagination. The scene comes *alive*.

- **Divine visions**: These are a flow of pictures that appear as I am praying for the eyes of my heart to be enlightened (Eph. 1:17-18) and I have my eyes fixed on Jesus (Heb. 12:1-2).
- **Dreams**: These are God's wisdom and counsel to us during the night (Num. 12:6; Ps. 16:7).

I choose to gaze *only* upon God's pictures (i.e., godly imagination, visions, and dreams)! Since *emotions are byproducts of pictures*, my emotions are automatically transformed into Kingdom emotions whenever I am gazing upon God's pictures. I *continue to watch* (am a witness of) God's power as it is healing and restoring me or a client.

Reasons I need to always be aware of what I am picturing:

1. **Pictures purify:** The intuitive, spontaneous flow comes from the vision being held before my eyes; therefore, I purify my reception of God's voice by having my spiritual eyes focused on Jesus who is present with me (Matt. 28:20).

2. **Jesus must always be central in the picture in my mind's eye. If He is not, then whatever is more predominate in my visionary capacity is an idol in my heart and will result in a distorted answer.** Seeing the thing I am praying for as a larger picture in my mind than the picture of the One I am coming to results in receiving a distorted answer from God (Ezek. 14:4; Num. 22:15-35). Proper prayer begins by lifting my eyes to the Lord and entering before Him with praise and worship (Matt. 6:9; Ps. 100:4). Praise and worship cause me to focus the eyes of my heart on Jesus. Then, Jesus is to remain dominant in the picture throughout the prayer.

3. **Pictures assist in spiritual transformation and establishing Christlikeness:** I am transformed by what I look upon. As I fix my eyes upon Jesus, I am transformed into His likeness (2 Cor. 3:18; 4:18; Heb. 12:2). This is called *"coming to the light"* or "abiding in Christ" (Jn. 15). This is God's method of establishing righteous behavior in my life. The opposite is religion's approach to transformation which is called *"stripping away"* where one focuses on their sinfulness and then begins whipping one's flesh (one example is laying on a bed of nails) in an attempt to beat the flesh into submission. While we no longer take such extreme measures, we do often try (usually unsuccessfully) to strip away the deeds of the flesh through our own self-effort and the power of our will. I choose "coming to the light."

4. **Wrong picturing weakens:** Looking at my sins and weaknesses and seeking to battle them does not provide victory. I am *not* instructed to do this in the Bible. This is a sin, simply because my eyes are not fixed on Jesus (Heb. 12:1-2).

5. **Proper picturing establishes true Christian spirituality:** Seeing and radiating Jesus is the only *true* approach to spiritual growth (Gal. 2:22-25; 1 Cor. 12:7-11; 2 Cor. 3:17-18; 4:17-18; Heb. 12:1-2).

6. **Jesus spoke this million-dollar truth in my journal:** "Whatever you focus on grows within you, and whatever grows within you, you become." That was the day I quit focusing on my weakness and

my sin and began focusing on Christ and His righteousness radiant within me.

7. **Proper picturing is part of throne room worship:** Throne room worship is defined as "seeing myself present with the heavenly chorus in the throne room in praise, worship, and adoration before my King." Since I am seated with Christ in heavenly places (Eph. 2:6), I am already present in the throne room. As I look into the heavens, I can see the worship taking place before my Lord. I see myself as a worshipper in the throne room where I join with the multitudes worshipping before His throne.[1]

8. **Proper pictures assist in soaking in God's presence:** To "soak" in God's presence is to rest in His love rather than to "strive" in prayer. Soaking is making a conscious decision to enter into God's presence to experience Him. It is two lovers sharing love. He is the Divine Lover of the universe; I am His espoused bride. When I soak, I enjoy His love and share the love back with Him. It is a divine encounter that utilizes the senses of my heart and spirit, meaning I am tuned to flowing thoughts, flowing pictures, flowing emotions, pondering, and meditation.[2]

C. I Move from Me Speaking to Speaking the Oracles of God

My speech must always be what the Spirit is telling me to say. "Death and life are in the power of the tongue" (Prov. 18:21 NASB95); therefore, I must only speak what Jesus is telling me to say when He is telling me to say it, and in the way He is telling me to say it. Speech I come up with on my own is by definition a "dead work" and to be forsaken (Heb. 6:1-2), as is evil speech, which is speech prompted by evil spirits who are injecting their ideas into my mind. Speak only words *edifying* for the need of the moment (Eph. 4:29).

Right confession:

Right confession is saying only what God tells me to say and continuing to say it and only it. Watch God correct man's negative confession in Jeremiah 1:6-10 (NASB95):

> *"Alas, Lord God! Behold, I do not know how to speak, because I am a youth." But the Lord said to me, "**Do not say**, 'I am a youth,' because everywhere I send you, you shall go, and all that I command you, you shall speak. Do not be afraid of them, for I am with you to deliver you," declares the Lord. Then the Lord stretched out His hand and touched my mouth, and the Lord said to me, "Behold, I have put My words in your mouth."*

The Lord has also promised to put His words into my mouth (Mk. 10:19-20).

D. I Know the Fuel That My Heart Is Designed to Run On

Man's heart/spirit consists of underlying *attitudes*, underlying *motivations*, and underlying *character traits*. For example, we should tune to God with:

- an *attitude* of reverence, awe, and respect;
- a *motivation* to seek Him diligently;
- and a *character trait* of humility and dependence upon Him.

Understanding the relationship of soul, heart, and spirit:

The spirit of a Christian is joined to the Holy Spirit (1 Cor. 6:17). In the Old Testament especially, an individual is described as only *two* parts, body and soul (Ps. 31:9). The word "soul" in this case is used to describe the *entire* non-material parts of man, so would include heart and spirit as parts of the soul. I suspect man's spirit is located within man's heart. Thus, I consider there to be a 95 percent overlap between man's soul, heart, and spirit.[3]

The centrality of the heart:

- The issues of life flow from our *hearts* (Prov. 4:23).
- We are to trust in the Lord with all our *heart*, and lean not on our own understanding (Prov. 3:5).
- Wisdom rests in our *hearts* (Prov. 14:33).
- A *healed heart* provides health to our entire body (Prov. 14:30 YLT).

The Bible emphasizes the heart:

The words *heart* and *spirit* show up 1,300 times, while *mind* and *think* are found less than 200 times. God wants us to live out of our hearts rather than our heads. Science has now proven that the electromagnetic field sent forth from our hearts, which is filled with information that helps coordinate the proper functioning of every part of our bodies, is many times larger than the electromagnetic field sent forth from our brains. Our hearts have a brain that sends *more* instructions to our brains than our brains send to our hearts.[4]

The language of the heart:

The language of the heart is experienced as flowing thoughts (Jn. 7:38), flowing pictures (Acts 2:17), flowing emotions (Gal. 5:22-23), pondering and meditation (Ps. 77:6). Sensing God's movement in our hearts can be called illumination, revelation, revelation knowledge, perception, discernment, word of wisdom, word of knowledge, or prophecy.

When seeking to bring healing to a heart wound, you must use the language of the heart (as stated above), not the language of the mind (i.e. reason/logic). Logic and reason *will not heal* heart wounds, nor does it instruct the heart as to how to behave. Pictures, flow, and emotions are what move the heart. Replacing pictures heals the emotions of the heart.

God's fuel, which my heart is designed to run on, is faith, hope, and love (1 Cor. 13:13). When I do two-way journaling, God automatically fills me up on this fuel so I can run smoothly throughout the day. If I tank up on anger, fear, doubt, and bitterness, I will run rough and mean all day.

E. I Honor God's Ongoing Passion for Fellowship with Me

Communion with Him was God's original intent for mankind. In the Garden, Adam walked and talked with God in the cool of the day (Gen. 3:8-9). Sadly, man believed and acted upon satan's lie that he did not need to listen to God's voice because he himself could be like God, knowing God and evil (see Gen. 3:5 NASB95). This caused mankind to be cut off from God's voice and the Tree of life, and communion with God was lost.

But God did not abandon His desire to have fellowship with man. At Jesus' death, the veil in the temple was torn allowing us direct access into the Holy of Holies. Once again, I have access to God's voice (Matt. 27:51) and the Tree of Life which restores continual fruitfulness to my life (Rev. 22:2). Communion was restored.

Jesus, the second Adam, modeled the lifestyle of fellowship that God intends for us. When I want to know for sure the lifestyle God intends, I look at Jesus.

> *His Son...is the radiance of His glory and the **exact representation of His nature*** (Heb. 1:2-3 NASB95).

> ***Be imitators** of me, just as I also am **of Christ*** (1 Cor. 11:1 NASB95).

Jesus modeled our new lifestyle by doing *nothing on His own initiative* but only what He heard and saw His Father doing (Jn. 5:19-20,30; 8:26,38,42; 10:18; 12:49; 14:10; 16:13). Jesus opened up to me the ability to hear God's voice: "My sheep hear My voice" (Jn. 10:27 NASB95). I can now live and *walk by the Spirit's* leading (Gal. 5:25).

In accepting Christ, I repent from doing dead works (Heb. 6:1-2). A *dead work* is doing things on my own initiative, outside of divine flow, outside of conversations with God.

I choose God's River over a broken cistern.

Supernatural provision (manna) is to be a *daily* activity; storing it up for tomorrow only results in it *spoiling* (Exod. 16:16-20).

> *For My people have committed two evils: they have forsaken Me, the **fountain of living waters**, to hew for themselves cisterns, **broken cisterns** that can hold no water* (Jer. 2:13 NASB95).

I am to daily drink from His River of the water of life, which produces continual fruit (Rev. 22:1-2). I understand that I cannot live out of the high of yesterday's spiritual experience, but I need to have fellowship with God today (Lam. 2:22-23; Mk. 1:35).

Jesus lived by the Spirit by being *indwelt*, just as we are. Jesus said, "The Father is *in* Me" (Jn. 10:38 NASB95), and:

> *I do nothing on **My own initiative**, but I speak these things as the Father **taught** Me. And He who sent Me is with Me; He **has not left Me alone, for I always** do the things that are pleasing to Him. ...I speak the things which I have **seen** with My Father; therefore you also do the things which you heard from your father* (Jn. 8:28-29,38 NASB95).

For Jesus, being in Spirit meant tuning to His Father's *voice* and *vision* within (flowing thoughts and flowing pictures). Jesus always did what His Father within was directing Him to do, so the Spirit was never grieved; and the Spirit's power was always available to Jesus. The religious leaders were listening instead to the voice of their father, satan (Jn. 8:44). We all are listening to some inner voice, either from the Holy Spirit, self, or an evil spirit.

Fellowship with God is easily restored when I use the four keys to hearing God's voice.[5] These allow me to have two-way conversations daily with God, which I capture in two-way journaling.

1. **Stillness**: I quiet myself in the presence of God (Ps. 46:10).
2. **Vision:** I picture Jesus Who is present with me (Heb. 12:1; Matt. 28:20; Eph. 1:17-18; Acts 2:25; Ps. 16:8).
3. **Flow**: I recognize His River which is within as flowing thoughts, flowing pictures, flowing emotions, flowing physical sensations which light upon me, and flowing power (Jn. 7:37-39).
4. **Record**: In faith, I write down what I am receiving and act on it (Hab. 2:2; Rev. 1:9-11).

Or simply, I quiet myself down, picture Jesus at my right hand, ask for His input, tune to flowing thoughts and pictures and emotions and feelings, and journal these out using childlike faith.

Another way to state the four keys is: 1) stop, 2) look, 3) listen, and 4) write. Many people in Scripture used these four keys (including Jesus), and together they wrote more than half the Bible.[6] So these four keys are the *standard biblical protocol* for communing with God.

Intimacy with Jesus precedes and supersedes miracles, deliverance, and prophecy.

> *Many will say to Me on that day, "Lord, Lord, did we not prophesy in Your name, and in Your name cast out demons, and in Your name perform many miracles?" And then I will declare to them, "I never **knew** [Greek: ginosko—was intimate with] you; depart from Me" (Matt. 7:22-23 NASB95).*

We need to restore the communion Adam had in the Garden, King David had in the Psalms, John had in the book of Revelation, and the prophets had throughout Scripture. *The 4 Keys to Hearing God's Voice* is the proven model used by Habakkuk, John, and others (Hab. 2:1-2; Rev. 1:9-11).

F. I Have Experienced the Six Foundational Experiences of a Spirit-Anointed Lifestyle (Heb. 6:1-2)

1. **Repentance from dead works**: A dead work is an Ishmael *I* create outside of God's leading and will be rejected by God. Therefore, there is no point in me creating it in the first place.

2. **Faith toward God**: I *believe* the flow within me is the River of the Spirit, and I intentionally tune to this flow at all times; as it is the Spirit that gives life, and the flesh profits nothing.

3. **Instruction about baptisms**: I have been baptized in water, into the body of Christ, in the Holy Spirit, and in fire.

4. **Laying on of hands**: God's flow of divine power and energy is transmitted through my hands. I expect this, and I can often feel the warmth and tingling as it flows (Mk. 16:18).

5. **The resurrection of the dead**: I have died to self (i.e. ego, self-effort, and the works of the flesh) and am alive in Christ, releasing the fruit and gifts of the Spirit (Gal. 2:20).

6. **Eternal judgment**: "Judge not, and ye may not be judged; condemn not, and ye may not be condemned; *release, and ye shall be released*" (Lk. 6:37 YLT). Judging brings condemnation and imprisonment to me. God's power is released to flow within me when I stop judging myself and others and express mercy, forgiveness, and compassion. I do not need to judge most things, nor do I have the capacity to do it properly.

When God sees that my foundation is solid, He grants me a building "permit" (Heb. 6:3) to go on to maturity, which includes Spirit-anointed fruitfulness and God's blessing (Heb. 6:1,7).

My new lifestyle is Jesus living His life out through me, through His indwelling Spirit. I see a new picture of Jesus joined to me:

*I have been crucified with Christ; and it is no longer I who live, but Christ lives in me; and the life which I now live in the flesh **I live by faith** in the Son of God* (Gal. 2:20 NASB95).

I see my puny efforts as worthless:

It is the Spirit who gives life; the flesh profits nothing (Jn. 6:63 NASB95).

I see myself always obeying:

*And He who sent Me is with Me; He has not left Me alone, for I **always do** the things that are pleasing to Him* (Jn. 8:29 NASB95).

I am always holding a picture of Jesus at my right hand (Acts 2:25), His Spirit joined to my spirit (1 Cor. 6:17), and His River flowing out from my innermost being (Jn. 7:37-39), causing me to feel and experience these spiritual realities (Gal. 5:22-23).

Summary of how I live and walk by the Spirit:

I am living by the Holy Spirit when I have quieted my thoughts, pictures, and emotions, and am envisioning Jesus present with me, asking for His input and tuned to His flowing pictures, flowing thoughts, flowing emotions, flowing physical sensations, and flowing power. I *believe* God is alive flowing within me through His River which is flowing from His throne (Rev. 22:1-2; Jn. 7:37-39).

G. I Know How to Prepare for a Healing Session

I am strengthened in the Spirit when I put on the full armor of God (Eph. 6:10-18). I pray and picture the following:

In Jesus' name, I present my entire being to God to be filled by the Spirit. I see You, Holy Spirit, in union with my spirit, filling every part of my being.

1. I speak to my **mind**: Be the mind of Christ by receiving God's flowing thoughts.
2. I speak to my **eyes**: Be enlightened by seeing God's flowing pictures.
3. I speak to my **vocal cords**: Speak the oracles of God by speaking what flows naturally.
4. I speak to my **heart**: Be compassionate by extending mercy to myself and others.
5. I speak to my **belly**: Release power, through my union with the Holy Spirit. Release God's creative flow.
6. I speak to my **feet**: Be a peacemaker by walking in peace toward all.

Thank You, Jesus. It is done, it is done, it is done!

Healing (and sanctification) is from the inside out.

*Now may the God of peace Himself sanctify you entirely; and may your **spirit and soul and body** be preserved complete, without blame at the coming of our Lord Jesus Christ* (1 Thess. 5:23 NASB95).

Faith *and* love must both be present for miracles to occur.

- **Principle: Faith** is energized by **love** (Gal. 5:6).
- **Love:** "So far as it depends on you, be at peace with all men" (Rom. 12:18).

- **Love** carries healing power: "Jesus felt **compassion** for them and **healed** their sick" (Matt. 14:14).
- **When there is no faith and love:** "[Jesus] could do no *miracle* (*dunamis*) there except that He laid His hands on a few sick people and *healed* (*therapeuo*: process healing) them. And He wondered at their unbelief" (Mk. 6:5-6 NASB95).
- **Faith energized by love** releases *dunamis* = the mighty working power of God.

Five ways God releases words of knowledge (these build faith by revealing what God is doing):

1. **Spontaneous feeling:** The pain is not my pain; it is sympathetic.
2. **Flowing thoughts:** The thoughts simply light upon my mind. They may be split-second or repetitive.
3. **Flowing inner pictures:** This can be similar to a daydream, or it can be an open vision where I do not see anything else, but see something like a large-screen TV open in front of me.
4. **Flowing outer pictures:** I see words on or over a person, or the words look like newspaper headlines or the captions at the bottom of a TV program.
5. **Flowing words:** This is like tongues in that I do not think of what I am saying. I simply speak words, trusting the flow of the Holy Spirit to be forming them. He is.

Tips for the healing process:

1. Ask what they want before offering to heal (Jn. 5:6-14).
2. Ask permission from the client to pray for their healing. This brings the client into the healing process, and through that, they are giving their body permission to heal.
3. "In Jesus' name, I command that this (specific illness) in (client's name) be resolved according to God's wisdom and power. Show me,

Lord, what You are doing. Selah (pause and listen). Thank You, Jesus! In faith, I receive Your revelation as to how to minister healing." Minister as Jesus has shown you to minister to the client.

4. Continuing to watch/witness the unfolding healing causes a continuing release of power, so keep watching until the miracle is complete.
   - I encourage the client to speak forth what they are seeing or feeling.
   - I obey any instructions God is giving me.
   - The longer I stay with this vision, the easier it is to give birth to the good things God has intended for me and thus experience His promises to me.
   - I do not let my mind wander. The healing may be instant or take several minutes.
   - As I sense God's miracle-working power engulfing me, I sense a perfect wholeness and balance.

5. Quantum physics affirms that simple observation changes the outcome.[7]
   - A witness in court tells what they have observed. We are witnesses (Acts 1:8).
   - In prophetic healing prayer, we are witnesses watching what the Spirit is doing as He heals, and we are telling what we are seeing, feeling, and observing.
   - I may prime the pump by setting the stage with this picture from Scripture: I see the River of the water of life, flowing clear as crystal, pouring out from the throne of God and of the Lamb. Next to this River, I see the Tree of Life whose leaves are bringing healing, breaking every curse (Rev. 22:1-4, paraphrased).

Being continually led by the Spirit:

Jesus uses many means and methods to heal, so always follow the Spirit's lead. Healing can be instantaneous, progressive, or a therapeutic cure.

Physical healing has occurred *when God says it has*. I speak what He tells me to speak. The full manifestation of the healing may appear *later*. For example: When my heart had an abnormal rhythm, I prayed and God said it was healed. He told me to speak this: "My heart beats in perfect sinus rhythm, and the symptoms are disappearing." Notice, God did not want me to even say the word of the infirmity, nor did He want me to focus on the symptoms, but to simply dismiss them. Since the root had been healed (my heartbeat), the fruit (symptoms) would take care of itself; and they were nothing for me to concern myself with. Remember, whatever you gaze upon grows within you. Whatever grows within you, you become.

Abraham, the father of faith, provides a model for incubating heart faith that births miracles.[8]

1. Faith begins with a **spoken word** from the Lord (Gen. 12:1-3).
2. God adds a **vision**, a picture of the promise fulfilled (Gen. 15:5-6).
3. I **ponder** this *rhema* and vision from God—nothing else (Rom. 4:20-21)!
4. I **speak** the *rhema* and vision God has spoken to me, according to His directions (Gen 17:5).
5. I **act** on the *rhema* and vision God has spoken to me (Gen. 17:23).
6. I **die to self-effort** (Gen. 16:2; 17:18-19).
7. In the **fullness of time, God brings forth** the miracle (Gen. 21:1-2; Gal. 4:4a).

H. I Use Inner Healing to Resolve Deep Heart Wounds

Inner healing is allowing God to replace the pictures in the art gallery of our minds, removing pictures that do not have Jesus in them, and replacing them with pictures that do. The steps for inner healing are:

1. Re-enter the scene where the hurt happened. (Glance at it for one second *only*.)

2. Ask Jesus to show you where He is and what He is saying and doing. Look for Him to appear.

3. Tune to flowing thoughts and flowing pictures and record what Jesus says and does.

4. Act in obedience to what Jesus is showing and speaking.

5. This new true picture now *replaces* the old pictures which contained the lie that Jesus was not present and was not doing anything.

As you cooperate with God in the inner healing process, you will be repenting of all unforgiveness and resentment and asking God to circumcise your heart, cutting out the anger, hatred, judgment, and unforgiveness, and granting you a new heart of mercy, love, compassion, and forgiveness. Lay your hands on your heart while you pray and watch and feel Him doing this.

*A hurt is healed when God has shown you the **gift** He has produced in your life through the experience.* Ask Him to show you the gift. Record it in your journal.

Whenever you view this event or tell of it in the future, you always *focus on* what Jesus did in it and *the gift* He produced in your life through it. You do not focus on the pain. This means that when you are sharing your testimony about this event, you spend the majority of your time talking about how Jesus was present guiding the healing process and the words and visions He gave you. Keep your focus on experiencing His light, not the time spent rummaging in darkness.

Remember, whatever you focus on grows within you, and whatever grows within you, you become!

I. Reviewing the Steps to Release Divine Power

Sensing God's power/energy flowing:

1. God's power (*dunamis* and *energeo*) energizes and heals.

2. God's power can be **seen** as light, fulfilling its purposes.

3. God's power can be **felt** as heat, vibration, and tingling.

4. I **watch** and **participate** in what I see/sense God's power is doing.

5. The act of **observing** the Spirit completing the healing helps create that reality. (Principles in quantum physics say the simple act of observing alters the end reality.)

6. The client should always **share** what they are sensing, feeling, hearing, or seeing, so that I can become more focused on exactly what God is doing in the moment.

Reviewing things that can *increase* the flow of God's power to heal:

1. I **invite the Spirit's healing power** to be present, and pray in Jesus' name.

2. I express Kingdom **emotions**: love, joy, peace, thankfulness.

3. I **increase faith**, which can be nurtured through praise, worship, testimonies, words of knowledge of what God wants to heal, and believing prayer.

4. I **listen** and am **obedient** to what God is speaking (Jn. 15:7: "words," in this verse is *rhema*).

5. I prefer **several coming together** in unity and agreement and laying hands on the individual (Ps. 133:1-3; Matt. 18:19; Lk. 4:40).

6. **I (we) will** confess sins so my (our) prayers can be energized (Jas. 5:15-16).

7. **I utilize** casting out demons (Acts 5:16), inner healing, breaking off generational sins and curses, ungodly soul ties, ungodly beliefs, inner vows, and word curses.[9]

Here are some examples of *beliefs that restrict* the flow of God's healing power and that must be repented of and replaced with God's truth and His pictures:

1. "I do not trust God" (which is code for one who is afraid of being disappointed). Those words are usually not said out loud; it is just to avoid getting to the nub of the problem.

2. "Miracles went out with the apostles! I have never seen a miracle."

3. "I am not righteous or good enough. I must be punished."

4. "God will do that for them, but not for me. What if God fails this time?"

5. "It is in my genes."

6. "The doctor told me I would die soon of this disease."

7. "I want to die."

Here are some samples of *emotions that restrict* the flow of God's healing power and that must be repented of and replaced with God's truth and His pictures:

1. Guilt, shame (is probably number one).

2. Unforgiveness or resentment, especially when aimed inward!

3. Afraid of getting honest with themselves or others.

4. "If Jesus takes this away, who will I be?" The problem/disease is so much a part of them, they are afraid of who they will be without it (lose my social security or military disability benefits).

5. "I am afraid of losing the *attention* that my addiction, sickness, etc. is bringing to my life."

6. "I am afraid to face life without my "crutch." What will the new me look like?"

7. "I am not ready to give up that part of me."

I remove blocks that hold back God's anointing:

1. Sin:

> *But your iniquities have made a separation between you and your God, and your sins have hidden His face from you so that He does not hear* (Isa. 59:1-2 NASB95).

> *There is **no health** in my bones **because of my sin**...and the light of my eyes, even that has gone from me* (Ps. 38:3,10 NASB95).

2. Legalism: yoke (Isa. 58:9)
3. Pointing the finger: critical attitude (Isa. 58:9)
4. Speaking vanity: speaking evil (Isa. 58:9)
5. Religious form: bowing like a reed (Isa. 58:5)

All the above are the outworkings of living by law rather than living in fellowship with God. God offered a relationship at Mt. Sinai, yet the Israelites chose laws. The above five problems are automatically removed every time I switch from living by laws to communing with God (stop, look, listen, write).

I remove inner discord by aligning my inner being:

- **Thinking** *only* what the Bible and the Spirit say (about self, others, life)
- **Speaking** *only* what the Bible and the Spirit say (about self, others, life)
- **Picturing** *only* what the Bible and the Spirit say (about self, others, life)
- **Believing** *only* what the Bible and the Spirit say (about self, others, life)
- **Feeling** *only* God's heart for the situation at hand (about self, others, life)

Demons manifest the energy/power of satan:

- Demons can be identified by a force within that pushes one toward evil.
- Demons can be *bound* (tied up) in Jesus' name (a stopgap measure we do if the client is not yet ready to have the demon cast out).

- Demons can be *cast out* in Jesus' name, and this occurs easily once we have removed their legal right to be there (repented of sins, false beliefs, inner vows, experienced inner healing, and broken off word curses).
- People can often feel demons moving and leaving their bodies, which is one reason why you want the client to be constantly communicating to you what they are sensing within them.

J. I Have Adopted Wimber's Relational Five-Step Healing Prayer Model

1) Interview, 2) diagnosis and prayer selection, 3) prayer ministry, 4) stop and re-interview, 5) post-prayer.

The most common roots of illness are below, and each requires a different prayer approach:

- **Psychosomatic issues**—emotional dis-ease is the main root of many diseases
- **Natural causes**—accidental injuries or cancer-causing carcinogens
- **Genetic causes**—often stemming from birth
- **Generational curses**—negative energies picked up while in the womb
- **Afflicting spirits**—demons, which require repentance and casting out
- **Lifestyle issues**—neglecting scriptural teaching regarding rest, diet, exercise, stress, etc.

Guidelines for group healing soaking prayer:

1. Gather around a client with one or more people laying their hands on the client.
2. Everyone receives and sends God's unconditional love, compassion, and healing power to the client, seeing it pulsate through every cell of the client's being, doing only and exactly what God desires to do.
3. Anyone can pray and/or share words of wisdom and words of knowledge. Silence is fine.

4. Now become a witness as you watch God's light, love, and life filling every cell.

5. Throughout this filling, have the client report what they are feeling and sensing.

6. The normal length is 15 minutes. Repeat as necessary.

K. I Recognize *Rhema* Is a Sub-Category of *Logos*

Logos (communication): One of the Greek words translated as "word" means "the *entire* communication process." One example of *logos* is the Bible, the Word of God. The Bible is to be meditated on (Josh. 1:8) and treasured in your heart (Ps. 119:11).

Rhema (speech): Another Greek word translated as "word" means "when *words leave one's lips*." The Spirit's voice in our hearts is one example of *rhema,* while verses leaping off the pages of Scripture and into our hearts is another example. *God's voice* is experienced as flowing, spontaneous thoughts that light upon our mind (Jn. 7:37-39). The Holy Spirit is sensed as a river that flows within.[10]

Rhema is a distinct sub-category of *logos,* just as *speech* is a sub-category of *communication. Rhema* is never used for written words. Thus, *rhema* is distinctive, as *logos* can and does include both written words, as well as spoken words. *Rhema* means *specifically* words leaving one's lips, so when the Bible uses *rhema,* it is specifically saying "speech." When the Bible uses the word *logos,* it includes speech as well as every other form that communication can take. *If a promise in the Bible is connected with rhema, then know that spoken words must be involved for this promise to work.*

Naba is a Hebrew word translated as "prophecy"; it means "bubbling up." When I want to prophesy, I ask to see Jesus present in the situation (Acts 2:25; Ps. 16:8) and picture Him present. Then I ask for His thoughts. I speak the thoughts and words that are *bubbling up* within me. "Seeing Jesus" can begin with a godly imagination from which I can step into a flowing vision by asking for the Spirit to take over the godly imagination, and then I tune to flow. Keep everything simple and childlike. Make sure it is simple enough for children to do. Then it is Christianity.

Paga is a Hebrew word translated as "intercession"; it is God's voice leading me in prayer. One literal definition of *paga* is "to strike or light upon by chance," or "an *accidental intersecting.*" Spirit-led intercession is sensed as spontaneous thoughts that light upon my mind while I am praying. I honor these thoughts, as they have been sent by God. So I fix my eyes upon Jesus, tune to flow and pray, being guided by the flow (Heb. 12:1-2; Jn. 7:37-39). Childlike faith allows me to comfortably live this way.

L. I Know How to Stay Safe So My Life Will Not Be Derailed

I achieve safety and success by utilizing my spiritual advisors. God's paradigm or system for success is not the brilliance of my mind or theology, but rather the multitude of counselors, specifically, the confirmation from two or three others (Prov. 11:14; 2 Cor. 13:1).

Who are my spiritual counselors? They are people who are *alongside* or *ahead* of me in the area being explored. I turn to them for spiritual confirmation of the leadings I have from the Lord. They are willing to seek God with me and share with me, for my prayerful consideration, what they sense in their hearts. I do not ask them what they think. I ask them *what God is speaking in their **hearts** concerning the issue.*

A definition of submission: "Submission is openness to the Spirit-led counsel and correction of several others while keeping a sense of personal responsibility for my discernment of God's voice within."

Spirit-led counsel means I am not asking what they think, but what they sense God is speaking in their hearts. *Multiple counselors* means I am going to three, not just one.

I am responsible for discerning the final decision. I ask God in prayer to show me how to properly fit together the counsel that my three advisors have provided; for I know that when I stand before God, I have to give an account for my actions, and I cannot blame anyone else.

"The Leader's Paradigm"

Make wise decisions by using "The Leader's Paradigm." Use this for big decisions especially. "The Leader's Paradigm" involves *confirming* God's guidance through six ways He speaks.

1. **Illumined Scriptures**: "They said one to another, 'Were not our hearts burning within us while He was speaking to us on the road, while He was explaining the Scriptures to us?'" (Lk. 24:32 NASB95). This pillar is experienced as the Holy Spirit illuminates Scriptures to me—I sense them leaping off the page or just coming to my attention spontaneously.

2. **Illumined Thoughts in One's Mind**: "It seemed fitting for me as well, having investigated everything carefully from the beginning, to write it out for you in *consecutive* order, most excellent Theophilus" (Lk. 1:3 NASB95). This pillar is experienced as the Holy Spirit guides my reasoning process through flow.

3. **Illumined Witness in One's Heart**: "And immediately when Jesus *perceived* in His spirit that they so reasoned within themselves, He said unto them, Why reason ye these things in your hearts?" (Mk. 2:8 KJV). This pillar is experienced as an impression perceived in my spirit. Deep inner peace or unrest is often part of this experience.

4. **Illumined Counsel of Others**: "Where no counsel is, the people fall: but in the multitude of counsellors there is safety" (Prov. 11:14 KJV). This pillar is experienced as I ask my spiritual advisors to seek God for confirmation, additions, or adjustments in the guidance I sense God has given me.

5. **Illumined Understanding of Life's Experiences**: "Ye shall know them by their fruits. Do men gather grapes of thorns, or figs of this-tles?" (Matt. 7:16 KJV). This pillar is experienced as I ask God to give

me insight and understanding concerning the fruit that life is demonstrating. God gives me revelation as to what has caused the fruit I am experiencing.

6. **Illumined Revelation from God Through Dreams, Visions, Prophecy, and Journaling**: "And it shall come to pass in the last days, saith God, I will pour out of My Spirit upon all flesh: and your sons and your daughters shall prophesy, and your young men shall see visions, and your old men shall dream dreams" (Acts 2:17 KJV). This pillar is experienced as I receive direct revelation from God through dreams, visions, and journaling. Journaling is writing out my prayers and God's answers.

I want all of the above six to be flashing green lights. If one is flashing a red light, I will hold off and not move forward. Red is a warning that something is not right. Seek the Lord and adjust until there are no red lights. I might have five green lights and one neutral. That would be fine. I just do not want any lights flashing red, as I want to avoid danger and making mistakes. I do not want to die in the wilderness. I want to arrive at my promised land!

I want to acquire well-rounded input so I discern the full counsel of God. I want to ask God who the team is that He has placed around me who have the various heart motivations listed below. Then I seek out their input, especially for all major decisions. I ask them what God is speaking to them in their *hearts*, not what they *think* about a situation being discussed.

1. **Apostle**: heart for the *whole* (sees the whole picture and where this idea fits)
2. **Prophet**: heart for *creativity* (senses what is right for this moment)
3. **Evangelist**: heart for *sharing* (is passionate to see that my idea gets proper marketing)
4. **Pastor**: heart for *loving* (ensures that love is at the center of the project)
5. **Teacher**: heart for *truth* (ensures that ideas are clearly communicated)

M. Since Healing Is *Progressive*, I Relax and Enjoy the Ride

We all get healed in layers.

> *But the path of the righteous is like the light of dawn, that shines* **brighter and brighter** *until the full day. The way of the wicked is like darkness; they do not know over what they stumble. My son, give attention to my words; incline your ear to my sayings. Do not let them depart from your sight; keep them in the midst of your heart. For they are life to those who find them and health to all their body. Watch over your heart with all diligence, for from it flow the springs of life. Put away from you a deceitful mouth and put devious speech far from you. Let your eyes look directly ahead and let your gaze be fixed straight in front of you. Watch the path of your feet and all your ways will be established. Do not turn to the right nor to the left; turn your foot from evil* (Prov. 4:18-27 NASB95).

The simplest way I know to receive healing:

1. **Ask**, "God, what would You like to heal today?" Tune to flow and receive His answer.

2. **Ask**, "Lord, show me the root cause of this infirmity, specifically what occurred in my life at the time this infirmity appeared." Tune to flow and receive His answer.

3. **Ask**, "What specific step(s) am I to take to remove this root cause?" Tune to flow and receive His answer. Remember, Jesus may address wrong attitudes and beliefs and a need to forgive self, others, or events that happened, and may offer therapeutic remedies or power healings.

4. **Take the step**(s) He has told you to take. When confirmation is needed, submit your leadings to spiritual advisors who are ahead of you in the area of health and healing.

What walking and living in divine health looks like:

1. I delight and meditate in the law of the Lord (Ps. 1).
2. I repent quickly and easily, and I put on Christ's robe of righteousness by faith.
3. I live in joy: "a joyful heart is good medicine" (Prov. 17:22 NASB95).
4. Love, forgiveness, and compassion are energizers of God's healing power.
5. I increase Kingdom emotions, intimacy, and power through daily interaction with my King.

My suggestion about reviewing these spiritual laws is that any time the Spirit prompts you to review this chapter on spiritual laws, follow His lead. He often wants to remind or deepen a truth within us, so He asks us to meditate upon it.

Going Deeper

- "How to Keep Your Healing"[11]
- "When Reason Challenges Faith...What Am I to Do?"[12]
- Please read "Supplement I" for additional resources to let you continue deeper with how-to, revelation-based training modules for Spirit-filled living.

Journaling Application

- Lord, what would You speak to me concerning laws of the Spirit?
- Is there any law of the Spirit You want me to focus on applying now?

Mark's journaling: There is only *one* universal law to follow.

"Lord, thank You for helping me complete this book on hearing Your voice for healing."

"You are welcome, My son. This book *will help* many. Just because you were looking for a magic bullet and do not think you have found it, does not mean that you have not.

"Since it is confirmed that 85 percent of disease is emotional at its root, you have confirmed where 85 percent of one's prayer for healing should be focused. And that has been your focus over the years, and so it shall continue to be. Through it, many have been healed. Many have been healed. Many have been healed.

"Mark, you want a *law* that will release My power at all times. *The law is to walk and live by the Spirit, as My Son Jesus did. That is the **universal** law.* Everything else flows from this law.

"Health and healing require a life of love and trust, faith, and obedience. These are things *any child can do.* Childlikeness is what releases My power to heal. So keep it simple and do not make it complicated.

"Behold I have spoken. Behold it is done!"

"Yes, Lord."

> *Then he showed me **a river of the water of life**, clear as crystal, coming from the throne of God and of the Lamb, in the middle of its street. On either side of the river was the tree of life, bearing twelve kinds of fruit, yielding its fruit every month; and the leaves of the tree were for the healing of the nations* (Rev. 22:1-2 NASB95).

God has a constantly flowing river whose sparkling streams bring joy and delight to His people. *Life will flourish wherever this water flows* (Eph. 5:25; Ezek. 47:9; Ps. 46:4 TPT; Rev. 22:1-2).

Appendices

Supplements Introduced: An In-Depth Exploration of Eight Greek Words Related to Healing

Introduction to the Appendices by Dr. Don Paprockyj

These appendices are a wonderful and fascinating treatise on the subject of *instantaneous healing* versus *therapeutic healing*.

Dr. Virkler's normal, systematic breakdown of each subject he meditates on and publishes is evident here, with a definition of each subject word, and then presenting all the Scriptures for each of these Greek words. The appendices provide a great reminder and encouragement of the amazing identity and the enormous blessings that we have in Christ.

Some of the truths presented here that impacted me the most:

- The chart on authority and power of a policeman and the analogous attributes we have reinforced that we have a mighty stature in Christ.
- That satan lost *all* authority at the cross, "So we are the ones in the power seat, and satan is in the doghouse."
- The emphasis that healing cannot occur without faith working through love.
- I was convicted to avoid Christians who deny the power of God—signs, wonders, and gifts—for today.
- We are further encouraged to appreciate and develop the gifts that the Holy Spirit has energized each of us with, and not be envious of others.

- It is always great to be reminded to be at rest from our labors and live by the flow and the River within us.
- The Relational Five-Step Prayer notes are very helpful references. I remember learning this prayer model years ago at a Randy Clark conference, but Dr. Virkler has enhanced this model with added interview questions and greater emphasis on the client stating if anything is happening during prayer. This is very helpful.
- Knowing the different types of words of knowledge that can confirm hearing from the Lord—albeit in a peculiar manner (e.g., pain in a certain part of your body, hearing or vision of a number, etc.)—which can help ensure that healing takes place.
- Dr. Mark's journaling was beautiful (no surprise). I used part of it to minister to someone in prayer, "to see yourself seated with Me in heaven...and then release it on earth."
- We always need God's compassion to work through us and should continually pray that it be manifested in us.
- Another great reminder is to know the names of the demons, so it is easier for them to be cast out. Jesus asked the name of the demons in the Gadarene demoniac and also commanded as He was ministering to the child with the evil spirit, "You deaf and mute spirit...come out."
- It makes sense that the religious have always resisted deliverance.
- Deliverance is considered *therapeuo* healing, since it is a process.

This exhaustive work will serve as a continual source of encouragement, as well as a comprehensive reference.

Supplement A

Opening the Door to God's Blessings Through Salvation

The big questions we can answer in this meditation are, "What must I do to be saved?" and "What do I receive when I am saved?"

Let's define the Greek words *sozo* (G4982, "saved") and *soteria* (G4991, "salvation"). *Sozo* is a verb translated "to save." There are 120 occurrences in the King James Version. *Soteria* is the noun form of the above word: "salvation." It has 44 occurrences in the King James.

In *Kittle Theological Dictionary of the New Testament*, *sozo* means "to save, i.e., deliver or protect." *For soteria*, it says "the state of safety, preservation from harm and danger, rescuing or saving, saving from moral failure."

So for a working definition of *sozo*/*soteria* we could say "to save, deliver, protect, heal, preserve, and make well."

Overview of *Sozo* and *Soteria*

There are over 160 verses in the New Testament that contain *sozo* or *soteria*. Salvation *opens the door* for the power, anointing, healing, and blessings of God to flow in unprecedented ways in our lives. The future appendices will explore numerous words specifically discussing God's power to receive healing and deliverance. May we see the wonder of these magnificent promises He has made to us!

For example, here are a few verses with *sozo* and *soteria* in them:

1. Salvation involves *power*:

*For I am not ashamed of the gospel, for it is the **power** [__dunamis__] of God for salvation [__soteria__] to everyone who **believes**, to the Jew first and also to the Greek* (Rom. 1:16 NASB95).

2. Salvation is through Jesus Christ:

*And there is **salvation** [__soteria__] in no one else; for there is no other name under heaven that has been given among men by which we must be saved [__sozo__]* (Acts 4:12 NASB95).

3. Being saved involves *laying down your life* for Jesus:

*If anyone wishes to come after Me, he must **deny himself, and take up his cross and follow Me**. For whoever wishes to **save** [__sozo__] his life will lose it, but whoever loses his life for My sake and the gospel's will **save** [__sozo__] it. For what does it profit a man to gain the whole world, and forfeit his soul? For what will a man give in exchange for his soul? For whoever is ashamed of Me and My words in this adulterous and sinful generation, the Son of Man will also be ashamed of him when He comes in the glory of His Father with the holy angels* (Mk. 8:34-38 NASB95).

4. Being saved involves believing in Jesus, being baptized, and having signs following:

*And He said to them, "Go into all the world and preach the gospel to all creation. He who has **believed** and has been **baptized** shall be **saved** [__sozo__]; but he who has disbelieved shall be condemned. These signs will accompany those who have believed: in My name they will cast out demons, they will speak with new tongues; they will pick up serpents, and if they drink any deadly poison, it will not hurt them; they will lay hands on the sick, and they will recover"* (Mk. 16:15-18 NASB95).

5. *Saved* **includes the healing touch of Jesus:**

> *And a woman who had been suffering from a hemorrhage for twelve years, came up behind Him and touched the fringe of His cloak; for she was saying to herself, "If I only touch His garment, I will* **get well** *[*sozo*]." But Jesus turning and seeing her said, "Daughter, take courage; your faith has* **made you well** *[*sozo*]." At once the woman was* **made well** *[*sozo*]* (Matt. 9:20-22 NASB95).

Salvation is *free*, yet proof of salvation is that we *obey* Christ. You cannot earn salvation, as it is a *gift!*

> *For by grace, you have been* **saved** *[*sozo*] through faith; and that not of yourselves, it is the gift of God; not as a result of works, so that no one may boast* (Eph. 2:8-9 NASB95).

> *If you love Me, you will keep My commandments* (Jn. 14:15 NASB95).

The apostle Paul, in Ephesians 2:8-9, does not say that works are not required at all. The purpose of his statement is to show that works do not save us, but that grace and faith do! The very next verse, verse 10, shows that God calls members of His church for the very purpose of *performing good works*:

> *For we are His workmanship, created in Christ Jesus for good works, which God prepared beforehand so that we would walk in them* (Eph. 2:10 NASB95).

The apostle's language is very clear. God desires us to walk in good works, and He has prepared our spiritual educational process so that we will learn to do them. Doing good works in the name of Jesus Christ is a major part of the purpose of the life of each true Christian. We cannot truly be Christians without them!

*He who says, "I know him," and does not keep His command-ments, is a liar, and the **truth is not in him*** (1 Jn. 2:4 NKJV).

The Holy Spirit given to those who *obey* Christ:

*And we are His witnesses to these things, and so also is the **Holy Spirit** whom God has given to those who **obey** Him* (Acts 5:32 NKJV).

Enduring to the end is necessary to be saved:

*You will be hated by all because of My name, but the one who **endures to the end**, he will be **saved** [sozo]* (Mk. 13:13 NASB95).

Salvation culminates in our future hope where we will live together with Jesus in heaven:

*But since we are of the day, let us be sober, having put on the breastplate of faith and love, and as a helmet, **the hope of salvation** [soteria]. For God has not destined us for wrath, but for obtaining **salvation** [soteria] through our Lord Jesus Christ, who died for us, so that whether we are awake or asleep, we **will live together** with Him* (1 Thess. 5:8-10 NASB95).

All verses with *sozo*[1] and *soteria*[2] in them are available from BibleTools.org.

Summary: Salvation is the door-opening experience for all of God's blessings.

Salvation refers to our initial acceptance of Jesus as our Lord and Savior, as well as the ongoing process of spiritual transformation and the future process of the glorification of our bodies in heaven. So, *salvation* is a big enough word to include an event in our *past*, our *present* growth in

Christ, and our *future* glorification in heaven. Salvation is free, but obeying Christ is evidence we are followers of Him. This is a huge topic that can be explored in much more depth at another time.

For now, let's just say that salvation involves a work of the Spirit and opens us up to the various ways the power of God transforms us. We will explore a number of these different ways in the upcoming appendices.

Personal Application

1. Know who you are in Christ and confess the powerful truth.[3]
2. Lord, what would You speak to me concerning salvation?

Supplement B

Receiving Authority *(Exousia)* from God

***Kittle Theological Dictionary of the New Testament* definition of *exousia* (G1849):**

1. authority, privilege, permission, and the right to do something
2. (subjectively) force, capacity, competency, and freedom
3. (objectively) mastery, delegated influence

Overview of *Exousia*

There are approximately 100 occurrences of G1849, the word normally translated as "authority" in the New American Standard Bible; but in the King James Version it is more often translated as "power." However, there is another Greek word for "power," which is *dunamis,* and the King James translates *dunamis* as "power" 71 times. I do not know why the King James also chooses to translate *exousia* as "power" the majority of times. I guess this helps confirm my decision that my favorite version for accuracy is the New American Standard Bible.

Numerous verses say that Jesus has granted us both *authority* and *power* to heal diseases and cast out demons.

> *And He called the twelve together, and gave them **power** [duna-mis] and **authority** [exousia] over all the demons and to heal*

diseases. And He sent them out to proclaim the kingdom of God and to perform healing (Lk. 9:1-2 NASB95).

The big question I wanted to answer in this meditation is *who* has authority in the spiritual realm—Jesus, satan, or us? I have made a summary of eight verses at the end of this meditation.

I came away believing that satan lost all his authority when Jesus took it from him as He rose from the dead. Jesus is now seated in heavenly places, ruling and reigning, and we are at His side as co-rulers. Jesus has given all authority to us to use in healing diseases and casting out demons. So, we are the ones in the power seat, and satan is in the doghouse. When demons attack us with ungodly thoughts, we take them captive. We rule over satan and any attack he may choose to throw at us.

The vast majority of verses containing *exousia* (G1849) are listed below (NASB95):

1. Authoritative teaching is different from head teaching:

*He was teaching them as one having **authority** [exousia], and not as their scribes* (Matt. 7:29).

2. Earthly and heavenly authority structures are similar:

*For I also am a man under **authority** [exousia], with soldiers under me; and I say to this one, "Go!" and he goes, and to another, "Come!" and he comes, and to my slave, "Do this!" and he does it* (Matt. 8:9).

3. Jesus has the spiritual authority to forgive sins:

*"But so that you may know that the Son of Man has **authority** [exousia] on earth to forgive sins"—then He said to the paralytic, "Get up, pick up your bed and go home"* (Matt. 9:6).

4. Results of exercising spirituality can bring glory to God:

*But when the crowds saw this, they were awestruck, and glorified God, who had given such **authority** [underline]exousia[/underline] to men* (Matt. 9:8).

5. Jesus has given us authority to cast out demons and heal all diseases:

*Jesus summoned His twelve disciples and gave them **authority** [underline]exousia[/underline] over unclean spirits, to cast them out, and to heal every kind of disease and every kind of sickness* (Matt. 10:1).

6. Authority structures can easily conflict with one another:

*When He entered the temple, the chief priests and the elders of the people came to Him while He was teaching, and said, "By what **authority** [underline]exousia[/underline] are You doing these things, and who gave You this **authority** [underline]exousia[/underline]?"* (Matt. 21:23)

7. Challenging questions about authority:

*Jesus said to them, "I will also ask you one thing, which if you tell Me, I will also tell you by what **authority** [underline]exousia[/underline] I do these things"* (Matt. 21:24).

*And answering Jesus, they said, "We do not know." He also said to them, "Neither will I tell you by what **authority** [underline]exousia[/underline] I do these things"* (Matt. 21:27).

8. Through Jesus' death and resurrection, *all* authority has been given to Jesus:

*And Jesus came up and spoke to them, saying, "All **authority** [underline]exousia[/underline] has been given to Me in heaven and on earth. Go therefore and make disciples of all the nations, baptizing them in the* *name of the Father and the Son and the Holy Spirit, teaching them to observe all that I commanded you; and lo, **I am with you always, even to the end of the age**" (Matt. 28:18-20).*

9. You can tell when teaching is filled with authority, anointing, and life:

*They were amazed at His teaching; for He was teaching them as one having **authority** [exousia], and not as the scribes (Mk. 1:22).*

10. What makes teaching authoritative is when you back it up with real-life examples of power encounters:

*They were all amazed, so that they debated among themselves, saying, "What is this? A new teaching with **authority** [exousia]! He commands even the unclean spirits, and they obey Him" (Mk. 1:27).*

*"But so that you may know that the Son of Man has **authority** [exousia] on earth to forgive sins"—He said to the paralytic (Mk. 2:10).*

11. Disciples given authority to cast out demons:

*And He appointed twelve, so that they would be with Him and that He could send them out to preach, and to have **authority** [exousia] to cast out the demons (Mk. 3:14-15).*

*And He summoned the twelve and began to send them out in pairs, and gave them **authority** [exousia] over the unclean spirits (Mk. 6:7).*

12. Threatened authorities often clash with new authorities:

*Answering Jesus, they said, "We do not know." And Jesus said to them, "Nor will I tell you by what **authority** [exousia] I do these things"* (Mk. 11:33).

13. We set up authority structures so things can run smoothly:

*It is like a man away on a journey, who upon leaving his house and putting his slaves in **charge** [exousia], assigning to each one his task, also commanded the doorkeeper to stay on the alert* (Mk. 13:34).

14. The devil felt he had authority:

*And the devil said to Him, "I will give You all this **domain** [exousia] and its glory; for it has been handed over to me, and I give it to whomever I wish"* (Lk. 4:6).

15. Jesus backed up his sermons with a practical demonstration of spiritual authority:

*They were amazed at His teaching, for His message was with **authority** [exousia]. In the synagogue there was a man possessed by the spirit of an unclean demon, and he cried out with a loud voice, "Let us alone! What business do we have with each other, Jesus of Nazareth? Have You come to destroy us? I know who You are—the Holy One of God!" But Jesus rebuked him, saying, "Be quiet and come out of him!" And when the demon had thrown him down in the midst of the people, he came out of him without doing him any harm. And amazement came upon them all, and they began talking with one another saying, "What is this message? For with **authority** [exousia] and power He commands the unclean spirits and they come out"* (Lk. 4:32-36).

*"But, so that you may know that the Son of Man has **authority** [underline]exousia[/underline]] on earth to forgive sins,"—He said to the paralytic—"I say to you, get up, and pick up your stretcher and go home"* (Lk. 5:24).

16. Understanding the power of being under authority creates great faith:

*"For I also am a man placed under **authority** [underline]exousia[/underline]], with soldiers under me; and I say to this one, 'Go!' and he goes, and to another, 'Come!' and he comes, and to my slave, 'Do this!' and he does it." Now when Jesus heard this, He marveled at him, and turned and said to the crowd that was following Him, "I say to you, not even in Israel have I found such **great faith**"* (Lk. 7:8-9).

17. We proclaim the Kingdom and demonstrate it by casting out demons and healing diseases:

*And He called the twelve together, and gave them **power** [underline]dunamis[/underline]] and **authority** [underline]exousia[/underline]] over all the demons and to heal diseases. And He sent them out to proclaim the kingdom of God and to perform healing* (Lk. 9:1-2).

18. Demons must obey the name of Jesus; and when they are cast out and sickness healed, satan is falling from heaven:

*The seventy returned with joy, saying, "Lord, even the demons are subject to us in Your name." And He said to them, "I was watching Satan fall from heaven like lightning. Behold, I have given you **authority** [underline]exousia[/underline]] to tread on serpents and scorpions, and over all the power of the enemy, and nothing will injure you. Nevertheless do not rejoice in this, that the spirits are subject to you, but rejoice that your names are recorded in heaven"* (Lk. 10:17-20).

19. God has the authority to kill and to cast into hell:

*But I will warn you whom to fear: fear the One who, after He has killed, has **authority** [exousia] to cast into hell; yes, I tell you, fear Him!* (Lk. 12:5)

20. Tune to the Spirit and speak when in tight circumstances:

*When they bring you before the synagogues and the rulers and the **authorities** [exousia], do not worry about how or what you are to speak in your defense, or what you are to say; for the Holy Spirit will teach you in that very hour what you ought to say* (Lk. 12:11-12).

21. Being faithful in small things frees God to grant you authority for greater things:

*The first appeared, saying, "Master, your mina has made ten minas more." And he said to him, "Well done, good slave, because you have been faithful in a very little thing, you are to be in **authority** [exousia] over ten cities"* (Lk. 19:16-17).

22. Authority will be challenged, and you need to be ready to give an anointed response:

*They spoke, saying to Him, "Tell us by what authority You are doing these things, or who is the one who gave You this **authority** [exousia]?" Jesus answered and said to them, "I will also ask you a question, and you tell Me: Was the baptism of John from heaven or from men?" They reasoned among themselves, saying, "If we say, 'From heaven,' He will say, 'Why did you not believe him?' But if we say, 'From men,' all the people will stone us to death, for they are convinced that John was a prophet." So they answered that they did not know where it came from. And Jesus said to them, "Nor will I tell you by what **authority** [exousia] I do these things"* (Lk. 20:2-8).

23. Earthly rulers have authority. Discern when a question is a trick question and always tune to the Spirit, so you can give anointed answers to *all* questions:

> So they watched Him, and sent spies who pretended to be righteous, in order that they might catch Him in some statement, so that they could deliver Him to the rule and the **authority** [_exousia_] of the governor. They questioned Him, saying, "Teacher, we know that You speak and teach correctly, and You are not partial to any, but teach the way of God in truth. Is it lawful for us to pay taxes to Caesar, or not?" But He detected their trickery and said to them, "Show Me a denarius. Whose likeness and inscription does it have?" They said, "Caesar's." And He said to them, "Then render to Caesar the things that are Caesar's, and to God the things that are God's" (Lk. 20:20-25).

24. Darkness is a time when evil has more power, conversely meaning there is more power when in the light:

> While I was with you daily in the temple, you did not lay hands on Me; but this hour and the **power** [_exousia_] of darkness are yours (Lk. 22:53).

Note: The Modern KJV uses the word *authority* rather than *power* in this verse.

> And when he learned that He belonged to Herod's **jurisdiction** [_exousia_], he sent Him to Herod, who himself also was in Jerusalem at that time (Lk. 23:7).

25. Receiving and believing in Jesus' name grants you the authority to be born of God:

> But as many as received Him, to them He gave the **right** [_exousia_] to become children of God, even to those who believe in His name,

who were born, not of blood nor of the will of the flesh nor of the will of man, but of God (Jn. 1:12-13).

26. Jesus has been given authority to execute judgment, which will be based on if you did good or evil:

*And He gave Him **authority** [exousia] to execute judgment, because He is the Son of Man. Do not marvel at this; for an hour is coming, in which all who are in the tombs will hear His voice, and will come forth; those who did the good deeds to a resurrection of life, those who committed the evil deeds to a resurrection of judgment* (Jn. 5:27-29).

27. Jesus was given authority by His Father to lay down His life and to take it up again:

*No one has taken it away from Me, but I lay it down on My own initiative. I have **authority** [exousia] to lay it down, and I have authority to take it up again. This commandment I received from My Father* (Jn. 10:18).

28. God gave Jesus authority to give eternal life to those whom His Father had given to Him:

*Even as You gave Him **authority** [exousia] over all flesh, that to all whom You have given Him, He may give eternal life. This is eternal life, that they may know You, the only true God, and Jesus Christ whom You have sent* (Jn. 17:2-3).

29. Earthly rulers have no authority over believers unless God gives it to them. There are greater and lesser sins:

*So Pilate said to Him, "You do not speak to me? Do You not know that I have **authority** [exousia] to release You, and I have authority to crucify You?" Jesus answered, "You would have no **authority*** [_exousia_] over Me, unless it had been given you from above; for this reason he who delivered Me to you has the greater sin" (Jn. 19:10-11).

30. God does not reveal to us the times or seasons:

He said to them, "It is not for you to know times or epochs which the Father has fixed by His own **authority** [_exousia_]; but you will receive **power** [_dunamis_] when the Holy Spirit has come upon you; and you shall be My witnesses both in Jerusalem, and in all Judea and Samaria, and even to the remotest part of the earth" (Acts 1:7-8).

31. We have authority over our resources:

While it remained unsold, did it not remain your own? And after it was sold, was it not under your **control** [_exousia_]? Why is it that you have conceived this deed in your heart? You have not lied to men but to God (Acts 5:4).

32. You cannot purchase spiritual authority with money:

Now when Simon saw that the Spirit was bestowed through the laying on of the apostles' hands, he offered them money, saying, "Give this **authority** [_exousia_] to me as well, so that everyone on whom I lay my hands may receive the Holy Spirit." But Peter said to him, "May your silver perish with you, because you thought you could obtain the gift of God with money!" (Acts 8:18-20)

33. God's prophetic leading can protect one from the authority of evil men:

But Ananias answered, "Lord, I have heard from many about this man, how much harm he did to Your saints at Jerusalem; and here he has **authority** [_exousia_] from the chief priests to bind all who call on Your name." But the Lord said to him, "Go, for he is a chosen instrument of Mine, to bear My name before the Gentiles and kings and the sons of Israel; for I will show him how much he must suffer for My name's sake" (Acts 9:13-16).

Note: Acts 26:10,12 is a recounting of this event.

34. Believers turn from being under the authority of satan to being under the authority of God:

*To open their eyes so that they may turn from darkness to light and from the **dominion** [_exousia_] of Satan to God, that they may receive forgiveness of sins and an inheritance among those who have been **sanctified by faith in Me** (Acts 26:18).*

35. God has the authority to create each person with the gifts, calling, and destinies He desires. Therefore, be happy with the gifts and call and destiny God has for you and do not seek to emulate others:

*Or does not the potter have a **right** [_exousia_] over the clay, to make from the same lump one vessel for honorable use and another for common use? (Rom. 9:21)*

36. Governing authorities are ordained by God for good. They are to bear the sword to bring wrath to the one practicing evil:

*Every person is to be in subjection to the governing **authorities** [_exousia_]. For there is no **authority** [_exousia_] except from God, and **those which exist are established by God.** Therefore whoever resists **authority** [_exousia_] has opposed the ordinance of God; and they who have opposed will receive condemnation upon themselves. For rulers are not a cause of fear for good behavior, but for evil. Do you want to have no fear of **authority** [_exousia_]? Do what is good and you will have praise from the same; for it is a **minister*** *of God to you for good. But if you do what is evil, be afraid; **for it does not bear the sword for nothing;** for it is a **minister of God, an avenger who brings wrath on the one who practices evil*** (Rom. 13:1-4).

37. You have authority over your own will:

*And he who hath stood stedfast in the heart—not having necessity—and hath **authority** [exousia] over his own will, and this he hath determined in his heart—to keep his own virgin—doth well* (1 Cor. 7:37 YLT).

38. I have authority over my beliefs, decisions, and actions, but be careful not to wound another who is weaker in faith than I:

*But take care that this **liberty** [exousia] of yours does not somehow become a stumbling block to the weak* (1 Cor. 8:9).

*Do we not have a **right** [exousia] to eat and drink? Do we not have a **right** [exousia] to take along a believing wife, even as the rest of the apostles and the brothers of the Lord and Cephas? Or do only Barnabas and I not have a **right** [exousia] to refrain from working?* (1 Cor. 9:4-6; see also 1 Cor. 9:12,18)

39. Jesus is reigning until He has put all His enemies under His feet, so we are engaged in a mop-up operation which Jesus is winning. We need to put all things under our own feet, since we are His body and His feet:

*Then comes the end, when He hands over the kingdom to God, when He has abolished all rule and all **authority** [exousia] and **power** [dunamis]. For He must reign until He has put all His enemies under His feet. The last enemy that will be abolished is death. For He has put all things in subjection under His feet. But when He says, "All things are put in subjection," it is evident that*

He is excepted who put all things in subjection to Him. When all things are subjected to Him, then the Son Himself also will be subjected to the One who subjected all things to Him, so that God may be all in all (1 Cor. 15:24-28).

40. We have been given authority by God for the mission and destiny He has for our lives:

*For this reason I am writing these things while absent, so that when present I need not use severity, in accordance with the **authority** [*exousia*] which the Lord gave me for building up and not for tearing down* (2 Cor. 13:10).

41. It takes revelation by the Spirit to see the authority and power that we currently have:

*I pray that the eyes of your heart may be enlightened, so that you will know what is the hope of His calling, what are the **riches of the glory of His inheritance in the saints**, and what is the surpassing greatness of His **power** [*dunamis*] toward us who believe. These are in accordance with the **working of the strength of His might** which He brought about in Christ, when He raised Him from the dead and seated Him at His right hand in the heavenly places, **far above all** rule and **authority** [*exousia*] and **power** [*dunamis*] and dominion, and every name that is named, not only in this age but also in the one to come. And **He put all things in subjection under His feet**, and gave Him as head over all things to the church, which is His body, the fullness of Him who fills all in all* (Eph. 1:18-23).

42. Satan is the prince of the power of the air, and we are freed from his authority and seated with Christ in heavenly places:

*In which you formerly walked according to the course of this world, according to the prince of the **power** [*exousia*] of the air, of the* *spirit that is now working in the sons of disobedience. Among them we too all formerly lived in the lusts of our flesh, indulging the desires of the flesh and of the mind, and were by nature children of wrath, even as the rest. But God, being rich in mercy, because of His great love with which He loved us, even when we were dead in our transgressions,* **made us alive together with Christ** *(by grace you have been saved), and* **raised us up with Him, and seated us with Him in the heavenly places in Christ Jesus,** *so that in the ages to come He might show the surpassing riches of His grace in kindness toward us in Christ Jesus* (Eph. 2:2-7).

For He rescued us from the **domain** [*exousia*] *of darkness, and transferred us to the kingdom of His beloved Son* (Col. 1:13).

43. We, the Church, are to demonstrate the wisdom of God to the rulers in heavenly places:

So that the manifold wisdom of God might now **be made known through the church** *to the rulers and the* **authority** [*exousia*] *in the heavenly places* (Eph. 3:10).

44. We are throwing down the spiritual forces of darkness:

For our **struggle** [root Greek meaning is "throw down"] *is not against flesh and blood, but against the rulers, against the* **powers** [*exousia*], *against the world forces of this darkness, against the spiritual forces of wickedness in the heavenly places* (Eph. 6:12).

45. The fullness of God dwells in us, so we join with our Lord Jesus Christ who is head over *all* authority:

For in Him all the fullness of Deity dwells in bodily form, and in Him you have been made complete, and He is the head over all rule and **authority** [*exousia*] (Col. 2:9-10).

46. Jesus is now at the right hand of God, in heaven, and all are subjected to Him:

> *Who is at the right hand of God, having gone into heaven, after angels and **authorities** [_exousia_] and **powers** [_dunamis_] had been subjected to Him* (1 Pet. 3:22).

47. Jesus Christ has all authority before time, now, and forever:

> *To the only God our Savior, through Jesus Christ our Lord, be glory, majesty, dominion and **authority** [_exousia_], before all time and now and forever. Amen* (Jude 1:25).

I skipped the 19 verses on authority in the book of Revelation, as Revelation is a symbolic book, and many scholars believe it was written in 68 AD and was essentially all fulfilled except perhaps parts of the last two chapters by 70 AD. In 70 AD Rome flattened Jerusalem because of their rebellion against Rome. Others, of course, project Revelation into the future. We are not going to address this entire debate at this time.

> *The Revelation **of Jesus Christ** which God gave unto him, to shew unto his servants things which must **shortly** come to pass; and he sent and **signified** it by his angel unto his servant John* (Rev. 1:1 KJV; the NKJV is almost identical).

Note: Verse 1 says this book is revealing Jesus, not the antichrist, and the word "antichrist" *never* shows up in the book of Revelation.

He uses the word *signified*. He could have used *write, written, reveal, revealed, disclose, disclosed, tell,* and *told*, which are words used hundreds of times in the New Testament. Instead, he uses a word that shows up only six times and is always translated *signified* in the King James Version.

Summary of key verses as to *who* currently has authority—Christ or Antichrist:

One big question I wanted to answer is *who* has the authority in the spiritual realm—Jesus, satan, or us. I have made a summary of nine verses, which are listed below. I come away believing that satan lost all his authority when Jesus took it from him and rose from the dead (Col. 2:14-15; Matt. 16:19; Rev. 1:18). Jesus is now seated in heavenly places, ruling and reigning, and we are at His side. Jesus has given all authority to us to use in healing diseases and casting out demons.

1. Through Jesus' death and resurrection, *all* authority has been given to Jesus (Matt. 28:18-20).
2. Jesus is reigning—we are engaged in a mop-up operation as we put all things under our feet (1 Cor. 15:24-28; Eph. 1:18-23).
4. We, the Church, are to demonstrate the wisdom of God to the rulers in heavenly places (Eph. 3:10).
5. We are throwing down the spiritual forces of darkness (Eph. 6:12).
6. The fullness of God dwells in us, so we join with our Lord Jesus Christ Who is head over *all* authority (Col. 2:9-10).
7. Jesus is now at the right hand of God, in heaven, and all are subjected to Him (1 Pet. 3:22).
8. Jesus Christ has all authority before time, now, and forever (Jude 1:25).

Personal Application

- Write out your summary of who has power, and your role in defeating any remaining pockets of darkness you find.
- "Lord, what do You want to speak to me about authority?"

Supplement C

Dunamis Is the Power of God and Is Occasionally Translated as "Miracle"

There is no unique Greek word for "miracle." A miracle is one way the Greek word *dunamis* (Strong's #G1411) and the word *semeion* were translated. *Dunamis* is found 123 times in the King James Version and is translated as "power" 79 times in the King James Version. On 20 occasions in the New American Standard Bible it is translated as "miracle."

The other main words used to translate *dunamis* in the King James Version are *might, mighty, mightily, powers,* and *strength.* Young's Literal Translation never uses the word *miracle.* Instead, it uses *mighty works, mighty deeds, mighty energies,* and *powers.*

Kittle Theological Dictionary of the New Testament defines *dunamis* as "force, miraculous power, a miracle." *Force* is defined as the interaction between two bodies, or it can also be defined as the push or pull experienced by an object when an external force acts on it. The other way of explaining *force* is, it is a responsible factor for an object to be either in the state of motion or state of rest until an external force acts on it.

Conclusion: A miracle of healing is experiencing a mighty *force* of God's power acting upon a disease, infirmity, or demon, and it results in an immediate transformation of one's health.

All 20 occurrences of *miracle* in the New Testament (NASB95):

1. Lawless performing miracles:

*Not everyone who says to Me, "Lord, Lord," will enter the Kingdom of heaven, but he who does the will of My Father who is in heaven will enter. Many will say to Me on that day, "Lord, Lord, did we not prophesy in Your name, and in Your name cast out demons, and in Your name perform many miracles (dunamis)?" And then I will declare to them, "I never **knew** [ginosko] you; depart from Me, you who practice lawlessness"* (Matt. 7:21-23).

2. Do not attack those not in your close-knit group:

*But Jesus said, "Do not hinder him, for there is no one who will perform a **miracle** [dunamis] in My name, and be able soon afterward to speak evil of Me"* (Mk. 9:39).

3. Rebuked:

*Then He began to denounce the cities in which most of His **miracles** [dunamis] were done, because they did not repent* (Matt. 11:20).

*Woe to you, Chorazin! Woe to you, Bethsaida! For if the **miracles** [dunamis] had occurred in Tyre and Sidon which occurred in you, they would have repented long ago in sackcloth and ashes* (Matt. 11:21).

*And you, Capernaum, will not be exalted to heaven, will you? You will descend to Hades; for if the **miracles** [dunamis] had occurred in Sodom which occurred in you, it would have remained to this day* (Matt. 11:23).

*Woe to you, Chorazin! Woe to you, Bethsaida! For if the **miracles** [__dunamis__] had been performed in Tyre and Sidon which occurred in you, they would have repented long ago, sitting in sackcloth and ashes* (Lk. 10:13).

4. Jesus was limited by their unbelief:

*And He did not do many **miracles** [__dunamis__] there because of their unbelief* (Matt. 13:58).

Even though there was the force/power of the Holy Spirit present in Jesus to do miracles, this power needs something to interact with. That something is "faith working through love" (Gal. 5:6). Since *dunamis* is a force, it can only be called into action when it interacts with faith and love. So, *dunamis* flows when faith and love are present, and these were *not* present in his hometown, so no mighty works occurred.

Principle: Faith + Love + *dunamis* release a miracle/mighty work of God.

5. Jesus was limited in power miracles, but still able to do therapeutic healings:

*He could do no **miracle** [__dunamis__] there except that He laid His hands on a few sick people and **healed** [__therapeuo__] them* (Mk. 6:5).

The definition of *therapeuo* is "to heal, cure, restore to health," according to *Thayer's Greek-English Lexicon of the New Testament*.

6. Miracles as a sign:

*When the Sabbath came, He began to teach in the synagogue; and the many listeners were astonished, saying, "Where did this man get these things, and what is this wisdom given to Him, and such **miracles** [__dunamis__] as these performed by His hands?"* (Mk. 6:2)

*As soon as He was approaching, near the descent of the Mount of Olives, the whole crowd of the disciples began to praise God joyfully with a loud voice for all the **miracles** [dunamis] which they had seen (Lk. 19:37).*

*Men of Israel, listen to these words: Jesus the Nazarene, a man attested to you by God with **miracles** [dunamis] and wonders and signs which God performed through Him in your midst, just as you yourselves know (Acts 2:22).*

*Even Simon himself believed; and after being baptized, he continued on with Philip, and as he observed signs and great **miracles** [dunamis] taking place, he was constantly amazed (Acts 8:13).*

*The signs of a true apostle were performed among you with all perseverance, by signs and wonders and **miracles** [dunamis] (2 Cor. 12:12).*

*God also testifying with them, both by signs and wonders and by various **miracles** [dunamis], and by gifts of the Holy Spirit according to His own will (Heb. 2:4).*

7. Over the top:

*God was performing extraordinary **miracles** [dunamis] by the hands of Paul (Acts 19:11).*

8. The miracle in Acts 4:16 is powered by *dunamis* according to Acts 4:7:

But Peter, along with John, fixed his gaze on him and said, "Look at us!" And he began to give them his attention, expecting to receive something from them. But Peter said, "I do not possess silver and gold, but what I do have I give to you: In the name of Jesus Christ the Nazarene—walk!" And seizing him by the right *hand, he raised him up; and **immediately his feet and his ankles were strengthened. With a leap he stood upright and began to walk;** and he entered the temple with them, walking and leaping and praising God* (Acts 3:4-8).

*By what **power** [_dunamis_], or in what name, have you done this?* (Acts 4:7)

*A noteworthy **miracle** [_semeion_, "sign"] has taken place* (Acts 4:16).

*The man was more than forty years old on whom this **miracle** [_semeion_, "sign"] of **healing** [the Greek is _iasis_, "cure"] had been performed* (Acts 4:22).

9. Miracles are different from gifts of healings:

*To another faith by the same Spirit, and to another gifts of healing by the one Spirit, and to another the effecting of **miracles** [_duna-mis_], and to another prophecy, and to another the distinguishing of spirits, to another various kinds of tongues, and to another the interpretation of tongues* (1 Cor. 12:9-10).

*And God has appointed in the church, first apostles, second prophets, third teachers, then **miracles** [_dunamis_], then gifts of **healings** [_iama_], helps, administrations, various kinds of tongues* (1 Cor. 12:28).

Iama is "a means of healing, remedy, medicine."

10. Specialized ministries:

*All are not apostles, are they? All are not prophets, are they? All are not teachers, are they? All are not workers of **miracles** [_dunamis_], are they?* (1 Cor. 12:29)

11. Hear God's voice and believe as Abraham did:

*So then, does He who provides you with the Spirit and works **miracles** [__dunamis__] among you, do it by the works of the Law, or by hearing with faith? Even so Abraham believed God, and it was reckoned to him as righteousness* (Gal. 3:5-6).

Summary of the word *miracle* (NASB):

Out of twenty uses of the word *miracle*, two times mention actual miracles; Jesus rebukes those who witnessed them five times; six times say that miracles are signs; two times mention they are in a different category from gifts of healing; three times they are dependent on faith; one time mentions some have this ministry; one time says let other groups do miracles "in My name."

To release a *dunamis* miracle, you need faith working by love! Love and compassion are high-frequency emotions and are carrier waves of *dunamis* healing power. Faith is the switch that turns them on. There is *no mention* of prayer to release these miracles, nor of laying on hands, but the Bible does mention the commanding of a lame man to walk and grabbing him and lifting him up. The same passage also mentions commanding a person to look at them.

Personal Application

"Lord, what do You want me to see concerning miracles?" Record these revelations in a separate location.

Free Resources: Download, Experience, Distribute

1. Miracles—7 Step Model [1]
2. Miracles—7-Step Model (PowerPoint) [2]
3. Miracles—7-Step Model (Streaming Audio, 72 minutes) [3]
4. Miracles—7-Step Model (Wallet Card) [4]

Fifty-Eight Additional Verses Containing *Dunamis* (NASB95)

God rules over all powers, even giving the wicked the power they have.

There are evil powers present:

> *For I am convinced that neither death, nor life, nor angels, nor principalities, nor things present, nor things to come, nor **powers** [dunamis], nor height, nor depth, nor any other created thing, will be able to separate us from the love of God, which is in Christ Jesus our Lord* (Rom. 8:38-39).

God empowers evil men for His purposes:

> *For the Scripture says to Pharaoh, "For this very purpose I raised you up, to demonstrate My **power** [dunamis] in you, and that My name might be proclaimed throughout the whole earth"* (Rom. 9:17).

Evil workers will do *dunamis* signs and false wonders seeking to deceive:

> *That is, the one whose coming is in accord with the activity of Satan, with all with **power** [dunamis] and signs and false wonders, and with all the deception of wickedness for those who perish, because they did not receive the love of the truth so as to be saved. For this reason God will send upon them a deluding influence so that they will believe what is false* (2 Thess. 2:9-11).

Avoid people claiming to be believers but denying the power of God:

Holding to a form of godliness, although they have denied its **power** [*dunamis*]; *avoid such men as these* (2 Tim. 3:5).

Both God and the enemy can manifest power [*dunamis*]:

Demonic hosts have power, but we have more power:

Behold, I have given you authority to tread on serpents and scorpions, and over all the **power** [*dunamis*] *of the enemy, and nothing will injure you* (Lk. 10:19).

Man practicing magic manifesting *dunamis*:

Now there was a man named Simon, who formerly was practicing magic in the city and astonishing the people of Samaria, claiming to be someone great; and they all, from smallest to greatest, were giving attention to him, saying, "This man is what is called the Great **Power** [*dunamis*] *of God"* (Acts 8:9-10).

The power to do a miracle does not come from us, but from God:

Jesus was anointed by the Spirit with *dunamis*:

You know of Jesus of Nazareth, how God anointed Him with the **Holy Spirit** *and with* **power** [*dunamis*] *and how He went about doing good and healing all who were oppressed by the devil, for God was with Him* (Acts 10:38).

Peter declares the power is not from him, but from Jesus:

But when Peter saw this, he replied to the people, "Men of Israel, why are you amazed at this, or why do you gaze at us, as if by our own **power** [*dunamis*] *or piety we had made him walk?"* (Acts 3:12-13)

We need to be clothed with power (*dunamis*), as that is when we receive the power to do miracles:

After a 40-day fast and resisting temptations, Jesus receives power:

> *And Jesus returned to Galilee in the* **power** [*dunamis*] *of the Spirit, and news about Him spread through all the surrounding district* (Lk. 4:14).

God's power clothes us and covers us:

> *And behold, I am sending forth the promise of My Father upon you; but you are to stay in the city until you are clothed with* **power** [*dunamis*] *from on high* (Lk. 24:49).

God's power is the Holy Spirit resting upon us:

> *You will receive* **power** [*dunamis*] *when the Holy Spirit has come upon you; and you shall be My witnesses both in Jerusalem, and in all Judea and Samaria, and even to the remotest part of the earth* (Acts 1:8).

Another filling with the Holy Spirit making them bold when they were in prayer, in one accord, praising God:

> *They lifted their voices to God with one accord and said, "O Lord, it is You who made the heaven and the earth and the sea, and all that is in them, who by the Holy Spirit, through the mouth of our father David Your servant, said, 'Why did the Gentiles rage, and the peoples devise futile things? The kings of the earth took their stand, and the rulers were gathered together against the Lord and against His Christ.'*

"For truly in this city there were gathered together against Your holy servant Jesus, whom You anointed, both Herod and Pontius Pilate, along with the Gentiles and the peoples of Israel, to do whatever Your hand and Your purpose predestined to occur. And now, Lord, take note of their threats, and grant that Your bond-servants may speak Your word with all confidence, while You extend Your hand to heal, and signs and wonders take place through the name of Your holy servant Jesus." And when they had prayed, the place where they had gathered together was shaken, and they were all filled with the Holy Spirit and began to speak the word of God with boldness (Acts 4:24-31).

Note: *Dunamis* is not specifically mentioned here.

The phrase "miraculous powers" is *dunamis* repeated twice in succession:

*This is John the Baptist; he has risen from the dead, and that is why **miraculous** [dunamis] **powers** [dunamis] are at work in him* (Matt. 14:2).

*He came to His hometown and began teaching them in their synagogue, so that they were astonished, and said, "Where did this man get this wisdom and these **miraculous** [dunamis] **powers** [dunamis]?"* (Matt. 13:54)

His hometown's lack of faith meant Jesus could do no power miracles, but only *therapeuo* miracles:

Therapeuo is the word we get *therapeutic* from, indicating perhaps healings that did not require works of power but herbs, anointing with oil, or other more natural healing approaches:

*And He could do no **miracle** [dunamis] there except that He laid His hands on a few sick people and **healed** [therapeuo] them. And*

He wondered at their unbelief. And He was going around the villages teaching (Mk. 6:5-6).

Dunamis power was released through touch, faith, the forgiveness of sins, unity, and spoken command that is acted on, and the results were *iaomai* healing.

An *iaomai* healing references power (*dunamis*) being involved, flowing from Jesus to the woman who reached out and touched Him in faith:

> *Immediately the flow of her blood was dried up; and she felt in her body that she was **healed** [iaomai] of her affliction. Immediately Jesus, perceiving in Himself that the **power** [dunamis] proceeding from Him had gone forth, turned around in the crowd and said, "Who touched My garments?"* (Mk. 5:29-30)

Healing is part of salvation (*sozo*), and *hugies* is often translated as "made well."

> *And He said to her, "Daughter, **your faith** has made you **well** [sozo]; go in peace and be **healed** [hugies] of your affliction"* (Mk. 5:34).

Note: *Dunamis* is not specifically mentioned in this verse. Power was present:

> *The **power** [dunamis] of the Lord was present for Him to perform healing [iaomai]* (Lk. 5:17).

Power was present, and touch transferred it:

> *And all the people were trying to touch Him, for **power** [dunamis] was coming from Him and **healing** [iaomai] them all* (Lk. 6:19).

It is possible to perceive when *dunamis* leaves your body:

> *Immediately Jesus, perceiving in Himself that the* **power** [*duna-mis*] *proceeding from Him had gone forth, turned around in the crowd and said, "Who touched My garments?"* (Mk. 5:30)

The focus of eyes as a precursor to a miracle:

Eye contact, grabbing, and lifting:

> *But Peter, along with John, fixed his gaze on him and said, "Look at us!" Peter said, "In the name of Jesus Christ the Nazarene— walk!" And seizing him by the right hand, he raised him up; and immediately his feet and his ankles were strengthened* (Acts 3:4-7).

Note: Acts 4:7 references this miracle with the word *power* (*dunamis*).

Casting out demons requires either *exousia* or *dunamis* (I suspect it is *exousia*):

Jesus manifested *exousia* and *dunamis*:

> *And amazement came upon them all, and they began talking with one another saying, "What is this message? For with* **author-ity** [*exousia*] *and* **power** [*dunamis*] *He commands the unclean spirits and they come out"* (Lk. 4:36).

We are given *exousia* and *dunamis*:

> *And He called the twelve together, and gave them* **power** [*duna-mis*] *and* **authority** [*exousia*] *over all the demons and to heal diseases* (Lk. 9:1).

Demons come out through *exousia* and *dunamis*:

*And amazement came upon them all, and they began talking with one another saying, "What is this message? For with **authority** [exousia] and **power** [dunamis] He commands the unclean spirits and they come out"* (Lk. 4:36).

The role of power/*dunamis* in salvation and preaching the gospel:

When we preach the gospel, it is done in the *dunamis* of the Holy Spirit.

> *For our gospel did not come to you in word only, but also in **power** [dunamis] and in the Holy Spirit and with full conviction; just as you know what kind of men we proved to be among you for your sake* (1 Thess. 1:5).

We have received the divine nature which contains divine power.

> *Seeing that His divine **power** [dunamis] has granted to us everything pertaining to life and godliness, through the true knowledge of Him who called us by His own glory and excellence. For by these He has granted to us His precious and magnificent promises, so that by them you may become partakers of the divine nature, having escaped the corruption that is in the world by lust* (2 Pet. 1:3-4).

Salvation is an empowering and transforming experience:

> *For I am not ashamed of the gospel, for it is the **power** [dunamis] of God for salvation to everyone who believes, to the Jew first and also to the Greek* (Rom. 1:16).

Our union with God's Spirit and our spirit is an empowering, transforming experience (1 Cor. 6:17):

> *But we have this treasure in earthen vessels, so that the surpassing greatness of the **power** [dunamis] will be of God and not from ourselves* (2 Cor. 4:7).

The message of the cross is *dunamis* to us:

> *To preach the message of the cross seems like sheer nonsense to those who are on their way to destruction, but to us who are on our way to salvation, it is the mighty **power** [dunamis] of God released within us* (1 Cor. 1:18 TPT).

Overcoming thankfulness for the greatness of what He has provided us:

> *I pray that the God of our Lord Jesus Christ, the Father of glory, may give to you a spirit of wisdom and of revelation in the knowledge of Him. I pray that the eyes of your heart may be enlightened, so that you will know what is the hope of His calling, what are the riches of the glory of His inheritance in the saints, and what is the surpassing greatness of His **power** [dunamis] toward us who believe. These are in accordance with the working of the strength of His might which He brought about in Christ, when He raised Him from the dead and seated Him at His right hand in the heavenly places, far above all rule and authority and **power** [dunamis] and dominion, and every name that is named, not only in this age but also in the one to come. And He put all things in subjection under His feet, and gave Him as head over all things to the church, which is His body, the fullness of Him who fills all in all* (Eph. 1:17-23).

Preaching *must* be demonstrated with power:

> *My message and my preaching were not in persuasive words of wisdom, but in demonstration of the Spirit and of **power** [dunamis], so that your faith would not rest on the wisdom of men, but on the **power** [dunamis] of God* (1 Cor. 2:4-5).

The fabric of the Kingdom is power experiences, rather than words:

*For the kingdom of God does **not consist in words** but in **power**
[<u>dunamis</u>]* (1 Cor. 4:20).

Ultimately all powers will be abolished by the power of the Spirit:

*Then comes the end, when He hands over the kingdom to the God
and Father, when He has abolished all rule and all authority and
power [<u>dunamis</u>]* (1 Cor. 15:24).

The Kingdom of God, God's world, and *dunamis*:

God's Kingdom includes God's power and glory.

*And do not lead us into temptation, but deliver us from evil. (For
Yours is the kingdom and the **power** [<u>dunamis</u>] and the glory forever. Amen)* (Matt. 6:13).

God is referred to as *dunamis*.

*Jesus said to him, "You have said it yourself; nevertheless I tell you,
hereafter you will see the Son of Man sitting at the right hand of
Power [<u>dunamis</u>], and coming on the clouds of heaven"* (Matt.
26:64).

Reflection: Well, we know God is *light* (1 Jn. 1:5), and *love* (1 Jn.
4:16), and *Spirit* (Jn. 4:24); and according to Matthew 26:64, God is
also *power* (*dunamis*).

Every atom is infused and upheld by God, so in this, everything is connected in God:

*In these last days has spoken to us in His Son, whom He appointed
heir of all things, through whom also He made the world. And
He is the radiance of His glory and the exact representation of His*

*nature, and upholds all things by the word of His **power** [duna-mis]. When He had made purification of sins, He sat down at the right hand of the Majesty on high* (Heb. 1:2-3).

The power of God is revealed in the physical world He has created:

*For since the creation of the world His invisible attributes, His eternal **power** [dunamis] and divine nature, have been clearly seen, being understood through what has been made, so that they are without excuse* (Rom. 1:20).

Angels, authorities, and powers are *now* subjected to Jesus:

*Who is at the right hand of God, having gone into heaven, after angels and **authorities** [exousia] and **powers** [dunamis] had been subjected to Him* (1 Pet. 3:22).

Some would be alive when the Kingdom came with power:

*And Jesus was saying to them, "Truly I say to you, there are some of those who are standing here who will not taste death until they see the kingdom of God after it has come with **power** [dunamis]"* (Mk. 9:1).

The Kingdom promised came in power in Acts 1:8:

*You will receive **power** [dunamis] when the Holy Spirit has come upon you; and you shall be My witnesses both in Jerusalem, and in all Judea and Samaria, and even to the remotest part of the earth* (Acts 1:8).

The Holy Spirit came in power in Acts 2:1-4.
Jesus returns with great *dunamis*:

> *And the stars will be falling from heaven, and the* **powers** [*duna-mis*] *that are in the heavens will be shaken. Then they will see the Son of Man coming in clouds with great* **power** [*dunamis*] *and glory* (Mk. 13:25-26).

Angels also have *dunamis*:

> *And to give relief to you who are afflicted and to us as well when the Lord Jesus will be revealed from heaven with His* **mighty** [*dunamis*] *angels in flaming fire* (2 Thess. 1:7).

The Kingdom lifestyle, including Kingdom emotions, is empowered by *dunamis*.

Kingdom emotions are empowered by the Spirit:

> *Now may the* **God of hope fill you with all joy and peace in believing**, *so that you will* **abound in hope** *by the* **power** [*duna-mis*] *of the Holy Spirit* (Rom. 15:13).

Dunamis works in our inner man creating faith, love, and revelation:

> *I pray that He would grant you, according to the riches of His glory, to be strengthened with* **power** [*dunamis*] *through His Spirit in the inner man, so that Christ may dwell in your hearts through faith; and that you, being rooted and grounded in love, may be able to comprehend with all the saints what is the breadth and length and height and depth, and to know the love of Christ which surpasses knowledge, that you may be filled up to all the fullness of God* (Eph. 3:16-19).

My laboring now involves laboring with His power/*dunamis* within:

*For this purpose also I labor, striving according to His **power** [<u>dunamis</u>], which mightily works within me* (Col. 1:29).

The equipping and anointing to fulfill our destiny and call are provided through *dunamis*:

*I was made a minister, according to the gift of God's grace which was given to me according to the working of His **power** [<u>dunamis</u>]* (Eph. 3:7).

Glorifying the One who empowers us beyond our wildest imagination:

*Now to Him who is able to do far more abundantly beyond all that we ask or think, according to the **power** [<u>dunamis</u>] that works within us, to Him be the glory in the church and in Christ Jesus to all generations forever and ever. Amen* (Eph. 3:20-21).

The goal is to die to self and be resurrected by the power of the Spirit into a new lifestyle of intimate knowing of Christ (i.e., hearing, seeing, feeling Jesus through the Spirit):

*That I may **know** [<u>ginosko</u>] Him and the **power** [<u>dunamis</u>] of His resurrection and the fellowship of His sufferings, being conformed to His death; in order that I may attain to the resurrection from the dead* (Phil. 3:10-11).

We are protected by the *dunamis* of God when we apply faith:

*Who are protected by the **power** [<u>dunamis</u>] of God through faith for a salvation ready to be revealed in the last time* (1 Pet. 1:5).

My new life in Christ is now strengthened by *dunamis*:

*Strengthened with all **power** [dunamis], according to His glorious might, for the attaining of all steadfastness and patience; joyously* (Col. 1:11).

Each of us is empowered with a unique *dunamis* from God:

*To one he gave five talents, to another, two, and to another, one, each according to his own **ability** [dunamis]; and he went on his journey* (Matt. 25:15).

Perhaps we could say, each of us are called and anointed from birth by God with the power to fulfill the destiny God has called us to. Stephen was specially anointed with power:

*And Stephen, full of grace and **power** [dunamis], was performing great wonders and signs among the people* (Acts 6:8).

We pray for God to fulfill every good work of faith with *dunamis*:

*To this end also we pray for you always, that our God will count you worthy of your calling, and fulfill every desire for goodness and the work of faith with **power** [dunamis]* (2 Thess. 1:11).

The voice of false guilt, false shame, inferiority, insecurity, and accusation is demonic and is cast down by the *dunamis* of God, because we speak with our mouths what the blood of Jesus has accomplished for us:

*Then I heard a loud voice in heaven, saying, "Now the salvation, and the **power** [dunamis], and the kingdom of our God and the authority of His Christ have come, for the accuser of our brethren has been thrown down, he who accuses them before our God day and night. And they overcame him because of the blood of the Lamb and because of the word of their testimony, and they did not love their life even when faced with death"* (Rev. 12:10-11).

Impregnated by *dunamis*:

Mary was impregnated by the *dunamis* of God.

> *The angel answered and said to her, "The Holy Spirit will come upon you, and the **power** [*dunamis*] of the Most High will over-shadow you; and for that reason the holy Child shall be called the Son of God"* (Lk. 1:35).

Sarah's conception was by the *dunamis* of God.

> *By faith even Sarah herself received **ability** [*dunamis*] to conceive, even beyond the proper time of life, since she considered Him faithful who had promised* (Heb. 11:11).

Personal Application

Review these verses on *dunamis* and jot down the insights God is showing you, and then journal asking God, "What do You want to speak to me from these verses?"

Summary of Power

1. *Dunamis* miracles are power encounters, facilitated by faith riding on the carrier wave of love.
2. Satan has *dunamis* and will seek to deceive people through signs and wonders.
3. Avoid people who claim to be believers but minimize the power of God.
4. The power to do miracles does not come from man, but from God.
5. Wait until you are clothed with the power of God. The disciples waited in one accord, praying, waiting until the manifest presence of the Spirit came *upon* them (Acts 2:1-4).

6. Jesus' keys to receiving God's power included being *full* of the Spirit (Lk. 4:1). Jesus was led by the Spirit into the wilderness to fast for 40 days. There He overcame the big temptations—food and fame. He returned in the *power* of the Spirit (Lk. 4:14) and began doing miracles.

7. An *iaomai* healing involved *dunamis* flowing from the healer into the client.

8. You can perceive the flow of this power if you are sensitive and tuned to it.

9. *Dunamis* healings can be precipitated by a touch of faith and eye contact.

10. Casting out unclean spirits utilizes commands.

11. At salvation, through the union of our spirits with the Holy Spirit, we receive *dunamis*.

12. We need revelation knowledge to *see* that we have this indwelling power that enlightens our spirits, souls, and bodies and brings healing to all.

Supplement D

Iaomai and *Iama* Are Words
for Power Healing

The *dunamis* of God can produce instantaneous miracles (Acts 3:4-8). *Iaomai* is a Greek word that indicates on numerous occasions the miracle was instantaneous. Often these miracles occur by simply a spoken word by Jesus, and this can be done from a distance. There is a lot to discover in these 32 uses of *iaomai* and *iama*.

Definition of *Iaomai*

The Kittle Theological Dictionary of the New Testament defines *iaomai*: "to heal, healing, a cure." A working definition of *iaomai*: the power of God that releases healing. It is often coupled with casting out demons.

Strong's Exhaustive Concordance Numbers for the Greek Words Researched

- G2390 ἰάομαι *iaomai (ee-ah'-om-ahee)*: total KJV occurrences: 29 in 26 verses
- G2386 ἴαμα *iama (ee'-am-ah)*: total KJV occurrences: 3 (1 Cor. 12:9, 28, 30)

The above two words have been identified as *iaomai* in the verses below.

All verses with *iaomai* or *iama* from the NASB:

1. Great faith—instant healing:

*But the centurion said, "Lord, I am not worthy for You to come under my roof, but just say the word, and my servant will be healed. For I also am a man under authority, with soldiers under me; and I say to this one, 'Go!' and he goes, and to another, 'Come!' and he comes, and to my slave, 'Do this!' and he does it." Now when Jesus heard this, He marveled and said to those who were following, "Truly I say to you, I have not found such **great faith** with anyone in Israel...." And Jesus said to the centurion, "Go; **it shall be done for you as you have believed.**" And the servant was **healed** [iaomai] **that very moment** (Matt. 8:8-13; see also Lk. 7:7-10).*

2. Jesus withholds revelation from those with dull hearts so they do not get healed:

*For the heart of this people has become dull, with their ears they scarcely hear, and they have closed their eyes, otherwise they would see with their eyes, hear with their ears, and understand with their heart and return, and I would **heal** [iaomai] them (Matt. 13:15).*

3. The passionate and persistent demonstrate great faith and receive instant healing:

*Then Jesus said to her, "O woman, your faith is great; it shall be done for you as you wish." And her daughter was **healed** [iaomai] at once (Matt. 15:28).*

4. Touched garments in faith, a flow of power, immediate healing:

*For she thought, "If I just touch His garments, I will get well." Immediately the flow of her blood was dried up; and she felt in her body that she was **healed** [iaomai] of her affliction. Immediately Jesus, perceiving in Himself that the power [dunamis] **proceeding*** *from Him had gone forth, turned around in the crowd and said, "Who touched My garments?" And His disciples said to Him, "You see the crowd pressing in on You, and You say, 'Who touched Me?'" And He looked around to see the woman who had done this. But the woman fearing and trembling, aware of what had happened to her, came and fell down before Him and told Him the whole truth. And He said to her, "Daughter, your faith has made you well; go in peace and be **healed** [hugiēs, G5199, "made sound"] of your affliction"* (Mk. 5:28-34; Lk. 8:47).

5. Heart healing:

*The Spirit of the Lord is upon me, because he hath anointed me to preach the gospel to the poor; he hath sent me to **heal** [iaomai] the brokenhearted, to preach deliverance to the captives, and recovering of sight to the blind, to set at liberty them that are bruised* (Lk. 4:18 KJV).

6. Power of the Lord present to perform healing:

*One day He was teaching; and there were some Pharisees and teachers of the law sitting there, who had come from every village of Galilee and Judea and from Jerusalem; and the **power** [dunamis] of the Lord was present for Him to perform **healing** [iaomai]* (Lk. 5:17).

7. Healed by *iaomai* and delivered by *therapeuo*:

*A great throng of people...who had come to hear Him and to be **healed** [iaomai] of their diseases; and those who were troubled with unclean spirits were being **cured** [therapeuo]* (Lk. 6:17-18).

8. Healing power flows through touch:

*And all the people were trying to touch Him, for power was coming from Him and **healing** [iaomai] them all* (Lk. 6:19).

9. Proclaiming the Kingdom of God is coupled with full equipping of every form of power and authority to heal and deliver:

*And He called the twelve together, and gave them **power** [duna-mis] and **authority** [exousia] over all the demons and to **heal** [therapeuo] diseases. And He sent them out to proclaim the kingdom of God and to perform **healing** [iaomai] (Lk. 9:1-2).*

10. Jesus used various methods to heal:

*He began speaking to them about the kingdom of God and **curing** [iaomai] those who had need of **healing** [therapeia] (Lk. 9:11).*

The American Standard Version reverses the words in the translation, which appears to me to be a more correct translation: "and them that had need of healing (*iaomai*) he cured (*therapeia*)."

11. It appears that deliverance occurred first and healing second, with both occurring fairly quickly:

*While he was still approaching, the demon slammed him to the ground and threw him into a convulsion. But Jesus rebuked the unclean spirit, and **healed** [iaomai] the boy and gave him back to his father (Lk. 9:42).*

12. Healing occurred as they obeyed and walked—a *process* healing:

*Now one of them, when he saw that he had been **healed** [iaomai], turned back, glorifying God with a loud voice (Lk. 17:15).*

13. Healed instantly by touch and creative healing:

*But Jesus answered and said, "Stop! No more of this." And He touched his ear and **healed** [iaomai] him (Lk. 22:51).*

14. Healing began through a spoken word:

> *When he heard that Jesus had come out of Judea into Galilee, he went to Him and was imploring Him to come down and **heal** [iaomai] his son; for he was at the point of death. So Jesus said to him, "Unless you people see signs and wonders, you simply will not believe." The royal official said to Him, "Sir, come down before my child dies." Jesus said to him, "Go; your son lives." The man **believed the word that Jesus spoke** to him and started off. As he was now going down, his slaves met him, saying that his son was living. So he inquired of them the hour when he **began** to get better. Then they said to him, "Yesterday at the seventh hour the fever left him." **So the father knew that it was at that hour in which Jesus said to him, "Your son lives";** and he himself believed and his whole household. This is again a second sign that Jesus performed when He had come out of Judea into Galilee* (Jn. 4:47-54).

15. Begin by asking what the person wants; healing through a simple command of action which is obeyed; being warned not to sin so that something worse would not happen to him; and three different words for healing are used to describe this healing.

> *When Jesus saw him lying there and knew that he had already been a long time in that condition, He said to him, **"Do you wish to get well?"** The sick man answered Him, "Sir, I have no man to put me into the pool when the water is stirred up, but while I am coming, another steps down before me." Jesus said to him, **"Get up, pick up your pallet and walk."** Immediately the man became **well** [hugiēs], and picked up his pallet and began to walk. Now it was the Sabbath on that day. So the Jews were saying to the man who was **cured** [therapeuo], "It is the Sabbath, and it is not permissible for you to carry your pallet." But he answered them, "He who made me **well** [hugiēs] was the one who said to me, 'Pick*

213

*up your pallet and walk.'" They asked him, "Who is the man who said to you, 'Pick up your pallet and walk?'" But the man who was **healed** [iaomai] did not know who it was, for Jesus had slipped away while there was a crowd in that place. Afterward Jesus found him in the temple and said to him, "Behold, you have become **well** [hugiēs]; **do not sin anymore**, so that nothing worse happens to you"* (Jn. 5:6-14).

16. God blinds the eyes and hardens the hearts of those who love the approval of men rather than the approval of God, and God will not heal them:

*"He has blinded their eyes and he hardened their heart, so that they would not see with their eyes and perceive with their heart, and be converted and I **heal** [iaomai] them." These things Isaiah said because he saw His glory, and he spoke of Him. Nevertheless many even of the rulers believed in Him, but because of the Pharisees they were not confessing Him, for fear that they would be put out of the synagogue; **for they loved the approval of men rather than the approval of God**￼* (Jn. 12:40-43).

17. Healing was spoken and a command to act which was obeyed:

*Peter said to him, "Aeneas, Jesus Christ **heals** [iaomai] you; get up and make your bed." Immediately he got up* (Acts 9:34).

18. Anointing with the Holy Spirit and power prepare one to heal all oppressed by the devil.

*You know of Jesus of Nazareth, how God anointed Him with the Holy Spirit and with **power** [dunamis], and how He went about doing good and **healing** [iaomai] all who were oppressed by the devil, for God was with Him* (Acts 10:38).

19. Prayer, laying on of hands:

*And it happened that the father of Publius was lying in bed afflicted with recurrent fever and dysentery; and Paul went in to see him and after he had prayed, he laid his hands on him and **healed** [iaomai] him (Acts 28:8).*

20. There are gifts (plural) of healing:

*And to another gifts of **healing** [iaomai] by the one Spirit (1 Cor. 12:9).*

21. Miracles are separated from gifts of healings (all plural):

*And God has appointed in the church, first apostles, second prophets, third teachers, then **miracles** [dunamis], then gifts of **healing** [iaomai] (1 Cor. 12:28).*

22. Gifts and healings are *both* plural:

*All do not have gifts of **healings** [iaomai], do they? (1 Cor. 12:30)*

23. Live righteously so you do not get infirmity:

*And make straight paths for your feet, so that the limb which is lame may not be put out of joint, but rather be **healed** [iaomai] (Heb. 12:13).*

24. Removing sin removes roadblocks to healing; corporate prayer may accomplish more than praying on your own:

*Therefore, confess your sins to one another, and pray for one another so that you may be **healed** [iaomai]. The effective prayer of a righteous man can accomplish much (Jas. 5:16).*

25. Christ has already purchased our healing:

*And He Himself bore our sins in His body on the cross, so that we might die to sin and live to righteousness; for by His wounds you were **healed** [iaomai] (1 Pet. 2:24).*

Personal Application

Review these verses above and jot down the insights God is showing you, and then journal asking God, "What do You want to speak to me from these verses?"

Reflective Thoughts About *Iaomai* Healing

Things healed through *iaomai* (NASB):

1. All who are *oppressed* by the devil (Acts 10:38—perhaps oppressed is different than casting out?)
2. Diseases (Lk. 6:18)
3. Brokenhearted (Lk. 4:18 KJV)
4. Creative miracle (Lk. 22:51)

What is the *speed* of *iaomai* healings (NASB)?

1. The Greek word is *hora* in the following verses: Matt. 8:8-13; 15:28. *Hora* definition from *Thayer's Greek Dictionary* is "day, hour, instant, season."
2. The following verses use Greek works meaning "straightway": Mk. 5:28-34; Lk. 8:47; 22:51; Jn. 5:6-14; Acts 9:34.
3. Three healings occur quickly after *acting* on a command (Jn. 5:6-14; Acts 9:34; Lk. 17:15).
4. When deliverance was involved, healing appeared to be more *immediate.*
5. *Most healings do not specify any timetable* concerning how long the healing takes to fully manifest.

***Dunamis* power is indicated to be energizing *iaomai* healings.**

1. Anointed with power (*dunamis*, Acts 10:38)
2. Power was present (*dunamis*, Lk. 5:17)
3. Power flowed (*dunamis*, Mk. 5:28-34; Lk. 8:47; Lk. 6:19)

Things that hinder *iaomai* healings:

Dull hearts, as Jesus withholds revelation and healing (Matt. 13:15; Jn. 12:40-43)

Things that precipitate *iaomai* healings:

1. Faith (Matt. 8:13; Lk. 7:7; Mk. 5:28-34; Lk. 8:47; 1 Pet. 2:24): Faith can be demonstrated by passionate persistence (Matt. 15:28). Since faith works by love (Gal. 5:6), you need love also; so ask for God's love for the person.
2. Reaching out and touching in faith (Mk. 5:28-34; Lk. 8:47; Lk. 6:19; 22:51).
3. Prayer and laying on of hands (Acts 28:8).
4. Righteous living and repenting of sins (Heb. 12:13; Jas. 5:16).

Healing combos:

- Jesus uses curing (*iaomai*) and healing (*therapeia*) (Lk. 9:11).
- Jesus uses deliverance followed by *iaomai* healing (Lk. 9:42).

Christians have received a *total* healing package which includes these various ways to heal—*dunamis, exousia, therapeuo, iaomai*.

> *And He called the twelve together, and gave them **power** [duna-mis] and **authority** [exousia] over all the demons and to **heal** [therapeuo] diseases. And He sent them out to proclaim the **king-dom of God** and to perform **healing** [iaomai] (Lk. 9:1-2).*

Supplement E

Therapeuo Healing Is More Often *Process* Healing

Definitions

- *Therapeuo* defined by *Thayer's Greek-English Lexicon of the New Testament*: G2323 *therapeuo* 1) to serve, do service 2) to heal, cure, restore to health.
- Therapeuo defined by *Kittle Theological Dictionary of the New Testament*:
  - o G2323, *therapeuo*: to wait upon menially, to relieve (of disease)— total KJV occurrences: 44 (38 times "heal")
  - o G2322, *therapeia*: attendance (especially medical, i.e., cure)— total KJV occurrences: 4

We get the word "therapeutic" from *therapeuo*.[1] Merriam-Webster defines "therapeutic" as "the treatment of disease or disorders by remedial agents or methods.[2] Drawing these definitions together, we can say that a working definition of *therapeuo* could be "caring for the sick and attending to their needs by providing various healing modalities that restore them to health."

The above Greek words are noted below with (*therapueo*) inserted.

A Complete Listing of Verses with *Therapeuo* or *Therapeia* from the NASB95

1. Jesus used *therapeuo* to heal every kind of disease and cast out demons:

*Jesus was going throughout all Galilee, teaching in their synagogues and proclaiming the gospel of the kingdom, and **healing** [therapeuo] every kind of disease and every kind of sickness among the people* (Matt. 4:23).

*The news about Him spread throughout all Syria; and they brought to Him all who were ill, those suffering with various diseases and pains, demoniacs, epileptics, paralytics; and He **healed** [therapeuo] them* (Matt. 4:24).

*When evening came, they brought to Him many who were demon-possessed; and He cast out the spirits with a word, and **healed** [therapeuo] all who were ill* (Matt. 8:16).

*Jesus said to him, "I will come and **heal** [therapeuo] him"* (Matt. 8:7).

*Jesus was going through all the cities and villages, teaching in their synagogues and proclaiming the gospel of the kingdom, and **healing** [therapeuo] every kind of disease and every kind of sickness* (Matt. 9:35).

*But Jesus, aware of this, withdrew from there. Many followed Him, and He **healed** [therapeuo] them all* (Matt. 12:15).

*When He went ashore, He saw a large crowd, and felt compassion for them and **healed** [therapeuo] their sick* (Matt. 14:14).

And large crowds came to Him, bringing with them those who were lame, crippled, blind, mute, and many others, and they laid them down at His feet; and He **healed** [*therapeuo*] *them* (Matt. 15:30).

And large crowds followed Him, and He **healed** [*therapeuo*] *them there* (Matt. 19:2).

And the blind and the lame came to Him in the temple, and He **healed** [*therapeuo*] *them* (Matt. 21:14).

And He **healed** [*therapeuo*] *many who were ill with various diseases, and cast out many demons; and He was not permitting the demons to speak, because they knew who He was* (Mk. 1:34).

But the news about Him was spreading even farther, and large crowds were gathering to hear Him and to be **healed** [*therapeuo*] *of their sicknesses* (Lk. 5:15).

2. Disciples are given authority (*exousia*) to cast out demons and *therapeuo* every kind of disease and sickness:

Jesus summoned His twelve disciples and gave them **authority** [*exousia*] *over unclean spirits, to cast them out, and to* **heal** [*therapeuo*] *every kind of disease and every kind of sickness* (Matt. 10:1).

Heal [*therapeuo*] *the sick, raise the dead, cleanse the lepers, cast out demons. Freely you received, freely give* (Matt. 10:8).

Departing, they began going throughout the villages, preaching the gospel and **healing** [*therapeuo*] *everywhere* (Lk. 9:6).

3. Legalists oppose the working with power to heal:

*And a man was there whose hand was withered. And they questioned Jesus, asking, "Is it lawful to **heal** [therapeuo] on the Sabbath?" so that they might accuse Him* (Matt. 12:10).

*They were watching Him to see if He would **heal** [therapeuo] him on the Sabbath, so that they might accuse Him* (Mk. 3:2).

*And He said to them, "No doubt you will quote this proverb to Me, 'Physician, **heal** [therapeuo] yourself! Whatever we heard was done at Capernaum, do here in your hometown as well'"* (Lk. 4:23).

*The scribes and the Pharisees were watching Him closely to see if He **healed** [therapeuo] on the Sabbath, so that they might find reason to accuse Him* (Lk. 6:7).

*But the synagogue official, indignant because Jesus had **healed** [therapeuo] on the Sabbath, began saying to the crowd in response, "There are six days in which work should be done; so come during them and get **healed** [therapeuo], and not on the Sabbath day"* (Lk. 13:14).

*And Jesus answered and spoke to the lawyers and Pharisees, saying, "Is it lawful to **heal** [therapeuo] on the Sabbath, or not?"* (Lk. 14:3)

4. Deliverance fell under *therapeuo*, and faith and fasting are required to be fully effective:

*Then a demon-possessed man who was blind and mute was brought to Jesus, and He **healed** [therapeuo] him, so that the mute man spoke and saw* (Matt. 12:22).

"Lord, have mercy on my son, for he is a lunatic and is very ill; for he often falls into the fire and often into the water. I brought him to Your disciples, and they could not **cure** *[therapeuo] him."* *And Jesus answered and said, "You unbelieving and perverted generation, how long shall I be with you? How long shall I put up with you? Bring him here to Me." And Jesus rebuked him, and the demon came out of him, and the boy was* **cured** *[therapeuo] at once. Then the disciples came to Jesus privately and said, "Why could we not drive it out?" And He said to them, "Because of the littleness of your faith; for truly I say to you, if you have faith the size of a mustard seed, you will say to this mountain, Move from here to there, and it will move; and nothing will be impossible to you. [But this kind does not go out except by prayer and fasting]"* (Matt. 17:15-21).

Who had come to hear Him and to be **healed** *[iaomai] of their diseases; and those who were troubled with unclean spirits were being* **cured** *[therapeuo]* (Lk. 6:18).

At that very time He **cured** *[therapeuo] many people of diseases and afflictions and evil spirits; and He gave sight to many who were blind* (Lk. 7:21).

And also some women who had been **healed** *[therapeuo] of evil spirits and sicknesses: Mary who was called Magdalene, from whom seven demons had gone out* (Lk. 8:2).

For in the case of many who had unclean spirits, they were coming out of them shouting with a loud voice; and many who had been paralyzed and lame were **healed** *[therapeuo]* (Acts 8:7).

Deliverance and anointing with oil were intertwined with *therapeuo* healing:

*And they were casting out many demons and were anointing with oil many sick people and **healing** [therapeuo] them* (Mk. 6:13).

5. *Therapeuo* is serving others well:

*Who then is the faithful and sensible slave whom his master put in charge of his **household** [therapeuo] to give them their food at the proper time?* (Matt. 24:45)

*And the Lord said, "Who then is the faithful and sensible steward, whom his master will put in charge of his **servants** [therapeuo], to give them their rations at the proper time?"* (Lk. 12:42)

*Nor is He **served** [therapeuo] by human hands, as though He needed anything, since He Himself gives to all people life and breath and all things* (Acts. 17:25).

*And it happened that the father of Publius was lying in bed afflicted with recurrent fever and dysentery; and Paul went in to see him and after he had prayed, he laid his hands on him and **healed** [iaomai] him. After this had happened, the rest of the people on the island who had diseases were coming to him and getting **cured** [therapeuo]* (Act 28:8-9).

*I saw one of his heads as if it had been slain, and his fatal wound was **healed** [therapeuo]. And the whole earth was amazed and followed after the beast* (Rev. 13:3).

*He exercises all the authority of the first beast in his presence. And he makes the earth and those who dwell in it to worship the first beast, whose fatal wound was **healed** [therapeuo]* (Rev. 13:12).

6. Touch is a part of *therapeuo*:

*For He had **healed** [therapeuo] many, with the result that all those who had afflictions pressed around Him in order to touch Him (Mk. 3:10).*

Jesus laid hands on each of them in *therapeuo* healing:

*While the sun was setting, all those who had any who were sick with various diseases brought them to Him; and laying His hands on each one of them, He was **healing** [therapeuo] them (Lk. 4:40).*

Therapeuo healing was instant, by a command to look at them, and then to participate in the commanded healing action in which touch was involved:

But Peter, along with John, fixed his gaze on him and said, "Look at us!" And he began to give them his attention, expecting to receive something from them. But Peter said, "I do not possess silver and gold, but what I do have I give to you: In the name of Jesus Christ the Nazarene—walk!" And seizing him by the right hand, he raised him up; and immediately his feet and his ankles were strengthened. With a leap he stood upright and began to walk; and he entered the temple with them, walking and leaping and praising God (Acts 3:4-8).

*And seeing the man who had been **healed** [therapeuo] standing with them, they had nothing to say in reply (Acts 4:14).*

Even though various therapies (*therapeuo*) by others did not heal her, the woman was instantly healed (*iaomai*) by touching Jesus' cloak in faith and experiencing a flow of power:

*And a woman who had a hemorrhage for twelve years, and could not be **healed** [therapeuo] by anyone, came up behind Him and*

*touched the fringe of His cloak, and **immediately** her hemorrhage stopped. And Jesus said, "Who is the one who touched Me?"
And while they were all denying it, Peter said, "Master, the people
are crowding and pressing in on You." But Jesus said, "Someone did
touch Me, for I was aware **that power had gone out of Me.**" When
the woman saw that she had not escaped notice, she came trembling
and fell down before Him, and declared in the presence of all the
people the reason why she had **touched Him**, and how she had been
immediately healed [iaomai]. And He said to her, "Daughter,
your faith has made you well; go in peace"* (Lk. 8:43-48).

7. Power to heal was restricted by lack of faith but could still heal some with *therapeuo*:

*And He could do no miracle there except that He laid His hands
on a few sick people and **healed** [therapeuo] them* (Mk. 6:5).

8. The total package: we are equipped with *dunamis* and *exousia* to heal through *therapeuo*:

*And He called the twelve together, and gave them **power** [duna-
mis] and **authority** [exousia] over all the demons and to **heal**
[therapeuo] diseases* (Lk. 9:1).

9. *Iaomai* and *therapeuo* worked together for Jesus:

*But when the multitudes knew it, they followed Him; and He
received them and spoke to them about the kingdom of God, and
healed [iaomai] those who had need of **healing** [therapeuo]*
(Lk. 9:11).

10. Healing is part of the Kingdom being manifested:

*And **heal** [therapeuo] those in it who are sick, and say to them,
"The kingdom of God has **come near to you**"* (Lk. 10:9).

11. Many things to learn: Begin by asking what the person wants; healing through a simple command of action which was obeyed; warned not to sin so that something worse would not happen to him; and three different words for healing are used to describe this healing.

*When Jesus saw him lying there, and knew that he had already been a long time in that condition, He said to him, "Do you wish to get **well** [hugiēs]?" The sick man answered Him, "Sir, I have no man to put me into the pool when the water is stirred up, but while I am coming, another steps down before me." Jesus said to him, **"Get up, pick up your pallet and walk."** Immediately the man became **well** [hugiēs], and picked up his pallet and began to walk. Now it was the Sabbath on that day. So the Jews were saying to the man who was **cured** [therapeuo], "It is the Sabbath, and it is not permissible for you to carry your pallet." But he answered them, "He who made me **well** [hugiēs] was the one who said to me, Pick up your pallet and walk." They asked him, "Who is the man who said to you, Pick up your pallet and walk?" But the man who was **healed** [iaomai] did not know who it was, for Jesus had slipped away while there was a crowd in that place. Afterward Jesus found him in the temple and said to him, "Behold, you have become **well** [hugiēs]; **do not sin anymore**, so that nothing worse happens to you" (Jn. 5:6-14).*

12. All healed through *therapeuo*:

*Also the people from the cities in the vicinity of Jerusalem were coming together, bringing people who were sick or afflicted with unclean spirits, and they were all being **healed** [therapeuo] (Acts 5:16).*

13. Leaves from the Tree of Life were part of *therapeuo*:

*On either side of the river was the tree of life, bearing twelve kinds of fruit, yielding its fruit every month; and the leaves of the tree were for the **healing** [therapeuo] of the nations* (Rev. 22:2).

Personal Application

Review these verses on *therapeuo* and jot down the insights God is showing you, and then journal asking God, "What do You want to speak to me from these verses?"

Reflections on *Therapeuo* Healing

1. Jesus used *therapeuo* alone to heal every kind of disease (mentioned 17 times)
   a. Matt. 4:23-24; 8:7,16; 9:35;12:15; 14:14;15:30;19:2; 21:1
   b. Mk. 1:34; 3:10; 6:5
   c. Lk. 5:15; 7:21; 8:2
   d. Acts 5:16

2. The disciples used *therapeuo* (Lk. 9:6).
3. *Iaomai* and *therapeia* are functioning together (Lk. 9:11; Acts 28:8-9).
4. Christians have received a *total* healing package which includes these various ways to heal (*dunamis, exousia, therapeuo, iaomai*) (Lk. 9:1-2; Matt. 10:8; Lk. 9:1).
5. *Therapeuo* healing is the Kingdom coming close (Lk. 10:9).
6. *Therapeuo* is serving well (Lk. 12:42; Acts 17:25).
7. Legalists oppose *therapeuo* healing (Matt. 12:10; Mk. 3:2; Lk. 4:23; 6:7; 13:14; 14:3).
8. Casting out demons is a part of *therapeuo* (Matt. 17:15-21; Acts 8:7; Lk. 6:18; 7:21 8:2; Acts 5:16; 8:7).
9. *Therapeuo* can involve a command of action that produces wellness (Jn. 5:6-14; Acts 4:14).

10. *Therapeuo* can involve seizing the right hand and pulling the lame man up (Acts 4:14).

11. Ask what they want before offering to heal (Jn. 5:6-14).

12. Most of the time there is no indication of how long the healing process took; however, it appears to be immediate when deliverance is involved.

Modalities specifically mentioned in the verses where *therapeuo* is found include:

1. Laying on of hands (Lk. 4:40): Could this include a chiropractor? The word "chiropractor" is a compound word based on "chiro" which means "hand." I recommend you find a quality Christian chiropractor in your area.

2. Anointing with oil (Mk. 6:13): Could this include essential oils? I recommend you explore the book *Essential Oils of the Bible: Connecting God's Word to Natural Healing* by Randi Minetor.

3. Leaves of trees (Rev. 22:2): Could this include herbology? God gave herbs for the service of mankind (Ps. 104:14). For years I have used the book *Prescription for Nutritional Healing* by Phyllis A. Balch CNC. It is currently in its sixth edition and has sold 8 million copies. I even saw it in bookstores in Malaysia when I was ministering there. For each ailment, this book lists causes and solutions, including herbs, nutrition, and more. I have sent remedies from this book to a pastor in Uganda, and in applying them, their baby was able to come home from the hospital. It is a wealth of good information.

4. Casting out demons (Matt. 17:15-21).

A few final thoughts on *therapeuo*:

When you pray for healing and you don't receive the miracle you seek, the Lord may want to heal you through *therapeuo*. This will involve a process that takes time and requires your cooperation and active participation. The first and most important part of this process is hearing from God. You must daily hear His instructions to you so you can daily move along the path to health. Learn to listen for God in spontaneous thoughts, pictures, and emotions. These are words of knowledge that you must respond to with appropriate prayers and actions.

When faced with a persistent health issue, I intensely search out, discover, and remove the root cause(s). I ask the Lord, "When did this infirmity begin? What happened in my life just before this struck?" Expect Him to answer you either directly in your heart or through the input of others.

Seek insight from your spiritual and health advisors. Explore trusted websites such as Life Extension,[3] Dr. Mercola,[4] Dr. Schulze,[5] and GreenMedInfo[6] (type in the name of the infirmity you are seeking solutions for). Also, you can look up a specific infirmity in the index in the books *A More Excellent Way*[7] and *Prescription for Nutritional Healing*.[8]

Finally, remember the importance of forgiving everyone for everything if you want to live in health. Ask the Lord if there is anyone you need to forgive. It could be yourself, or even God. Take any names or faces that flow into your mind, picture them, and state from your heart: "In the name of the Lord Jesus Christ and by His grace, I forgive you, and choose to honor you, to bless you, and to release you." True forgiveness from your heart removes any blockages that are preventing the healing power of the River of Life from flowing into your spirit, soul, and body.

Supplement F

I Release Divine Energy: *Energeo*

There are three Greek words translated as "power" in the New Testament. The summary below deals with *energeo*, which is the active flow of God's healing power out through our hands as we lay them on the sick.

> *Light flashes from his* [and our] ***hand**, there where his **power is hidden*** (Hab. 3:4 GNT).

Chart of *Exousia, Dunamis, Energeo*

The Greek word *energeo* defined by Bible dictionaries:

- *Kittle Theological Dictionary of the New Testament*: active energy, to be at work.
- *Robinson's Word Pictures*: to energize, God is the energizer of the universe.
- *Thayer's Greek-English Lexicon of the New Testament*: to put forth power, to work for one, to aid one, to effect.

A working definition of *energeo*: the power of God is available through the Holy Spirit and experienced as active, flowing energy that accomplishes God's works. We feel *energized* by it. It feels like *active energy*.

All Uses of *Energeo* and Its Various Forms

We know it is the release of God's power that brings healing and deliverance. We want to understand this power as well as we possibly can.

Our passionate question is: "What does the release of God's divine energy (*energeo*) feel like, and what does it accomplish?" We want to gain an understanding of how God uses the word *energeo*. Below are listed every time *energeo*, or the various forms of this word, appears in the Bible.

The Greek words researched:

- G1754 (ἐνεργέω) *energeo*: total KJV occurrences: 25
- G1756 ἐ(νεργής) *energes*: total KJV occurrences: 3
- G1755 (ἐνέργημα) *energema*: total KJV occurrences: 2
- G1753 (ἐνέργεια) *energeia*: total KJV occurrences: 10

I have inserted the word *energizes* into every verse where *energeo* (or its forms) was used, just to see how the verse would read with this key basic definition inserted. You may ponder this as you read and see how you feel the word *energizes* describes the meaning of *energeo* within each of the verses (from NASB95) below.

A summary of *energeo* is available on our website.[1] The summary also contains precise Greek dictionary definitions of *energeo*. *Kittle Theological Dictionary of the New Testament* defines *energeo* as "active energy" which, I agree, is *what it feels like in me* and through me as I lay my hands on people for healing. "Active energy" is my favorite definition.

1. The power of God (*dunamis*) when flowing as active energy (*energeo*) can cast out demons and heal the sick.

> *And they were casting out many demons and were anointing with oil many sick people and healing them. And King Herod heard of it, for His name had become well known; and people were saying, "John the Baptist has risen from the dead, and that is why these miraculous* **powers** [*dunamis*] *are at* **work** [energizing] *in Him"* (Mk. 6:13-14).

> *This is John the Baptist; he has risen from the dead, and that is why miraculous* **powers** [*dunamis*] *are at* **work** [energizing] *in him* (Matt. 14:2).

2. Sinful passions can energize us, producing sinful actions leading us to death. So, if this energy is spirit energy, it can flow from the Holy Spirit or my corrupted spirit or from demon spirits. Perhaps *energes* means "active spirit energy," *regardless* of the source.

> *For while we were in the flesh, the sinful passions, which were aroused by the Law, were at* **work** [energizing] *in the members of our body to bear fruit for death* (Rom. 7:5).

> *In which you formerly walked according to the course of this world, according to the prince of the* **power** [*exousia*] *of the air, of the spirit that is now* **working** [energizes] *in the sons of disobedience* (Eph. 2:2).

3. God's energizing underlies all Christians. Your passions, desires, and giftings come from the Lord. The word "effects" in the above verse is another form of the word *energeo*. So, the Spirit's energizing from within produces different results in each of us.

> *There are varieties of* **effects** [energizes], *but the same God who* **works** [energizes] *all things in all persons* (1 Cor. 12:6).

An interesting side note:

- **Gifts** come from the **Holy Spirit** (1 Cor. 12:4).
- **Ministries** are from the **Lord Jesus** (1 Cor. 12:5).
- **Energizing** comes from the **Father** (1 Cor. 12:6).

God is the author of all energizing, and the Holy Spirit administers various specific gifts to individuals, and Jesus forms these gifts into ministries within the Church and to the world. Neat!

4. The energizing by the Spirit produces miracles. So, as I minister God's grace for miracles, I need to honor the Holy Spirit by inviting Him, His presence, and His power to be manifest and flowing, and then

be sensitive to His flow of energy by noting such things as tingling or warmth in my hands, and pictures of light flowing into a person driving out darkness, etc.

> *To another the **effecting** [energizing] of miracles, and to another prophecy, and to another the distinguishing of spirits, to another various kinds of tongues, and to another the interpretation of tongues* (1 Cor. 12:10).

5. The energy of the Holy Spirit is what distributes the manifestation of the Holy Spirit to each Christian. So, we *each* have divine in-working energizing which we should honor and follow. In doing so, your life is fulfilling and prosperous. Copying someone else's giftings will not produce joy, peace, contentment, or effective ministry. Follow the leadings, giftings, and passions of *your* heart. They are placed there by the Holy Spirit.

> *But one and the same Spirit **works** [energizes] all these things, distributing to each one individually just as He wills* (1 Cor. 12:11).

6. It is the energy of God that makes our ministry and service to others effective. So, ask God to open doors. Know there will be obstacles and opposition, but that is all part of the process. Draw upon the strength of the Lord, not your abilities, as you serve.

> *A wide door for **effective** [energizing] service has opened to me, and there are many adversaries* (1 Cor. 16:9).

7. Our testimony and demonstration of the overcoming power of Christ's life within us during our trying times can inspire others to draw upon God's divine energy within when they face similar trials.

> *If we are afflicted, it is for your comfort and salvation; or if we are comforted, it is for your comfort, which is **effective** [energizing]*

in the patient enduring of the same sufferings which we also suffer
(2 Cor. 1:6).

8. When death is energizing us, we draw upon God's *zoe* life, and our
testimony of His saving grace brings life to the hearer as we share our
testimony. Our lives and our testimonies contain life for others. So, stand
tall and strong in the strength of the Lord, knowing others are being
blessed as they watch you. Know your shared testimony is to glorify God
and thus strengthen others.

> *For we who live are constantly being delivered over to death for
> Jesus' sake, so that the life of Jesus also may be manifested in our
> mortal flesh. So death* **works** [energizes] *in us, but life in you* (2
> Cor. 4:11-12).

9. *Energeo* occurs twice in this verse. Peter was energized by God to
be an apostle to the Jews. Paul was energized by God to be an apostle to
the Gentiles. We each have specific energizing (passions, anointings, and
gifts) by God for specific callings. Honor them. Do not mimic others'
lives.

> *But on the contrary, seeing that I had been entrusted with the gos-
> pel to the uncircumcised, just as Peter had been to the circumcised
> (for He who* **effectually** [energized] *worked for Peter in his apos-
> tleship to the circumcised* **effectually** [energized] *worked for me
> also to the Gentiles)* (Gal. 2:7-8).

10. The energizing release of power for a miracle is not a result of me
doing enough stuff right (keeping enough rules) but a hearing of God's
rhema word, coupled with faith to step forth and see a miracle. Abraham,
the Father of Faith, heard God's *rhema* word and saw God's promise fulfilled in a vision, and it resulted in faith erupting in his heart (Gen. 12:1-
3; 15:5-6).

*So then, does He who provides you with the Spirit and **works** [energizes] miracles among you, do it by the works of the Law, or by hearing with faith?* (Gal. 3:5)

11. Faith is energized by love/compassion, and vice versa; love energizes faith. Jesus, moved by compassion, healed (Matt. 14:14). Faith and love are two of God's abiding realities (1 Cor. 13:13). There probably will not be a healing ministry if compassion is not present.

*For in Christ Jesus neither circumcision nor uncircumcision means anything, but faith **working** [energized] through love* (Gal. 5:6).

12. God's energy causes all things to be worked together for good. That is why we can live in faith, hope, and love (1 Cor. 13:13).

*We have obtained an inheritance, having been predestined according to His purpose who **works** [energizes] all things after the counsel of His will* (Eph. 1:11).

13. God energized Jesus, bringing Him forth from the dead. We, too, can raise the dead as this power (*dunamis*) of God is available to believers and manifests as a release of spiritual energy (*energes*).

*And what is the surpassing greatness of His **power** [<u>dunamis</u>] toward us who believe. These are in accordance with the working of the strength of His might which He **brought about** [energized] in Christ, when He raised Him from the dead and seated Him at His right hand in the heavenly places* (Eph. 1:19-20).

14. God's *dunamis* is released as active energy which creates the gift of grace through which we minister to others. So, note your gifts, callings, and passions and follow them.

*Of which I was made a minister, according to the gift of God's grace which was given to me according to the **working** [energizing] of His **power** [<u>dunamis</u>] (Eph. 3:7).*

15. The power (*dunamis*) of the Holy Spirit is energizing (*energeo*) us from within and allows us to do things beyond our wildest imaginations, such as miracles, healings, and even raising the dead. These things are from God.

*Now to Him who is able to do far more abundantly beyond all that we ask or think, according to the **power** [<u>dunamis</u>] that **works** [energizes] within us (Eph. 3:20).*

16. When we operate in the divine gifts God has placed within each of us, and we serve one another with these gifts, we build up and energize the body of Christ. So, find your place and fill it.

*From whom the whole body, being fitted and held together by what every joint supplies, according to the proper **working** [energizing] of each individual part, causes the growth of the body for the building up of itself in love (Eph. 4:16).*

17. God is energizing us from within to accomplish His good pleasure.

*For it is God who is at **work** [energizes] in you, both to will and to **work** [energizes] for His good pleasure (Phil. 2:13).*

18. God's active energy and power are so great that He can subdue all things to Himself.

*Who will transform the body of our humble state into conformity with the body of His glory, by the **exertion** [energizing] of the **power** [<u>dunamis</u>] that He has even to subject all things to Himself (Phil. 3:21).*

19. This verse contains two forms of *energeo* plus *dunamis*, and it was easiest to see these using the King James Version of the Bible. As I labor, I choose to draw upon the inner energizing of the Holy Spirit, whose power is working within me. So, it is all about calling upon, sensing, and releasing the in-working energy of the Holy Spirit.

> *I also labor, striving according to his **working** [energia, energizing], which **worketh** [energeo, energizes] in me mightily [dunamis]* (Col. 1:29 KJV).

20. Faith in the energizing power of God's Spirit provides the divine energy to raise the dead and provides a quickening in our hearts and lives as we go through water baptism in faith that a transformation is taking place.

> *Having been buried with Him in baptism, in which you were also raised up with Him through faith in the **working** [energizing] of God, who raised Him from the dead* (Col. 2:12).

21. The word of God has God's energy to change us from within if we believe it. Anointed preaching can energize and transform those who believe.

> *For this reason we also constantly thank God that when you received the word of God which you heard from us, you accepted it not as the word of men, but for what it really is, the word of God, which also performs its **work** [energizes] in you who believe* (1 Thess. 2:13).

22. Demons can energize under the limitations of Almighty God; and although they may have times of expanded activity, they will be consumed ultimately by the power of God at the end of the age.

*For the mystery of lawlessness is already at **work** [energize]; only he who now restrains will do so until he is taken out of the way (2 Thess. 2:7).*

*That is, the one whose coming is in accord with the **activity** [energizing] of satan, with all **power** [dunamis] and signs and false wonders (2 Thess. 2:9).*

23. If you want to be deceived, God will energize you with a strong delusion. Note: it is those who received a love for the truth who are saved (2 Thess. 2:10). Logic and reasoning will not work with one under a spirit of delusion. Prayer and the anointing of God will be required to set the captive free.

*For this reason God will send upon them a deluding **influence** [energizing] so that they will believe what is false (2 Thess. 2:11).*

24. We should pray for divine energizing of our words as we share our testimonies of Christ's work within us. Exploring the New Testament and discovering *all* that we have within us through Christ will cause an expansion of your faith. So, look up "in Christ" "Christ in us," and "in whom."[2]

*I pray that the fellowship of your faith may become **effective** [energized] through the knowledge of every good thing which is in you for Christ's sake (Philemon 1:6).*

25. The Bible is anointed and energized by God. It has the power to get down to the real issues—what your heart thinks and believes and intends to do.

*For the **word** [Logos] of God is living and **active** [energizing], and sharper than any two-edged sword, and piercing as far as the*

> *division of soul and spirit, of both joints and marrow, and able to judge the thoughts and intentions of the heart* (Heb. 4:12).

26. The Spirit-energized prayer of a righteous man is effective, as it imparts divine energy. Repentance of sins clears the way for the flow of God's energy and power. So, part of healing prayer will incorporate repentance of sin. Look especially for unforgiveness, anger, and resentment, and repent of these. I have seen deliverance and healing occur immediately when a person repents of these things.

> *Therefore, confess your sins to one another, and pray for one another so that you may be healed. The **effective** [energizing] prayer of a righteous man can accomplish much* (Jas. 5:16).

A Summary of the New Testament Uses of the Greek Word *Energeo*

This "active energy" (*energeo*) operates in the release of divine power for miracles and gifts of healings, the sustaining of the universe, the energizing of individual gifts within people, and the opening of doors God provides for us to minister, as well as when we preach under the Spirit's anointing. Our faith is "energized" by love. For faith to be effective, it must be coupled with God's heartbeat emotion, which is love and compassion. This "active energy" is also present in the experience of God's manifest presence (sometimes called the "glory" of God). This "active energy" illumines the Scriptures in our hearts and minds and ministers Spirit life to the hearts of those who hear the preaching of the Word. Below is a delineation of what is accomplished through *energeo* (i.e., the active flow of divine energy).

1. *God is energizing the Christian* and is working all things out for good:

God energizes Christians by His Spirit, to accomplish His good pleasure (Col. 1:29; Phil. 2:13). This energizing is done by the Holy Spirit (Col.

1:29; 1 Cor. 12:11). While demons can energize non-Christians, their energizing power is limited by God (Jn. 19:11) and will ultimately be overcome by God (Eph. 2:2; 2 Thess. 2:9, 11). For those who want to be deceived, God energizes them with a strong delusion (2 Thess. 2:11).

2. Both the *Bible* and *Spirit-anointed preaching* are energized by God:

The Bible is anointed and energized by God and transforming for those who receive its truths (1 Thess. 2:13; Heb. 4:12). Spirit-energized preaching can transform the lives of those who receive it and believe (Phil. 1:6).

3. The *gifts and ministry one has*, including the open doors to work and minister, come from divine energizing through the Holy Spirit:

The gifts one has, the ministry one is called to, and open doors to minister are "energizings" from God (1 Cor. 12:6, 10-11; Gal. 2:7-8; Eph. 3:7; 1 Cor. 16:9). We are to labor according to the energizing of the Holy Spirit working within us (Col. 1:29). When we operate in the divine gifts God has placed within us, serving one another with these gifts, we build up and energize the body of Christ (Eph. 4:16). As we draw upon Christ's life in trying situations, the testimony of His in-working power energizes others (2 Cor. 4:11-12). We should pray for divine energizing of our words as we share our testimonies of Christ's work within us (Phil. 1:6).

4. *Spirit-energized prayer* accomplishes supernatural results, including deliverance and healing:

The energized prayer of a righteous man is effective, as it imparts God's power (Jas. 5:17). Divine energizing brings forth divine works (Eph. 1:29; 3:20; Mk. 6:13-14). Faith is energized when coupled with love (Gal. 5:6). God's energy within us releases God's grace to us, and this is freely received (Gal. 3:5-7). The energizing release of power for a miracle comes from God and is not a result of the works of the law but a hearing with faith (Gal. 3:5). It was God's energy that brought forth Jesus from the dead (Eph. 1:20).

Defining the sensations of *energeo* (energizing) in and through you:

When our **hands** are energized by the Holy Spirit, it is sensed as warmth, fire, heat, tingling, and energy. This is often experienced as we lay hands on the sick (Lk. 5:17; Mk. 5:30).

When our **hearts** are energized by the Holy Spirit, it is sensed as an inner quickening resulting in a flow of faith, hope, love, compassion, joy, peace, mercy, and power. We are experiencing the manifestation and fruit of the Holy Spirit within us (Gal. 5:22-23; 1 Cor. 12:7-11).

When our **lips** are energized by the Holy Spirit, it is sensed as a flow of words that come through the instruction of the Holy Spirit (1 Cor. 2:13) and set the captive free (Lk. 4:32). We are "speaking the oracles of God" (1 Pet. 4:10-11). It is our hearts instructing our mouths and adding persuasiveness to our lips (Prov. 16:23); or another way to say this, the Holy Spirit within is teaching our lips what to say (1 Cor. 2:13).

When our **work** is energized by the Holy Spirit, it is sensed as working at ease, experiencing flow, creativity, and productivity, and is considered a "live work" rather than a dead work (Heb. 6:1-2).

When our **mind** is energized by the Holy Spirit, it is sensed as flowing, anointed, creative thoughts and is called "the mind of Christ" (1 Cor. 2:1-16).

We *receive* God's energizing (*energeo*) in each of the following situations:

When we *invite the Holy Spirit to be present*, we can look and see Him as light and glory shimmering around us, through us, and through His creation. One way we honor the Holy Spirit is by inviting Him to be present and stating our dependence upon His healing power to be released to perform the miracle at hand. This results in Him manifesting Himself in the ways we need—i.e., the power to heal, or any of the nine fruit or ninefold manifestation of the Spirit (Gal. 5:22-23; 1 Cor. 12:7-11).

When we *pray for healing*, we ask for the Holy Spirit's power and compassion to be present. We tune to God's compassion arising in our hearts and a sensation of energy being present in our hands which we may experience as trembling/tingling and often heat. As we touch the sick, we release that energy into their beings. The Holy Spirit's flow and power can be restricted when any of the following are present: any opposite of love, mercy, and compassion (i.e., unforgiveness, anger, bitterness, hatred, rage), unconfessed sin, not welcoming and drawing upon the Holy Spirit's presence, and speaking negative words (Eph. 4:29-32).

As we *worship in Spirit* (Jn. 4:23-24) we see ourselves gathered with the heavenly host before His throne in worship (Rev. 4). We find we are soaking up the atmosphere of heaven when we see the power of God streaming from His throne as rays of light penetrating our beings (Hab. 3:4). We soak up that power and light and then see it released out through us as we lay hands on people and pray for them to be healed by the power of the Holy Spirit and in the name of the Lord Jesus Christ.

You will note that in each of the above situations, you entered into a state of rest, ceasing your own labors and believing in the power of God to accomplish (Heb. 3 and 4). You honored the Holy Spirit by welcoming His presence, and then you tuned to the Holy Spirit, Who is experienced within as a river (Jn. 7:37-39). This means you are tuned to flowing thoughts, flowing pictures, flowing emotions, and flowing power which are all coming from our heavenly Father seated in the throne room of God.

All of this can become the natural way you live as you choose to "abide in Christ" (Jn. 15). King David also wrote about abiding (Ps. 15:1), and in the following chapter he says that the way he did this was to place the Lord at His right hand, all the time (Ps. 16:8; Acts 2:25). So, we can choose to do this. We can see Jesus at our right hand all the time, working on our behalf. As we tune to flow, what we see Him doing becomes visions of divine reality which we say "yes" to and do ourselves. Thus, we take on Jesus' actions, releasing Christ into our surroundings!

Seeing Spiritual Realities Energizes Heart Faith

Pictures are the language of our hearts. When our heart speaks to us in our sleep (Ps. 16:7), it does so in dreams which are composed of pictures. The Bible says the issues of life flow from our hearts (Prov. 4:23).

When Abram, "the Father of Faith," *saw* God's promised provision as a divinely imparted picture (i.e., "the stars of the sky"), the Bible says *then* Abram believed (Gen. 15:5-6). Seeing a spiritual reality with the eyes of our hearts enhances faith in our hearts. The Bible says that the one who does not doubt in his heart can cast mountains into the sea, and all things become possible to him who believes. Let us always see God's energy flowing everywhere.

We recommend that you look and see the flow of God's divine energy (*energeo*) as you pray for healing and that you practice tuning to flow so you can feel it, also.

Journaling from Mark Virkler About God's Power

"Mark, My power sustains all things. It is the manifestation of My power that releases creative miracles. When you come into My presence, you see Me. You see My power. You see My glory. And then you command My will on earth as you see it in heaven. The Kingdom comes to earth, because the one who has been breathing in the atmosphere of My heaven releases that atmosphere on My earth through his commands. So, it is all about Me. It is about being in My presence and releasing My presence on My earth. It is about breathing in My glory and then exhaling it on My earth. Behold I have spoken; behold it is to be done.

"Mark, you see My glory as light which shines forth from My Throne and My Presence. You breathe in My light and My power and My peace and My authority, and then you exhale. You breathe it out upon My earth, and it changes and transforms My earth. It brings My Kingdom to My earth. It releases Me and My power upon My earth. This is what I have chosen for My Church to do. This is your job."

Journaling from Mark Virkler About God's Glory

"Mark, do not make My manifest presence hard. It is not hard. Yes, it is true that I choose when to manifest Myself. I have chosen to manifest My presence and My glory when I am invited to do so. It is as simple as that. Do not make it any harder. When you ask according to My will, then you receive what you have asked for. It *is* My will to manifest My glory throughout the whole world. So, ask and receive that your joy be made full. My glory does arise over My people. It does protect and empower them. It is My will to do so and for My world to see this glory.

"Mark, the more you live and see yourself seated with Me in heaven, the more you are endued with heaven's atmosphere and are able to release heaven on earth; for that which you live in is what you see, breathe, and soak up. Then it is that which you release to others. So come and live in My heavens, for that is where I have placed you. You *are* seated with Me in heavenly places. Come up here often and see My glory and My Kingdom, and then release it on earth. Behold I have spoken; behold it is to be done."

"Lord, I come. Take me by the hand and show me around. I come to see Your glory and to breathe in Your atmosphere and to release it on earth."

We utilize the eyes, ears, and emotions of our hearts to sense God's power:

The **eyes and ears of our hearts** see and hear (Jn. 5:19-20, 30). We can ask God to show us the flow of His power and any blockages that may need to be removed. Tune to flowing pictures and flowing thoughts, and act on what you receive.

Emotions of our hearts sense/feel. We ask the Holy Spirit to manifest God's compassion on the person/situation to whom we are ministering, and then we sense that compassion supernaturally arising within us (Matt. 14:14).

Personal Application

Lord, what do You want to say to me concerning experiencing and releasing divine energy?

Supplement G

Hugies Means to Be Made Whole

This word describes the end result of a person being healed. He is made whole or made well. He is restored to normal.

Kittle Theological Dictionary of the New Testament defines *hugies* as healthy, well (in body). *Thayer's Greek-English Lexicon of the New Testament* defines *hugies*: "a man who is sound in body, to make one whole, to restore him to health."

All 13 Occurrences of G5199 (*Hugies*) in the NASB

*Then He said to the man, "Stretch out your hand!" He stretched it out, and it was restored to **normal** [hugies], like the other* (Matt. 12:13).

*So, the crowd marveled as they saw the mute speaking, the crippled **restored** [hugies], and the lame walking, and the blind seeing; and they glorified the God of Israel* (Matt. 15:31).

*And He said to her, "Daughter, your faith has made you well; go in peace and be **healed** [hugies] of your affliction"* (Mk. 5:34).

*For an angel of the Lord went down at certain seasons into the pool and stirred up the water; whoever then first, after the stirring up of the water, stepped in was made **well** [hugies] from whatever disease with which he was afflicted* (Jn. 5:4).

*When Jesus saw him lying there, and knew that he had already been a long time in that condition, He said to him, "Do you wish to get **well** [hugies]?"* (Jn. 5:6).

*Immediately the man became **well** [hugies] and picked up his pallet and began to walk. Now it was the Sabbath on that day* (Jn. 5:9).

*But he answered them, "He who made me **well** [hugies] was the one who said to me, 'Pick up your pallet and walk'"* (Jn. 5:11).

*Afterward Jesus found him in the temple and said to him, "Behold, you have become **well** [hugies]; do not sin anymore, so that nothing worse happens to you"* (Jn. 5:14).

*The man went away, and told the Jews that it was Jesus who had made him **well** [hugies]* (Jn. 5:15).

*If a man receives circumcision on the Sabbath so that the Law of Moses will not be broken, are you angry with Me because I made an entire man **well** [hugies] on the Sabbath?* (Jn. 7:23)

*Let it be known to all of you and to all the people of Israel, that by the name of Jesus Christ the Nazarene, whom you crucified, whom God raised from the dead—by this name this man stands here before you in **good** [hugies] **health** [hugies]* (Acts 4:10).

***Sound** [hugies] in speech which is beyond reproach, so that the opponent will be put to shame, having nothing bad to say about us* (Tit. 2:8).

Personal Application

Review these verses on *hugies* and jot down the insights God is showing you, and then journal asking God, "What do You want to speak to me from these verses?"

Supplement H

Every Example of Casting Out Demons in the New Testament

Definition

Strong's Hebrew and Greek dictionaries define (G1139) *daimonizomai* (dahee-mon-id'-zom-ahee) as "to be *exercised by* a *daemon*: have a (be *vexed with*, be *possessed* with) devil."

A person *has* a demon that has invaded him and is *affecting an area* of his life. Christians have their spirits joined to the Holy Spirit (1 Cor. 6:17), yet need to *work out* their salvation (Phil. 2:12). As they work the light of God out through their souls and bodies, they bump into pockets of darkness (evil spirits/demons) which need to be cast out in Jesus' name. I never use the word *possess,* as it paints an incorrect picture and makes people react to it.

Our book *Prayers That Heal the Heart* describes seven prayers which one can use in sequence, and the seventh prayer is deliverance. The first prayers remove the anchors a demon uses as their legal right to attach themselves to you. Once these anchors are removed, the demon comes out easily and quickly.[1]

The synergy of the complementary gifts of prophet and teacher ministering deliverance together produces awesome results.[2] Whenever possible, team up with another as you minister, and that other person should have gifts which are complementary to yours.

How Often Did Jesus Minister Deliverance?

The Bible lists 41 different times when it is recorded in the Gospels that Jesus prayed for people to be healed. Of these 41 times, 13 incorporated prayers for deliverance. That means that in almost one-third of Jesus' prayers for healing, the Gospel writers specifically mention the fact that they involved the casting out of demons. Additional healing prayers of Jesus may have involved deliverance which was just not specifically mentioned, so the proportion could be higher.

Therefore, if I am praying for people to be healed, I would assume that between one-fourth and one-third of my prayers would involve deliverance. After all, if I am not going to pattern my healing prayer ministry after Jesus, who am I going to pattern it after? Jesus is the greatest healer the world has ever known.

Evaluate your prayer ministry approach to see if you are minimizing or overdoing deliverance prayer.

The following occurrence is worthy of special mention, for it *specifically states* that this woman's infirmity was *caused by a spirit*. The woman was instantly healed of an 18-year sickness affecting her spine. Jesus spoke and laid hands on her:

> He was teaching in one of the synagogues on the Sabbath. And behold, there was a woman who for eighteen years had **a sickness caused by a spirit**; and she was bent double, and could not straighten up at all. And when Jesus saw her, He called her over and said to her, **"Woman, you are freed from your sickness."** And He **laid His hands upon her**; and immediately she was made erect again, and began glorifying God (Lk. 13:10-13 NASB95).

A Complete Listing of All Thirteen Examples of Deliverance (NASB95)

When the deliverance story is told in *multiple* gospels, I have included *each* version of that particular story in one grouping, so we can discover if there are additional details in the various telling of the stories. See what you can find. I have highlighted key words in each story that accentuate key truths about casting out of demons.

1. Man with an unclean spirit:

It is clear that the demon/spirit was inside and came out; and as it left, it manifested by causing convulsions and speaking in a loud voice. Deliverance was by command.

> *Just then there was a man in their synagogue **with** an unclean **spirit**; and he cried out, saying, "What business do we have with each other, Jesus of Nazareth? Have You come to destroy us? I know who You are—the Holy One of God!" And Jesus rebuked him, saying, "Be quiet, and **come out** of him!" Throwing him into convulsions, the unclean spirit cried out with a loud voice and **came out** of him. They were all amazed, so that they debated among themselves, saying, "What is this? A new teaching with authority! He commands even the unclean spirits, and they obey Him" (Mk. 1:23-27).*

> *In the synagogue there was a man **possessed by** the spirit of an unclean **demon**, and he cried out with a loud voice, "Let us alone! What business do we have with each other, Jesus of Nazareth? Have You come to destroy us? I know who You are—the Holy One of God!" But Jesus rebuked him, saying, "Be quiet and **come out** of him!" And when the demon had thrown him down in the midst of the people, he **came out** of him without doing him any harm. And amazement came upon them all, and they began talking with one another saying, "What is this message? For with authority and power He commands the unclean spirits and they **come out**" (Lk. 4:33-36).*

2. Multitudes:

Many demons were cast out. Jesus told them not to reveal who He was. The words *spirit* and *demon* are being used interchangeably.

> *When evening came, they brought to Him many who were demon-possessed; and He **cast out** the **spirits** with a word, and healed all who were ill. This was to fulfill what was spoken through Isaiah the prophet: "He Himself took our infirmities and carried away our diseases"* (Matt. 8:16-17).

> *When evening came, after the sun had set, they began bringing to Him all who were ill and those who were **demon-possessed**. And the whole city had gathered at the door. And He healed many who were ill with various diseases, and **cast out many demons**; and He was **not permitting the demons to speak**, because they knew who He was* (Mk. 1:32-34).

> *While the sun was setting, all those who had any who were sick with various diseases brought them to Him; and laying His hands on each one of them, He was healing them. **Demons also were coming out** of many, **shouting, "You are the Son of God!" But rebuking them, He would not allow them to speak**, because they knew Him to be the Christ* (Lk. 4:40-41).

3. Many demons:

Preaching and deliverance go hand in hand:

> *And He went into their synagogues throughout all Galilee, preaching and casting out the demons* (Mk. 1:39).

4. Gadarene demoniac:

Mark uses the Greek tense correctly when he states that Jesus *had been saying*, "Come out!" He was *continuously* commanding. And the man was so controlled by so many demons, this was a hard case. This lets me know some cases can be harder than others. Jesus got the demons' names, and that weakened the demons. They also need a body to inhabit, so they begged to be able to go into the swine, and Jesus permitted them. These things ended the battle, and out they came.

> When He came to the other side into the country of the Gadarenes, two men who were demon-possessed met Him as they were coming out of the tombs. They were so extremely violent that no one could pass by that way. And they cried out, saying, "What business do we have with each other, Son of God? Have You come here to torment us before the time?" Now there was a herd of many swine feeding at a distance from them. The demons began to entreat Him, saying, "If You are going to cast us out, send us into the herd of swine." And He said to them, "Go!" And they came out and went into the swine, and the whole herd rushed down the steep bank into the sea and perished in the waters. The herdsmen ran away, and went to the city and reported everything, including what had happened to the demoniacs. And behold, the whole city came out to meet Jesus; and when they saw Him, they implored Him to leave their region (Matt. 8:28-34).

> They came to the other side of the sea, into the country of the Gerasenes. When He got out of the boat, immediately a man from the tombs with an unclean spirit met Him, and he had his dwelling among the tombs. And no one was able to bind him anymore, even with a chain; because he had often been bound with shackles and chains, and the chains had been torn apart by him and the shackles broken in pieces, and no one was strong enough to subdue him. Constantly, night and day, he was screaming among the tombs and in the mountains, and gashing himself with stones. Seeing Jesus from a distance, he ran up and bowed down before Him; and shouting with a loud voice, he said, "What business

do we have with each other, Jesus, Son of the Most High God? I implore You by God, do not torment me!" **For He had been saying to him, "Come out of the man, you unclean spirit!"** *And He was asking him, "What is your name?" And he said to Him, "My name is Legion; for we are many." And he began to implore Him earnestly not to send them out of the country. Now there was a large herd of swine feeding nearby on the mountain. The demons implored Him, saying, "Send us into the swine so that we may enter them." Jesus gave them permission. And coming out, the unclean spirits entered the swine; and the herd rushed down the steep bank into the sea, about two thousand of them; and they were drowned in the sea.*

Their herdsmen ran away and reported it in the city and in the country. And the people came to see what it was that had happened. They came to Jesus and observed the man who had been demon-possessed sitting down, clothed and in his right mind, the very man who had had the "legion"; and they became frightened. Those who had seen it described to them how it had happened to the demon-possessed man, and all about the swine. And they began to implore Him to leave their region. As He was getting into the boat, the man who had been demon-possessed was imploring Him that he might accompany Him. And He did not let him, but He said to him, "Go home to your people and report to them what great things the Lord has done for you, and how He had mercy on you." And he went away and began to proclaim in Decapolis what great things Jesus had done for him; and everyone was amazed (Mk. 5:1-20).

Then they sailed to the country of the Gerasenes, which is opposite Galilee. And when He came out onto the land, He was met by a man from the city who was possessed with demons; and who had not put on any clothing for a long time, and was not living in a house, but in the tombs. Seeing Jesus, he cried out and fell before Him, and said in a loud voice, "What business do we have with each other, Jesus, Son of the Most High God? I beg You, do not torment me." For **He had commanded the unclean spirit to come out of the man.** *For it had seized him many times; and he was bound with chains and shackles and kept under guard, and yet he would break his bonds and be driven by the demon into the desert. And Jesus asked him, "What is your name?" And he said, "Legion"; for many demons had entered him. They were imploring Him not to command them to go away into the abyss.*

Now there was a herd of many swine feeding there on the mountain; and the demons implored Him to permit them to enter the swine. And He gave them permission. And the demons came out of the man and entered the swine; and the herd rushed down the steep bank into the lake and was drowned.

When the herdsmen saw what had happened, they ran away and reported it in the city and out in the country. The people went out to see what had happened; and they came to Jesus, and found the man from whom the demons had gone out, sitting down at the feet of Jesus, clothed and in his right mind; and they became frightened. Those who had seen it reported to them how the man who was demon-possessed had been made well. And all the people of the country of the Gerasenes and the surrounding district asked Him to leave them, for they were gripped with great fear; and He got into a boat and returned. But the man from whom the demons had gone out was begging Him that he might accompany Him; but He sent him away, saying, "Return to your house and describe what great things God has done for you." So he went away, proclaiming throughout the whole city what great things Jesus had done for him (Lk. 8:26-39).

5. Syrophoenician's daughter:

Deliverance was a verbal response to faith, and deliverance was accomplished at a distance with instant results.

> *And a Canaanite woman from that region came out and began to cry out, saying, "Have mercy on me, Lord, Son of David; my daughter is cruelly demon-possessed." But He did not answer her a word. And His disciples came and implored Him, saying, "Send her away, because she keeps shouting at us." But He answered and said, "I was sent only to the lost sheep of the house of Israel." But she came and began to bow down before Him, saying, "Lord, help me!" And He answered and said, "It is not good to take the children's bread and throw it to the dogs." But she said, "Yes, Lord; but even the dogs feed on the crumbs which fall from their masters' table." Then Jesus said to her, "O woman, **your faith is great; it shall be done for you as you wish." And her daughter was healed at once** (Matt. 15:22-28).*

> *Jesus got up and went away from there to the region of Tyre. And when He had entered a house, He wanted no one to know of it; yet He could not escape notice. But after hearing of Him, a woman whose little daughter had an unclean spirit immediately came and fell at His feet. Now the woman was a Gentile, of the Syrophoenician race. And she kept asking Him to cast the demon out of her daughter. And He was saying to her, "Let the children be satisfied first, for it is not good to take the children's bread and throw it to the dogs." But she answered and said to Him, "Yes, Lord, but even the dogs under the table feed on the children's crumbs." And He said to her, "Because of this answer go; the demon has gone out of your daughter." And going back to her home, she found the child lying on the bed, the demon having left (Mk. 7:24-30).*

6. Child with an evil spirit:

The deaf and mute spirit was causing episodes of destructive behavior and did so as Jesus was casting it out. Jesus asked how long this had been happening. Apparently, this information aided in gaining the upper hand in the deliverance struggle. His disciples did not have enough faith to cast it out, but Jesus did.

> When they came to the crowd, a man came up to Jesus, falling on his knees before Him and saying, "Lord, have mercy on my son, for he is a **lunatic** and is very ill; for he **often falls into the fire and often into the water**. I brought him to Your disciples, and they could not cure him." And Jesus answered and said, "You unbelieving and perverted generation, how long shall I be with you? How long shall I put up with you? Bring him here to Me." And Jesus rebuked him, and the **demon came out of him, and the boy was cured at once**.

> Then the disciples came to Jesus privately and said, "Why could we not drive it out?" And He said to them, "Because of the littleness of your faith; for truly I say to you, if you have faith the size of a mustard seed, you will say to this mountain, 'Move from here to there,' and it will move; and nothing will be impossible to you. [But this kind does not go out except by prayer and fasting]" (Matt. 17:14-21).

> When they came back to the disciples, they saw a large crowd around them, and some scribes arguing with them. Immediately, when the entire crowd saw Him, they were amazed and began running up to greet Him. And He asked them, "What are you discussing with them?" And one of the crowd answered Him, "Teacher, I brought You my son, possessed with a spirit which **makes him mute**; and whenever it seizes him, it slams him to the

*ground and he foams at the mouth, and grinds his teeth and stiffens out. I told Your disciples to cast it out, and they could not do it." And He answered them and said, "O unbelieving generation, how long shall I be with you? How long shall I put up with you? Bring him to Me!" They brought the boy to Him. When he saw Him, immediately the spirit threw him into a convulsion, and falling to the ground, he began rolling around and foaming at the mouth. And He asked his father, "How long has this been happening to him?" And he said, "From childhood. It has often thrown him both into the fire and into the water to destroy him. But if You can do anything, take pity on us and help us!" And Jesus said to him, "If You can? **All things are possible to him who believes.**" Immediately the boy's father cried out and said, "I do believe; help my unbelief." When Jesus saw that a crowd was rapidly gathering, **He rebuked the unclean spirit,** saying to it, "**You deaf and mute spirit,** I command you, come out of him and do not enter him again." After crying out and throwing him into terrible convulsions, it came out; and the boy became so much like a corpse that most of them said, "He is dead!" But Jesus took him by the hand and raised him; and he got up. When He came into the house, His disciples began questioning Him privately, "Why could we not drive it out?" And He said to them, "**This kind cannot come out by anything but prayer**" (Mk. 9:14-29).*

And a man from the crowd shouted, saying, "Teacher, I beg You to look at my son, for he is my only boy, and a spirit seizes him, and he suddenly screams, and it throws him into a convulsion with foaming at the mouth; and only with difficulty does it leave him, mauling him as it leaves. I begged Your disciples to cast it out, and they could not." And Jesus answered and said, "You unbelieving and perverted generation, how long shall I be with you and put up with you? Bring your son here." While he was still approaching, the demon slammed him to the ground and threw him into a convulsion. But Jesus rebuked the unclean spirit, and healed the boy and gave him back to his father (Lk. 9:38-42).

7. Mute demoniac:

A demon causing muteness was cast out, and the man spoke.

> *As they were going out, a mute, demon-possessed man was brought to Him. After the demon was cast out, the mute man spoke; and the crowds were amazed, and were saying, "Nothing like this has ever been seen in Israel"* (Matt. 9:32-33).

8. Blind and mute demoniac:

This deliverance from blindness and muteness was called *therapeuo* healing. This indicates that deliverance can be classified under the topic of therapeutic healing modalities. Religious people oppose deliverance. Casting out demons by the spirit/finger of God is one way the Kingdom of God comes *upon* you.

> *Then a demon-possessed man who was **blind and mute** was brought to Jesus, and He healed [therapeuo] him, so that the mute man spoke and saw. All the crowds were amazed, and were saying, "This man cannot be the Son of David, can he?" But when the Pharisees heard this, they said, "This man casts out demons only by Beelzebul the ruler of the demons."*

> *And knowing their thoughts Jesus said to them, "Any kingdom divided against itself is laid waste; and any city or house divided against itself will not stand. If Satan casts out Satan, he is divided against himself; how then will his kingdom stand? If I by Beelzebul cast out demons, by whom do your sons cast them out? For this reason they will be your judges. But **if I cast out demons by the Spirit of God**, then the kingdom of God has **come upon you**. Or how can anyone enter the strong man's house and carry off*

his property, unless he first binds the strong man? And then he will plunder his house. He who is not with Me is against Me; and he who does not gather with Me scatters. Therefore I say to you, any sin and blasphemy shall be forgiven people, but blasphemy against the Spirit shall not be forgiven. Whoever speaks a word against the Son of Man, it shall be forgiven him; but whoever speaks against the Holy Spirit, it shall not be forgiven him, either in this age or in the age to come" (Matt. 12:22-32).

*And He was casting out a demon, and it was mute; when the demon had gone out, the mute man spoke; and the crowds were amazed. But some of them said, "He casts out demons by Beelzebul, the ruler of the demons." Others, to test Him, were demanding of Him a sign from heaven. But He knew their thoughts and said to them, "Any kingdom divided against itself is laid waste; and a house divided against itself falls. If Satan also is divided against himself, how will his kingdom stand? For you say that I cast out demons by Beelzebul. And if I by Beelzebul cast out demons, by whom do your sons cast them out? So they will be your judges. **But if I cast out demons by the finger of God, then the kingdom of God has come upon you**"* (Lk. 11:14-20).

9. Multitudes:

It is all here in one big bundle: two different words for healing are used, plus deliverance.

*Jesus was going throughout all Galilee, teaching in their synagogues and proclaiming the **gospel of the Kingdom**, and **healing** [underline]therapeuo[/underline] **every kind of disease and every kind of sickness** among the people. The news about Him spread throughout all Syria; and they brought to Him all who were ill, those suffering with **various diseases and pains, demoniacs, epileptics, paralytics;** and He **healed** [underline]iaomai[/underline] them* (Matt. 4:23-24).

*Jesus came down with them and stood on a level place; and there was a large crowd of His disciples, and a great throng of people from all Judea and Jerusalem and the coastal region of Tyre and Sidon, who had come to hear Him and to be **healed** [iaomai] of their diseases; and those who were troubled with **unclean spirits** were being **cured** [therapeuo]. And all the people were **trying to touch Him**, for **power** [dunamis] **was coming from Him** and **healing** [iaomai] them all* (Lk. 6:17-19).

10. Multitudes:

Again, we find deliverance connected with *therapeuo*, so I tend to class deliverance as one of the therapeutic methods I can use in promoting healing.

At that very time He cured [therapeuo] many people of diseases and afflictions and evil spirits; and He gave sight to many who were blind (Lk. 7:21).

11. Mary Magdalene and others:

A person can have multiple demons within, which can be cast out, bringing restoration and health.

*Some women who had been **healed** [therapeuo] of **evil spirits and sicknesses**: Mary who was called Magdalene, from whom **seven demons had gone out*** (Lk. 8:2).

12. Crippled woman:

Deliverance is once again classed as *therapeuo* healing. It is specifically stated that the spirit was the one causing the infirmity. It was released with a command and the laying on of hands. Healing was immediate.

*And He was teaching in one of the synagogues on the Sabbath. And there was a woman who for **eighteen years had had a sickness caused by a spirit**; and she was **bent double**, and could not straighten up at all. When Jesus saw her, He called her over and said to her, "**Woman, you are freed from your sickness.**" And He **laid His hands on her**; and **immediately** she was made erect again and began glorifying God. But the synagogue official, indignant because Jesus had healed on the Sabbath, began saying to the crowd in response, "There are six days in which work should be done; so come during them and get **healed** [<u>therapeuo</u>], and not on the Sabbath day"* (Lk. 13:10-14).

13. Various persons:

Casting out demons is a cure.

*I cast out demons and perform **cures** [<u>iasis</u>] today and tomorrow, and the third day I reach My goal* (Lk. 13:32).

Personal Application

"Lord, what would You speak to me concerning ministering deliverance?"

Supplement I

Additional Resources

Links to Free Downloads

1. A Sea of Galilee visualized walk with Jesus using the four keys: cwgministries.org/galilee

2. CLU School of the Spirit Course Sampler: cluschoolofthespirit.com/free

3. Biblical Gift Mix Profile—14-page download: cwgministries.org/giftmix

4. PDF copy of our booklet *How to Receive the Baptism in the Holy Spirit*: cwgministries.org/baptism

5. *Are Chakras Demonic? Energy Medicine Is God's Idea* PDF: cwgmin istries.org/chakras

6. Downloadable Brain Preference Indicator Test: cwgministries.org/brain

7. Dreams Crash Course: glorywaves.org/dreams

8. EFT: Is "Emotional Freedom Technique" Effective and Biblical? glorywaves.org/eft

9. Video Training—*4 Keys to Hearing God's Voice*: cwgministries.org/4keys

10. Video Training—*Prayers That Heal the Heart*: cwgministries.org/prayers

11. A monthly free video event is announced in our monthly email newsletter: cwgministries.org/subscribe

Training Packages

Books, workbooks, PowerPoints, audio and video series for the following titles are available at cwgministries.org. These can be coupled with coaches,[1] e-learning School of the Spirit modules,[2] or online college degrees.[3]

1. *Hearing God's Voice for Healing*
2. *4 Keys to Hearing God's Voice*
3. *Counseled By God*
4. *Prayers That Heal the Heart*
5. *Go Natural*
6. *Living Naturally Supernatural—Revised*
7. *Overflow of the Spirit*
8. *Unleashing Healing Power Through Spirit-Born Emotions*
9. *God's Counsel Through Dreams*

Mark Virkler's blogs which relate to discussions in this book:

1. cwgministries.org/million
2. cwgministries.org/store/river-life-mp3-download
3. cwgministries.org/blogs/prayers-heal-heart-7-step-model
4. cwgministries.org/spirit-life-circles-explained
5. cwgministries.org/Miracles7StepModel
6. cwgministries.org/7-step-meditation-process-explored
7. cwgministries.org/blogs/heart-prayers-employing-language-your-heart
8. cwgministries.org/blogs/distinguishing-logos-rhema-communication-speech
9. cwgministries.org/blogs/logos_verses_rhema
10. cwgministries.org/all-uses-rhema-bible

11. cwgministries.org/blogs/speaking-your-journaling-back-lord -your-personal-present-tense-reality
12. cwgministries.org/blogs/your-stripes-i-am-healed-and-symptoms -are-dissapearing
13. cwgministries.org/blogs/perfect-peace-when-your-imagination
14. cwgministries.org/blogs/how-does-bible-say-we-discover-truth
15. cwgministries.org/i-h20

More blogs and how to sign up to receive all Mark Virkler's blogs: www.cwgministries.org/blogs/mark-virklers-top-blogs

Prophetic counseling ministers:

1. Dr. Don Paprockyj: cwgministries.org/blogs/rev-don-paprocky-highly -recommended-zoom-counselor-or-seminar-speaker
2. Bob Lucy—Freedom from DID: cwgministries.org/did

Training schools you can attend that focus on the supernatural:

1. Everlasting Love Academy[4]—Patricia King Ministries
2. Bethel School of Supernatural Ministry[5]—Bill Johnson
3. Global Awakening School of Ministry[6]—Randy Clark
4. Catch the Fire School of Ministry[7]—John Arnott

Blogs and websites for health and spirituality:

- Type into search bars at each link below an affliction, disease, or condition
- Dr Axe,[8] Life Extension,[9] Mercola,[10] GreenMedInfo,[11] Dr. Schulze,[12] CWGMinistries[13]
- A New Brand of Christians - Praying for Healing on the Streets![14]
- Vaccine Information[15]
- Christian Care[16] (an alternative to traditional health insurance)

Books for health and spirituality:

1. Go to Amazon.com and type in searches for: books by Bill Johnson, Randy Clark, and John Arnott. Additionally, these books:
   - *Confessions of a Medical Heretic* by Robert S. Mendelsohn
   - *Cancer: Why We're Still Dying to Know the Truth* by Phillip Day
   - *Power Healing* by John Wimber
   - *Healing* by Francis MacNutt
   - *The Power to Heal* by Francis MacNutt
   - *Deliverance from Evil Spirits: A Practical Manual* by Francis MacNutt

2. *Revival Phenomena and Healing Workbook*[17] and *The Healing River and Its Contributing Streams*[18] by Randy Clark. Go on an International Healing Ministry Trip[19] with Randy Clark, and you *will* see the sick healed as you lay hands on them.

3. *How to Release God's Healing Power Through Prayer*[20]—free ebook by Virkler, Greig, Gaydos

4. *Restoring Health Care as a Ministry*[21]

5. *Health Mastery Through MRT* book[22]

6. *Healthier Today Than Yesterday* ebook[23] by Mark and Patti Virkler

7. *When Everything Changes*[24] by Steve Stewart. Increase your faith with amazing stories. Go on a Journey of Compassion[25] with Steve Stewart where you *will* see the sick healed as you lay hands on them.

Endnotes

Chapter 1

1. Uta Milewski's ebook can be downloaded from: cwgministries.org/store/gods-heart-you-ebook.

2. I cover how I learned to hear God's voice in these 12-week training modules, which each include a book, workbook, and audio or video series: "4 Keys to Hearing God's Voice: (cwgministries.org/store/4-keys-hearing-gods-voice-dvd-package); "Counseled By God" (cwgministries.org/store/counseled-god-dvd-package); "Prayers That Heal the Heart" (cwgministries.org/store/prayers-heal-heart-dvd-package).

3. You can find expanded teaching on the four keys here: cwgministries.org/4keys.

4. See cwgministries.org/million.

5. Download at: cwgministries.org/galilee.

6. Going Deeper:
   - Explore the benefits of salvation (salvation touches every area of my life): cwgministries.org/experience-salvation-being-born-spirit; cwgministries.org/cross.
   - Explore more testimonies of healing: cwgministries.org/AllBlogs#TestimoniesOfHealing.
   - Explore vibrant health: cwgministries.org/blogs/restore-vibrant-health.
   - Healing Scriptures for confession and meditation: cwgministries.org/HealingScriptures.

Chapter 2

1. For more on this, see cwgministries.org/WholeStory.
2. For more on this, see cwgministries.org/blogs/ThreeNTWords Healing.
3. For more on this, see cwgministries.org/energeo.
4. Going Deeper: Examples of miracles of healing at cwgministries.org/ AllBlogs#miracles.

Chapter 3

1. For example prayers, cwgministries.org/7prayers.
2. See cwgministries.org/meditation.
3. See cwgministries.org/4keys.
4. Type in "imagination" in the search bar at CWGministries.org for more.
5. See cwgministries.org/galilee.
6. See cwgministries.org/tongues.
7. Going Deeper: Read these blog entries:
   - "Word of Faith: One Way God Heals—Meditating on Scriptures," cwgministries.org/AllBlogs#Word-of-Faith-One-Way-God -Heals.
   - "Loving Relationships: Marriage, Family, Body of Christ," cwgministries.org/AllBlogs#HealthyRelationships.

Chapter 4

1. Download the free Brain Preference Indicator Test at cwgministries .org/brain.
2. See glorywaves.org/10-ways-to-get-in-spirit.
3. Download a free copy of "How to Receive the Baptism in the Holy Spirit" and the gift of speaking in tongues at: cwgministries.org/ baptism.

4. Going Deeper:
   - "Worshipping in Spirit Releases the Manifest Presence of the Holy Spirit" at cwgministries.org/AllBlogs#WorshippingInSpirit.
   - "Baptism in the Holy Spirit" at cwgministries.org/AllBlogs#BaptismInHolySpirit.
   - "Easily Learn How to Hear God's Voice": at cwgministries.org/AllBlogs#God'sVoice.

Chapter 5

1. Mohd Razali Salleh, "Life event, stress and illness," *The Malaysian journal of medical sciences*, vol. 15,4 (2008): 9-18; www.ncbi.nlm.nih.gov/pmc/articles/PMC3341916.
2. The information in this section is a summary from this article: Ann Pietrangelo, "The Effects of Stress on Your Body," Healthline, March 21, 2023, healthline.com/health/stress/effects-on-body.
3. These topics are covered more in-depth in some of our other books such as *Unleashing Healing Power Through Spirit Born Emotions* and *Prayers that Heal the Heart*.
4. Bill Johnson and Randy Clark, *The Essential Guide to Healing* (Chosen Books, 2011), 175.
5. Additional books: *4 Keys to Hearing God's Voice* and *Unleashing Healing Power Through Spirit Born Emotions* expand your understanding of these principles.
6. For more information, type "imagination" in the search bar of CWGministries.org.
7. You may download our free video training on *Prayers That Heal the Heart* at cwgministries.org/prayers. If you are looking for a list of what the emotional roots *might be* and a *new posture* we could take to offset this emotional root, there is such a list in the book, *Exposing the Spiritual Roots of Disease: Powerful Answers to Your Questions About Healing and Disease Prevention* by Dr. Henry Wright, which is available on Amazon. If you would like to hear Dr. Wright, listen

to this online short teaching by him concerning panic: youtube
.com/watch?v=eN26j0magds.

8. See our training module "Hearing God's Voice" at cluschoolofthespirit
.com/hear.

9. See our training module "Counseled by God" at cluschoolofthe
spirit.com/counsel.

10. See our training module "Prayers That Heal the Heart" at cluschool
ofthespirit.com/prayers.

11. See our training module "Hearing God Through Your Dreams" at
cluschoolofthespirit.com/dreams. Note: Our training modules are
also available at cwgministries.org.

12. Going Deeper: "Restoring Emotions by Hearing the Voice of the
Wonderful Counselor" at cwgministries.org/AllBlogs#Restoring
Emotions.

Chapter 6

1. A more detailed description of this process is here: cwgministries
.org/blogs/inner-healing-methods-virkler-and-lehman.

2. For more teaching on this step see this link: cwgministries.org/
7prayers.

3. See cwgministries.org/7prayers.

4. For more teaching on this step, see this link: cwgministries.org/store/
take-charge-your-health-complete-discounted-package.

5. "John Wimber Signs Wonders1985 1/12 (Personal Pilgrimage),"
YouTube, youtube.com/watch?v=wGkob0n363Aandlist=PLXn3620
-8oTwczfBREgL1UlNRgdyBik6a.

Chapter 7

1. Explore more about words of knowledge through dreams in these
blogs by Charity Kayembe:

- glorywaves.org/dream-gifts-how-to-receive-a-word-of-knowledge
-while-you-sleep.
- glorywaves.org/annas-dream-words-of-wisdom-knowledge.
- glorywaves.org/when-neurosurgeons-dream-gods-dreams.

2. Check out this blog: Seven Steps to Mastery: cwgministries.org/
blogs/seven-steps-mastery.
3. Dreams are another way to get a Word from God: cwgministries.org/
AllBlogs#DreamInterpretation.

Chapter 8

1. For more guidance on this, see cwgministries.org/blogs/inner
-healing-methods-virkler-and-lehman.
2. Simple observation changes the outcome: cwgministries.org/
QuantumConnection.
3. See training: cwgministries.org/7prayers.
4. Going Deeper: blogs about casting out demons at cwgministries.org/
AllBlogs#CastingOutDemons.

Chapter 9

1. The best source to learn about Peg's method of healing more in-depth
is her book, *I Saw the Light—BUT He Saw Me First* available on
Amazon.com (note especially Chapter 22, "He Restores My Soul").
2. Check out Peg's website: locm.org.
3. Going Deeper: Restoring Vision: I Pray that the Eyes of My
Heart Be Enlightened (Eph. 1:17): cwgministries.org/AllBlogs#
RestoringVision.

Chapter 10

1. Discover more about who Peg Yarbrough is: locm.org/about-us.

2. Learn more about Margaret Cornell: hearinggodsvoiceuk.net/about-the-team.

3. As taught in *4 Keys to Hearing God's Voice*: cwgministries.org/store/results/topic/how-hear-gods-voice-325.

4. Did you notice that this vision from God was given in a dream? If you have not yet mastered Christian dream interpretation, you can access a Dreams Crash Course at glorywaves.org/dreams.

5. Additional resources are available at the end of the blog at this link (PowerPoint, 60-minute teaching, handout, etc.): cwgministries.org/WordOfFaith.

6. Explore more about what quantum physics can teach us about faith: glorywaves.org/quantum-physics.

7. Going Deeper: "Revelation-Based Learning: What, How, Why" at cwgministries.org/AllBlogs#RevelationBasedLearning.

Chapter 11

1. Here are 60-plus blogs that you can review which go into many of these therapeutic healing modalities in more depth: cwgministries.org/AllBlogs#Gifts-Of-Healings.

2. The free "Contributing Strands Worksheet" (https://www.cwgministries.org/store/contributing-strands-worksheet) can be downloaded to assist in removing demons' anchors so you can easily cast them out. Use this tool and the accompanying training in *Prayers That Heal the Heart* which teaches you to apply the following seven prayers to a heart wound: breaking generational sins and curses; severing ungodly soul ties; repenting of ungodly beliefs and inner vows; replacing ungodly beliefs and inner vows with godly beliefs and godly purposes; inner healing; breaking off word curses; and, finally, casting out demons (http://www.cwgministries.org/free-resources-prayers-that-heal-the-heart).

3. See the book: *Prayers That Heal the Heart*: cwgministries.org/store/prayers-heal-heart-package.

4. Read about Bob Lucy's ministry in this blog: cwgministries.org/did.

5. Discover herb use in *Prescription for Nutritional Healing* (available on Amazon.com), or by doing an internet search for "herbs as medicine." One excellent herb company is Nature's Sunshine (http://www .naturessunshine.com/us/shop).

6. Supporting link at: cwgministries.org/longevity

7. There is a chapter on the healing benefits of fasting in the book *Go Natural! Eden's Health Plan* (cwgministries.org/store/edens-health -plan-go-natural), by Mark and Patti Virkler. The Master Cleanse (cwgministries.org/MasterCleanse) provides an excellent healing fast. Various cleanses for specific body organs are available here: herbdoc .com/index.php/5-Day-Detox-Programs.

   After using all the above cleanses for years, I have switched to GIA's "Cleanse" (giawellness.com/markvirkler/products/nourishment/ cleanse). I take a capful of their "Cleanse" every morning mixed with a capful of their "Thrive." I put these together into a glass of their single-file aligned water. I have gotten my *best* results doing this, and it is also the *easiest* cleanse and *tastes* the best. My blog discussing this is here: cwgministries.org/I-H20.

   Detoxification is made easier when you use "natural" cleaning products. We have used Melaleuca (melaleuca.com) products for years. Toxic chemicals in your home enter your system and damage your health.

8. The excellent reference book *A More Excellent Way* (available on Amazon.com) lists the *emotional roots* of many diseases. You can skip the book if you want and learn to simply live in faith, hope, and love. The book *Counseled by God* (cwgministries.org/store/ counseled-god-dvd-package) offers a good tool for growing in faith, hope, and love and removing harmful emotional states. Also check out this blog: "A Thankful Heart" at cwgministries.org/blogs/ gift-appreciation-heals.

9. Explore the resource on how to have "Mountain Moving Faith": cwgministries.org/store/mountain-moving-faith.

10. Learn more about how to enter into and enjoy Throne Room worship: cwgministries.org/blogs/leading-worshipers-throne-room.

11. See ask.com/wiki/The_Relaxation_Response.

12. See cwgministries.org/blogs/gift-appreciation-heals.

13. See cwgministries.org/blogs/singing-for-immune-system.

14. See cwgministries.org/blogs/energized-sleep.

15. See cwgministries.org/blogs/speak-healing-promises.

16. Quality essential oils can be purchased from youngliving.com.

17. See cwgministries.org/roar.

18. See draxe.com/nutrition-category/diets.

19. See draxe.com/nutrition/budwig-diet-protocol-cancer.

20. Digestive enzymes available from rgarden.com/maximizer.

21. Vitamins available from rgarden.com.

22. See lifeextension.com. Also, read this blog: "Synthetic vs. Whole Food Vitamins: Is It a Life and Death Issue?" at cwgministries.org/blogs/vitamins.

23. See cwgministries.org/I-H20; giawellness.com/markvirkler.

24. See airpurifiers.com/product-reviews/austin-air-bedroom-machine-air-purifier.

25. To learn more about both the problem and the solutions, please see: giafreedom.com/lifestyle-energy; cwgministries.org/I-H20.

26. Is the "Emotional Freedom Technique" Effective and Biblical? Find out more at this free resource: glorywaves.org/eft.

27. See *4 Key's to Hearing God's Voice* at cwgministries.org/4keys.

28. Carl R. Peterson, M.D, "Medical Facts About Speaking In Tongues," June 14, 2011, beingunderthenewcovenant.wordpress.com/2011/06/14/medical-facts-about-speaking-in-tongues-%E2%80%93-carl-r-peterson-m-d.

29. See cwgministries.org/blogs/chiropractic-safe-and-effective.

30. Dr. Burzynski's cancer clinic: burzynskiclinic.com
    - Oasis of Hope Hospital: oasisofhope.com

- Removing Mercury Amalgams: amazon.com/Its-All-Your-Head-Amalgams/dp/0895295504
- Limiting Vaccines: drtenpenny.com
- The Buteyko Breathing Method: treatasthmaathome.com/buteyko-breathing-method-technique
- BEMER Mat: mark-virkler.bemergroup.com

31. At qest4.com.

32. cwgministries.org/store/mrt

33. cwgministries.org/mrt

34. lifelinescreening.com

35. herbdoc.com/blog

36. cwgministries.org/Health-directory

37. cwgministries.org/GiftsHealings7StepModel

38. activerelease.com

39. cwgministries.org/our-mission

40. Going Deeper:
    - "A 7-Step Model for Therapeutic Healing" at cwgministries.org/GiftsHealings7StepModel.
    - "Gifts of Healings: 7-Step Model" one-page handout: cwgministries.org/Miracles7StepModel.
    - "Holy Spirit, Which Prayer Approach Shall I Use Today?" at cwgministries.org/AllBlogs#PrayerApproaches.

Chapter 12

1. See cwgministries.org/throne.

2. See cwgministries.org/soaking.

3. See cwgministries.org/spirit.

4. See heartmath.com.

5. See cwgministries.org/4keys.

6. See cwgministries.org/million.

7. See glorywaves.org/quantum-physics.

8. See cwgministries.org/store/mountain-moving-faith-cddvd-set.

9. See cwgministries.org/blogs/prayers-heal-heart-7-step-model.

10. See cwgministries.org/all-uses-rhema-bible.

11. See cwgministries.org/blogs/how-keep-your-healing-pastors-jim-mark -and-kiwanda-redner.

12. See cwgministries.org/blogs/when-reason-challenges-faith-what-am -i-do.

Supplement A

1. A list of verses containing *sozo*: bibletools.org/index.cfm/fuseaction/ lexicon.show/ID/g4982/page/1.

2. A list of verses containing *soteria*: bibletools.org/index.cfm/ fuseaction/Lexicon.show/ID/G4991/soteria.htm.

3. See cwgministries.org/blogs/my-confession-concerning-who-i-am -christ.

Supplement C

1. Access at cwgministries.org/7StepHealing.

2. Access at cwgministries.org/free-christian-books-and -articles#MiraclesPowerPoint.

3. Access at cwgministries.org/free-christian-books-and -articles#MiraclesMP3.

4. Access at cwgministries.org/store/7-step-healing-model-cards-100 -pack.

Supplement E

1. See biblehub.com/greek/2323.htm.

2. *Merriam-Webster,* s.v. "therapeutic," merriam-webster.com/dictionary/ therapeutic.

3. See lef.org.

4. See mercola.com.

5. See herbdoc.com.

6. See greenmedinfo.com.

7. Henry W. Wright, *A More Excellent Way, Be in Health: Spiritual Roots of Disease, Pathways to Wholeness* (New Kensington, PA: Whitaker House, 2009).

8. Phyllis A. Balch, *Prescription for Nutritional Healing: A Practical A-to-Z Reference to Drug-Free Remedies Using Vitamins, Minerals, Herbs & Food Supplements* (New York, NY: Avery, 2010).

Supplement F

1. See cwgministries.org/ReleaseDivineEnergy.

2. We do this in our book *The Great Mystery*, available at cwgministries.org/store/great-mystery.

Supplement H

1. Our book is available at cwgministries.org/store/prayers-heal-heart.

2. For guidance, see cwgministries.org/blogs/example-prophet-and-teacher-teaming-minister-deliverance.

Supplement I

1. cwgministries.org/pst

2. cluschoolofthespirit.com/individual-courses

3. cluonline.com

4. everlastingloveacademy.com

5. bethel.com/ministries/bethel-school-of-supernatural-ministry

6. globalawakening.com

7. somtoronto.com

8. draxe.com

9. lifeextension.com/science-research

10. articles.mercola.com/sites/articles/archive/2022/08/08/search-is-back.aspx

11. greenmedinfo.com

12. herbdoc.com/blog

13. cwgministries.org/blogs/checklist-restore-maintain-health

14. cwgministries.org/blogs/new-brand-christians-praying-healing-streets

15. drtenpenny.com

16. mychristiancare.org

17. revivalcry.com/store/school-of-healing-and-impartation-1-manual-randy-clark/

18. globalawakeningstore.com/The-Healing-River-and-Its-Contributing-Streams.html

19. globalawakeningstore.com/International-Ministry-Trips/

20. cwgministries.org/sites/default/files/files/books/How-to-Release-Healing.pdf

21. cwgministries.org/store/restoring-health-care-ministry

22. cwgministries.org/store/health-mastery-through-mrt

23. cwgministries.org/store/healthier-today-yesterday-ebook

24. cwgministries.org/store/when-everything-changes-ebook

25. impactnations.com

About Mark and Patti Virkler

Mark and Patti Virkler have co-authored more than 50 books on hearing God's voice and spiritual growth. They are founders of Communion With God Ministries (www.CWGMinistries.org) and Christian Leadership University (www.CLUOnline.com), where the voice of God is at the center of every learning experience. Mark has taught on intimacy with God and spiritual healing for more than 40 years on six continents.

YOUR
Prophetic
C O M M U N I T Y

Sign up for a **FREE** subscription to the Destiny Image digital magazine and get awesome content delivered directly to your inbox!

destinyimage.com/signup

Sign up for Cutting-Edge Messages that Supernaturally Empower You

- Gain valuable insights and guidance based on biblical principles
- Deepen your faith and understanding of God's plan for your life
- Receive regular updates and prophetic messages
- Connect with a community of believers who share your values and beliefs

Experience Fresh Video Content that Reveals Your Prophetic Inheritance

- Receive prophetic messages and insights
- Connect with a powerful tool for spiritual growth and development
- Stay connected and inspired on your faith journey

Listen to Powerful Podcasts that Propel You into God's Presence Every Day

- Deepen your understanding of God's prophetic assignment
- Experience God's revival power throughout your day
- Learn how to grow spiritually in your walk with God

From
Mark & Patti Virkler

No interpreter necessary!

Use these four keys to unlock the mystery of hearing God's voice for yourself! Transform and deepen your relationship with your heavenly Father starting today.

Based on the highly popular and successful book, How to Hear God's Voice, this exciting new book emphasizes the *4 Keys to Hearing God's Voice*.

"When I learned to hear God's voice after 11 years as a believer without it, every part of me was radically transformed. Thousands have told me they have had this same metamorphosis, and I believe that this will become your testimony also," writes co-author, Mark Virkler.

Filled with insights from years of hearing from God, *4 Keys to Hearing God's Voice* also includes visual aids that enhance the teaching and learning experience. Very reader-friendly, you will find that the concepts and principles are easily adapted to your personal circumstances and lifestyle.

Purchase your copy wherever books are sold.

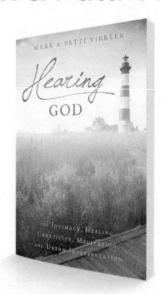

From
Mark & Patti Virkler

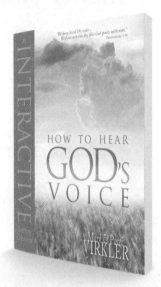

"But blessed are your eyes, because they see; and your ears, because they hear." Matthew 13:16

You can hear the voice of your Lord.

He is always speaking to you. In fact, every believer is called to have a one-on-one relationship with God because He longs to share sweet times of intimacy with all His children.

How to Hear God's Voice will teach you to discern His voice from all the other voices that clamor for your attention.

This book:

- Gives vital keys to increase the intimacy of your prayer time,
- Teaches you how to be still before the Lord,
- Helps you recognize His speech as spontaneous thoughts,
- Encourages you to seek vision while praying, and use a journal to record revelation.

Your communion with God will become a flow of His words springing forth from your heart. You will experience a depth of relationship you never thought possible!

Purchase your copy wherever books are sold.